*f*P

Expletive Deleted

$&#@*!

A GOOD LOOK AT BAD LANGUAGE

Ruth Wajnryb

FREE PRESS

New York London Toronto Sydney

FREE PRESS
A Division of Simon & Schuster, Inc.
1230 Avenue of the Americas
New York, NY 10020

FREE PRESS and colophon are trademarks of Simon & Schuster, Inc.

For information about special discounts for bulk purchases,
please contact Simon & Schuster Special Sales:
1-800-456-6798 or business@simonandschuster.com.

Book design by Ellen R. Sasahara

Manufactured in the United States of America

2 4 6 8 10 9 7 5 3 1

Library of Congress Cataloging-in-Publication Data

Wajnryb, Ruth.
Expletive deleted : a good look at bad language / Ruth Wajnryb.
p. cm.
The characters $&#@*! appear after the title on the t.p.
Includes bibliographical references (p.) and index.
1. English language—Obscene words. 2. Taboo, Linguistic.
3. Swearing. I. Title.
PE3724.03W35 2005
422—dc22   2005043786

ISBN-13: 978-0-7432-7434-0
ISBN-10:   0-7432-7434-2

To Mark Cherry and Barbara Lasserre

CONTENTS

Expletive Deleted

PROLOGUE

Until quite recently, swearing was a subject largely ignored by those who investigate the nature of language. Well, perhaps "ignored" is going too far. Let's say interest was lacking. Not a lot has changed since twelve years ago, when Timothy Jay, one of the few serious researchers in this field, wrote, "If all science on language stopped now, we would know very little about dirty word usage or how dirty word usage relates to more normal language use."

This lack of interest becomes glaringly obvious when you consider the massive amount of literature that has been generated analyzing discrete linguistic elements such as the past-tense inflection of "-ed" or present tense, third-person singular final "-s." While I'm happy to own up to my bias as an applied (that is, not pure) linguist, and while I'm loath to cast aspersions on other linguists' areas of expertise (we're a small academic community, and we have to live together peaceably), I need to ask here: Is there really any competition between swearing and the bits we put on the ends of verbs as topics for study? If you didn't vote for swearing, this is where you get off. *Bus stops here!*

The absence of research interest in swearing is itself intriguing. In 1975 the Australian linguist B. A. Taylor published a serious study of abusive language in the Australian context. He began his paper thus:

> If English were . . . a Germanic language spoken in Northern Delaware, and particularly if it were the language of some indigenous tribe, it is pretty certain that some enterprising anthropologist would long since have recognised and described the subsystem of taboo language contained within it.

Taylor and I share a partiality to the anthropological device, for I frequently invoke the services of the Visiting Anthropologist from Mars. Taylor goes on to say that because English is the language of most of the world's linguists, the subsystem of taboos on which swearing is based has been largely ignored or, where analyzed, undertaken in the spirit of fun, and not as a serious endeavor.

Nearly thirty years on, the situation has improved—a little. Yet the fact remains that I don't need two hands to count the number of dedicated books on the subject. One explanation may be found in the sociolinguist Erving Goffman's reference to "the most conventionalized and perfunctory doings we engage in . . . [that] traditionally have been treated by students of modern society as part of the dust of social activity, empty and trivial—routine formulae-fillers."

Others have commented on the academic avoidance of this domain of language. Australian researcher Angus Kidman treats as preposterous the notion that swearing is intuitively obvious and requires no further examination. He criticizes studies that treat swearing as nothing more than a linguistic category of words and fail to see that it is a culturally driven speech act. He claims that the very fact that different word labels are used in different varieties of English ("swearing" in Britain and Australia; both "swearing" and "cursing" in the United States) should tell us that we're not simply talking about an undifferentiated, invariant category of words.

Researcher Richard Dooling bemoans the lack of available access to the relevant literature:

> The Library of Congress classification system does not provide a selection of books . . . on swearing or dirty words. A researcher . . . must travel to the BF of psychoanalysis, the PE of slang, the GT of anthropology, the P of literature and literary theory, the N of art, the RC of medical psychiatry and back to the B of religion and philosophy.

Such a disorderly journey around the library shelves provides Dooling with the evidence that words such as "shit" are "inextricably bound up with almost everything."

The fact that this area of research continues to be undervalued as an academic pursuit is itself meaningful. I'm not moved by the contention that, since most linguists alive today speak English as a native language, they are therefore blind to much of their language. If this were the case, how should we explain the fascination with the morphology of the English verb system? Rather, I suspect that the taboo overlying the language of swearing has so stigmatized the subject that academics are hesitant to soil their hands even by association. They may take the view that an interest in this domain is likely to attract the raised eyebrow. At a practical level, it may not be deemed a specialization likely to win the esteem of their research fellows, a sine qua non for most academics.

1

FALLING FOUL

"How the fuck did I work that out?"

—PYTHAGORAS

For generations, children have chanted "Sticks and stones will break your bones / But names will never hurt you." But even if the child who was being bullied (the "bullee," if you like) used this ditty as a protective strategy, no one really believed the words. Names do hurt. We do worry about what other people think and say about us. Let's face it, even that earnest class of person known as a lexicographer was, until recently, unwilling to include swear words in the dictionary for fear of offending the literate public and, through that offense, negatively impacting on publishers' commercial interests. Notwithstanding its articulated mission "to chart every word in the language," the *Oxford English Dictionary* began including so-called four-letter words only in the early 1970s. The editors of *The Random House Dictionary of the English Language* agonized for decades over the same issue, with their four-letter inclusions not appearing until 1987.

Those who make decisions about what goes in or stays out of newspaper text have been similarly afflicted. It is perhaps one of the remaining vestiges of the Puritan influence that Americans are even more angst-ridden about such matters than the British. In his *New York Times* column, William Safire once resorted to the ludicrously oblique to make his point, referring to a certain scatological noun that was on the point of hitting the fan. The taboo exerts its influence in the most curious of places, such as the following transcript of the cockpit voice recordings in a 1989 airline crash in Iowa: "We're going to have to ditch this son of a [word deleted] . . ." Even in the context of disaster and imminent death, when one could argue that swearing might actually be completely appropriate, the squeamishness persists.

The fact that serious word people have been so hesitant to take the plunge perhaps carries a message for the would-be researcher. Part of the problem is that it's hard to write about SHIT, FUCK, CUNT, and their fellows without using the words themselves. Although it has been done. In 1948 one Burges Johnson succeeded in writing a book on swearing, rather romantically titled *The Lost Art of Profanity,* without once mentioning any of the naughty words. And Jesse Sheidlower wrote a famous book called *The F-Word,* but such an endeavor can't have been easy.

I had my own difficulties conducting interviews for this book. Once I was talking to an in-house journalist about the Australian Broadcasting Corporation's policy on using CUNT in radio and TV broadcasting. Said journalist was so uncomfortable using the word in our conversation that she eventually asked permission to say "the C-word." Things went swimmingly from that point on, but it took a while to get there and resolve the impasse. You can see why researching past-tense verb endings would offend no one and therefore seem a much less problematic avenue.

Nonetheless, I find it strange that linguists have allowed themselves to be affected by the taboo to the point that its exploration has been underresearched. After all, certain nether areas of the body are also not for polite company or *pas devant les enfants.* Yet we have urologists, proctologists, and gynecologists, who aren't afraid to put their particular "-ist" next to their name on a plaque. We don't ban snails from texts on biology simply because they are unsightly. Sociologists continue to study the criminal mind no matter how perverse the crime. If these specialists can investigate their chosen areas without imbuing the subjects with value or imposing others' aesthetic judgments, then why can't linguists?

Of course, in referring to the lack of interest in my topic, I mean the absence of academic investigative interest. Outside and beyond the ivory towers of academe, there's no shortage of interest. Indeed, it's a topic on which everyone seems to have a viewpoint. I have found that nearly everyone has a swearing story that they are keen to share. Mostly the views are extreme and, more often than not, judgmental and negatively so.

Moreover, as with many lay or folk notions, beliefs about swearing are riddled with myth. A major one is that swearing is destructive. Take, for instance, the Cuss Control Academy (I kid you not), a North American institute of nonreligious people dedicated to raising public awareness about the negative impact of swearing. These people have nothing good to say about swearing: It makes you look bad; it's a social ill; and it corrupts the language. The institute runs workshops for those keen to reduce their use of profanity, vulgarity, obscenity, and offensive slang. For a reasonable fee, you can learn "the ten tips for taming the tongue" and have the opportunity to practice them in pleasant surroundings where you can feel safe and understood, all the while knowing that you are improving both yourself and society.

James V. O'Connor, president of the Cuss Control Academy, is so concerned about the effect on children of their parents' swearing that his book *Cuss Control: The Complete Book on How to Curb Your Cursing* was written with the primary goal of getting parents to clean up their vocabulary. He argues that we swear because we're lazy, it's easy, and we mistakenly think it's okay. Our children, growing up in a cursing culture, hear it everywhere—at home, in the street, on television, at the movies—and they might be forgiven for failing to understand why it's "wrong." For them, "Don't cuss" may well be just another rule to be broken. O'Connor then goes on to contradict himself by claiming that while kids might take up swearing in rebellion, much as they take up smoking, the habit can become ingrained.

It's not only collectives of private citizens that are speaking out, often ignorantly, about swearing. In December 2003 California legislator Doug Ose became very upset over the fact that the rock star Bono had used a vulgarity (I believe the offensive phrase was "fucking brilliant") on live TV. The occasion was the presentation of the annual Golden Globe Awards, and the fact that Bono emerged from this incident unscathed upset a good many people. Apparently, the Federal Communications Commission deemed that Bono had used "fucking" as an adjective, so his wrists escaped an official slap.

It was at this point that Doug Ose introduced the Clean Airwaves Act, targeting eight swear words to be banned from the airwaves. (It's probably not without significance that I could not find one media report prepared to cite all eight of the words.) Ose asserted that these profanities should be outlawed whether they were used as verbs, adjectives, gerunds, participles, or infinitives.

The incident triggered worldwide media attention, although it seems to have been of no interest to anyone but me that when the FCC deemed Bono's indiscretion to be adjectival, they actually mistook an adverb for an adjective. However, one Australian journalist did speculate as to whether the FCC decision would motivate students to study grammar, "at least to know what they can get away with."

Knowing what I do, about both grammar and school students' attitude toward it, I have no doubt that the grammatical leeway granted to FUCKING as an adjective will make not a single iota's difference either to what people say or what they refrain from saying. In the words of Ashley Montagu, an early researcher of swearing, the fundamental truth is that "no people has ever abandoned its habits of swearing merely because the State . . . forbade it." Mussolini's campaign to eradicate swearing through posters and signs on public transport exhorting Italians *"Non bestemmiare per l'onore d'Italia"* ("Do not swear for the honor of Italy") had zero impact.

The taboo affects the microdomestic level as well. One

Web-based astrologist, appropriately named Luna, operates an e-mail-delivered Astro-Guide, including a personalized service to people who send in Dear Luna questions. I found this one, signed by Can't Take Her Anywhere:

> Dear Luna,
> I am an Aries man whose Libra wife has a mouth like a truck driver. I used to share her habit but have cleaned up my act since having kids. She still cusses a blue streak. Everywhere we go it's "the f-ing this" and "the f-ing that." . . . She is blind to the raised eyebrow, turned heads and angry looks. . . . I love her with all my heart, but her behaviour is extremely embarrassing. What can I do?

Luna's response probably didn't tell "Can't Take Her Anywhere" anything he didn't already know. The wife's cussing was seen as a possible cry for attention, and anger-management strategies were recommended, as well as the need for caution and self-commitment—in brief, in order for the cusser to change, the cusser has to want to change. In another advice column, an advice seeker is warned "not to swear on a date, because you wouldn't swear at a job interview and 'technically' this is the same thing."

Australian talk radio, newspapers, and television morning shows are more or less permanently interested in swearing, if only for the fracas that swearing often triggers in otherwise harmonious interchanges. In 1999 the then Victorian premier Jeff Kennett famously used the word "prick" on Australian radio. In the same year, the long-standing Australian current affairs program *Four Corners* allowed FUCK on the program on three separate occasions.

In 2003 the *Macquarie Dictionary*'s Sue Butler was being interviewed on an Australian television morning show. The matter being discussed was the acceptability of calling someone a "boofhead" in public. Butler explained that while the word "boofhead" was more affectionate than aggressive, it was really the *act* of calling someone a "something," whether "boofhead" or "fuckwit," that increasingly offends. Butler was cut off after "fuckwit"; the interview was terminated, and the channel subsequently issued an apology. I have no idea whether the incident had an impact on the show's ratings.

The topic of swearing generates extreme opinions. Writing for the British *Daily Mirror,* Melanie Phillips abhors and condemns swearing as "the sickness in society":

> We live . . . in an age defined by the smashing of taboos. It's all part of the assault on bourgeois codes of behaviour, on the suburban, the respectable. But as taboos get smashed, new ones . . . emerge. . . . So the frontiers of shockability get pushed ever outwards. . . . Laddishness is the new black.

For Phillips, profanity "embodies an absence of self-restraint," and its increasing casualization bespeaks an erosion of public values and consideration for others. Like the allegedly falling standards in literacy, swearing is becoming a universal scapegoat—it's the symptom, cause, and outcome of most of the evils of the new millennium. And, no doubt, those of previous millennia.

On the other hand, Phillips's extreme position can be

contrasted with a more general tolerance toward swearing. A young student journalist researching modern swearing suggested to me that the new tolerance may be the outcome of the "trickle-down effects of post-modernity destroying the wall between high culture and low culture, pushing the words traditionally occupying the vocabulary of the uneducated into mainstream media, politics and entertainment." She also suggested that the softening social attitude of the public toward swear words is a symptom of a general lightening up. People are realizing that swearing does not spell the end of civilization, that everyone does it at some time, that we all abuse an uncooperative computer or laugh at a raunchy joke at the bar. In short, the words aren't evil, and the universe does not come crashing down.

Talking about swearing can stimulate a great deal of hilarity, a fact well known to comedians, who use it to their advantage. There must be a basic handbook for wannabe stand-ups: When in doubt or in need of a quick laugh, dip into toilet humor or pull out a dick joke or throw in a few FUCKS. People laugh, almost by reflex. It's the result of the flouting of a taboo. The comic is allowed to say it, and we're allowed to laugh. It's a ritual. Everyone goes home feeling better for the laughter. Take, for instance, George Carlin's recital of his infamous list of seven major words you can't say on television. Audiences delighted in hearing Carlin say "shit, piss, fuck, cunt, cocksucker, motherfucker, and tits."

This attitude may explain websites such as Swear Away, at http://listen.to/swearing, and Swearotron at http://www.rathergood.com/swearotron.html, where you run your cursor (curser?) over a face with an angry expression and the face emits a swear word. Sometimes it's a standard swear word; sometimes it's delivered in a heavy foreign accent. Some of them are normal words such as "the" delivered with the same intensity as FUCK or SHIT. Some people have too much time on their hands.

Then there are those who take their right to swear just as seriously. There's Chip Rowe, for example (http://www. chiprowe.com/articles/swear.html), an American citizen who launched the Society to Highlight Ingrate Terms (SHIT). He compares his society with the National Rifle Association, which purports that "a good gun owner is an educated gun owner." So, too, Rowe reminds members of SHIT, do cuss words relieve a tremendous amount of tension, "but only if used with respect for their power." SHIT, therefore, with a zeal not unlike that of the Cuss Control Academy, will educate people in the proper use of swear words. Here is a sample of the curriculum:

> "Shit" is an all-purpose word; cussers should use it when failing an exam or watching a favorite team cost you $20 by blowing a huge lead. However, if you lose more than $20, that's a FUCK. If you're dealing with the IRS, that might be a shit or a fuck, depending on who did your taxes; if you're dealing with the FBI or ATF, that's always a fuck. Among other cuss words, "asshole" is good for the boss or moron co-workers or in-laws, but "motherfucker" should be reserved for more weighty situations, such as when a mugger who [sic] shoots you even after you give him your wallet, or you realize you're slipping off the edge of the Grand Canyon as you back

up for a family photo. I hear "motherfucker" invoked for the simplest of transgressions, such as a foul during a basketball game. No, no, no! "Fuck you" will suffice, or maybe "What the hell?" "Motherfucker" is a fairly serious accusation.

Inappropriate usage of "bad language" remains an ongoing point of public interest, as frequent media coverage attests. But most interest is in its sensationalist potential. Like the orchestrated photo opportunity, an attack of the swear words furnishes a good broadcast moment, a grab on the viewing public's attention. But this is not the kind of interest that will advance our knowledge of the language of swearing, which, as I have been at pains to point out, is of itself a valid and worthwhile pursuit. It is in this pursuit that the rest of this book has been written.

2

PRECISELY FOUL

"Fucking hell, Brutus, not you too?"

—Julius Caesar

Before we plunge any deeper into the linguistic badlands, let's make sure we are all using the same vocabulary. There are two potential points of confusion when it comes to understanding and talking about foul language. One has to do with the words used that commonly *constitute* "swearing." The other has to do with how we *refer* to "swearing."

The first point of confusion arises from the form–function relationship of swearing terms. The fact is that there are more swearing functions to perform than there are swear words to use; to put it differently, lots of targets but a scarcity of ammunition. This means that swearers have to use the same old words over and over again, though in different circumstances and for different purposes. They dip into the swear bank and use words that may be similar semantically (in their dictionary meaning) but different pragmatically (in their context of use). "Damn it!" and "Damn you!" both employ DAMN, but I'm sure you'll agree that each achieves a different meaning in context.

The second potential point of confusion concerns the *meta-language* of swearing. "Meta-language" is a term we linguists use for language that describes language—in this case, the language conventionally used to talk about swearing. Rather oddly, though perhaps appropriately, the meta-language of swearing also calls on a restricted bank of words.

Take the word "swear," for example, which itself has two very different meanings. There's the swearing you do in court when you promise to tell the truth, and there's the different swearing you do at home when, for the umpteenth time, the kids have left their dirty footprints on the hall carpet. We talk about "swearing," "cursing," and "using bad language," and the meanings differ even while, confusingly, the words we use are the same or similar. We commonly interchange "foul" language with "rude," "vulgar," and "obscene." And these words themselves splinter off into separate submeanings—as does "rude," which can mean impolite in the sense of not displaying the requisite amount of respect, or it can mean using an inappropriate word for a particular context (a gynecologist referring to the "pussy" instead of the "vagina," for example). Sometimes the words used to talk about swearing are interchangeable, but sometimes they're not. Almost always, they're being used loosely.

To explore foul language seriously, we need a meta-language that is precise and consistent. That's why I've put together a glossary of sorts.

abusive swearing
Swear words that are directed toward others ("You fucker"); derogatory in tone ("This is a shitty piece of work"); involve metaphoric curses ("Go to hell!"); or denigrate through name-calling ("You bastard").

blasphemy
A form of swearing that deliberately vilifies religion or anything associated with religious meaning. What's important here is the swearer's intention. "Jeez," for instance, is a common and, indeed, conventional word today and would not be regarded as blasphemous unless its use were intended to give particular offense to a Christian.

curse, cursing
In a curse, the curser usually invokes a higher being and calls down some evil upon a specifically defined target. "May you be damned for all eternity" is a curse. A number of aspects distinguish "cursing" from "swearing": Cursing invokes the aid of a higher being; it is more ritualistic and deliberately articulated; it is future-oriented, built on an understanding that the effect may be delayed; and it may not involve the use of foul language. Placing a curse on someone has traditionally been frowned on by church and society, and even today a curse such as "Eat shit and die!" is considered powerful, threatening behavior. Note that, while in the past, a particular deity or supernatural being of some description was usually explicitly invoked, in today's more secular times, it's possible for an enraged nonbeliever to shout "I hope you die!" without specifying divine intervention.

"Cursing" is loosely interchangeable with "swearing"

(using foul language), but in its precise meaning, it is a species within the generic form, "swearing." In more religious times, curses were serious and intended literally; in these more secular times, curses are more spontaneous and metaphoric ("Rot in hell!"), thus overlapping with conventional abusive swearing.

cuss, cussing

A term from American English that means "swearing" in the general sense of using foul language (for example, "bloody hell").

dysphemism

This is the substitution of an offensive or disparaging term for an inoffensive one. Most deliberately abusive swearing involves the use of dysphemisms (for example, using "ass" rather than "fanny").

epithet

Often used interchangeably with "expletive," this is a defamatory or abusive word or phrase.

euphemistic swearing

This involves the substitution of an inoffensive term, or one that is seen as acceptable ("Goodness gracious") for one that is considered indelicate or taboo-breaking ("Good God Almighty!").

expletive

This is the exclamatory swear word or phrase said in emotional circumstances; it betrays a letting off of pent-up steam. Literal surface-level meaning is secondary ("Great balls of fire!," "Mother of God!," "Fucking hell!," "Blow me down!"). What is being signaled is the release of emotion. The word(s) tend to be prefabricated in the sense of being fixed and invariant: "Blow me down," for instance, never becomes "Blow you down." Expletives are frequently uttered without addressing anyone specifically. In this sense, they are reflexive—that is, turned in on the user.

foul language (see "swearing")

In a meta-linguistic sense, using "foul language" generally equates with "swearing." Swear words are examples of foul language. The term "foul" recognizes that much swearing trespasses on topics and domains generally deemed appropriate in personal but not social language—that is, bodily functions and body products (or effluvia). Foul language used in social settings can be equated with abuse or aggression, but while this is often the case, it is not exclusively so. You can use foul language without abusing anyone ("Shit, I forgot to bring my report") or as an indication that you are relaxed and feeling comfortable ("Fuck! So good to get out of the office and relax"). Appropriate use of foul language is complicated by the fact that the various functions of foul language are all furnished from the same limited supply of words.

insult

Loosely speaking, in an abusive context, when you swear at someone, you intend to insult them. In more precise terms, "insult" is reserved for an abusive term that is meant literally ("You ugly, fat, pimply idiot"), rather than in the metaphoric sense of most swear words ("You're fucked!"). In practice, swear words and insults coexist comfortably ("Fuck you, you ugly shithead"), combining their abusive power, usually to good effect.

invective
This is a refined version of the insult used in formal contexts, a notable example being the Australian Parliament, where it might be considered a minor art form. It can vary in its degree of subtlety, involving any or all of biting irony, wit, puns, and wordplay. It has the character of insulting rather than swearing, because it tends to steer clear of conventional swear words in the sense of expletives or foul language. It often allows the user to insult his or her victim without using taboo words or breaching social protocol (for example, spoonerisms such as "You shining wit").

oath
The word "oath" has two meanings that parallel the two broad contexts of use of "swear." One is the formal promise you make when you swear by the Bible or by Jove, or by whatever you fancy. Here the oath is the actual text that you recite in the swearing act. Oaths are no longer a common feature of daily life. The second meaning is rather like the loose metaphoric curse, for example, "He muttered an oath when the hammer hit his finger."

obscenity
Swearing through the explicit use of indecent or taboo words to refer to intimate parts of the body and the body's functions and products (for example, "shit" or "fuck").

profanity

Swearing through the use of words that abuse anything sacred. "Profanity" is a wider term than "blasphemy" and distinct in that there may be no intention to vilify. Profanity may simply involve the use of religious terminology such as "God" or "Jesus" in a secular and indifferent manner. It is sometimes confused with obscenity (see, for example, the Viz Profanosaurus, a listing of "profane" words that are, in fact, vulgar or obscene at http://www.funbunch.co.uk/breaking/viz.htm).

swear

The verb "to swear" has two distinct meanings. One is a regular word in the ordinary language; the other is a meta-linguistic term used to describe a kind of language. The first meaning is the making of a formal promise or oath, such as swearing to tell the truth, the whole truth, and nothing but the truth. In these cases, "swear" is often followed by an infinitive verb—*to tell* the truth, *to do* my best, *to honor* my school, *to fight* for my country, etc. This sense of "swear" can also be followed by the prepositions "by" or "on": "I swear *by* my mother's grave" or "I swear *on* the Bible." The second meaning of "swear" is entirely distinct. Here "swear" is not the actual word used, in the way we say "I swear to . . ." but a meta-linguistic word that describes the use of foul language for a particular purpose. This kind of swearing is normally followed by "at" or "about"—"He was swearing wildly at his wife"; "He was swearing about the mortgage." This kind of swearing is characterized by reference to taboo or stigmatized material and by its strong nonliteral force. It is usually associated with strong attitude or emotion.

taboo words

These are words that have been prescribed by a particular
culture as being off-limits. They may be words that disrespect religion, or that make public reference to intimate
acts. They may also include stigmatized topics such as
mental illness, birth defects, or a person's detention in
prison. Topics such as death, income, or a person's religious affiliation also carry taboos. A whole vocabulary of
euphemisms now exists (for example, "passing away," "re-
muneration," "faith") to allow people to discuss these topics in public.

vulgarity

A form of swearing that makes use of foul language by
breaking taboos related to intimate language. It is broader
than "obscenity" but is loosely used interchangeably. It often amounts to calling a spade a shovel or being deliberately
dysphemistic: "I have to take a crap" or "Wow, look at those
tits."

3

FOUL IS AS FOUL DOES

"I don't suppose it's gonna fucking rain, is it?"

—JOAN OF ARC

If ever we needed to justify an exploration of swearing, it should surely be enough to note that it is almost universal as a human activity. The taboos and, of course, the words are different, and the circumstances, settings, and rules vary. But nearly every collective of people does it. I say "nearly" because I will take up this intriguing matter in more detail later, in "Cross-Culturally Foul."

Of course, this doesn't mean that everyone in a particular culture engages in the same outpourings under the same provocations. Some of the differences, such as those involving gender, will also be explored later. But others are outside of such broad categories as class or gender. There are individual differences. Who among us doesn't remember a maiden aunt, or even a married one, whose sensibilities were so easily offended that everyone in her presence minded their p's and q's and f's? Similarly, who among us doesn't have a family member who swears like a trooper?

My parents rarely swore and, when they did, it was sotto voce and in another language; my brother never swore as a child, certainly not in my presence. I swore profusely and indiscriminately. So out of kilter with my surroundings was I that I could have been dropped into the family home from another planet. Clearly, if cultures differ one to another, they also differ abundantly internally.

Why do we swear? The answer to this question depends on the approach you take. As a linguist—not a psychologist, neurologist, speech pathologist, or any other -ist—I see swearing as meaningful verbal behavior; patterned; systematic; and readily lending itself to a functional analysis. Pragmatically, swearing can be understood in terms of the meanings it is taken to have in particular circumstances and what it achieves in any particular circumstance.

My mind map of foul language involves three concentric circles. If you like, you can think of these in geological terms: the earth's core, its crust, and the atmosphere around it. The inner circle or core is constituted of the actual foul words. There are about a dozen of these (I like to think of them as the Dirty Dozen)—FUCK, CUNT, SHIT, PISS, BITCH, BASTARD, and ASS (with DAMN, HELL, FART, CRAP, and DICK)—and they provide the resources for a number of different speech acts.

As I've said earlier, these dozen words are rather overworked, serving a range of different masters. I've placed these masters—speech acts—in the next circle, or the crust level. I like to think of these speech acts in infinitive terms: *to* swear, *to* curse, *to* insult, *to* intensify, *to* be vulgar, *to* be obscene, *to* blaspheme, etc. Again, there are about a dozen of these, although there is no strict linear correspondence between them and the core foul words in the foul-word bank.

For example, you can use SHIT to insult ("You're a shithead") or intensify ("It's a shitty deal"). In the infinitive form, these speech acts roam around, as it were, looking for a particular circumstance to ground them. Without context (our outer circle), the speech acts are only theoretical; they haven't yet achieved a meaning.

In the outer circle, or atmosphere, we have the context of use in which, finally, we can attribute some meaning to our chosen words. It is only when a word is located in a particular context—participants interacting in a shared place and time, with a shared understanding of their interconnection—that we can speak of meaning and achievement. The outer circle is made up of three broad domains of achievement—catharsis, aggression, and social connection—in which most uses of foul language can be classified. Given that life and language are complex phenomena, the dividing lines among these three domains are permeable. But it's a special kind of permeability, one that enables leakage to happen without mandating that it must.

It might be easier to think of the three components of the outer domain as the three reasons people swear. The first is catharsis: the almost instinctive "bastard!" emitted when you stub your toe. The second is abusive: the "bastard" that you snarl at the driver who just sneaked into your parking spot. The third is social: the "bastard" in "you old bastard" when you hail a friend you haven't seen for a while.

Our small reservoir of swear words services all three categories freely, if not completely equally. In addition, the emotional dimension may either dominate (as in cathartic and abusive swearing) or be incidental (social swearing). Despite these overlapping and integrated elements, the complexity is really only academic. Out there in the "real" world, we have no trouble distinguishing between the different kinds of swearing, because each swearing episode is so embedded in its own context of action that we don't need a user's manual to tell us whether that big guy over there with the red face who's calling something out has a problem with his stubbed toe, or with us, or whether he just recognized us from our school days and is coming over to get reacquainted.

Cathartic swearing is the most straightforward. This is the stub-your-toe, bump-your-head, lose-a-race, get-caught-going-through-a-red-light kind of swearing, which henceforth I will refer to with a catchall label as the "stub-your-toe" variety. In his massive survey, *The Cambridge Encyclopedia of the English Language,* David Crystal places toe-stubbing swearing firmly within the expressive or emotional function of language. He sees it as a visceral means of releasing excessive nervous energy and, as such, one of the commonest forms of language. If life is a pressure cooker, stub-your-toe swearing allows steam out in measured, manageable bursts. It's a loss of decorum to which we can all relate—a lowest common denominator, ringing true no matter how preposterous the circumstance.

The following joke is an example of humor capitalizing on the universality of pent-up frustration.

In Jerusalem, a female journalist heard about a very old Jewish man who had been going to the Western

Wall to pray, twice a day, every day, for a long, long time. So she went to check it out. She went to the Western Wall, and there he was! She watched him pray, and after about forty-five minutes, when he turned to leave, she approached him for an interview.

"I'm Rebecca Smith from CNN. Sir, how long have you been coming to the Western Wall and praying?"

"For about fifty years."

"Fifty years! That's amazing! What do you pray for?"

"I pray for peace between the Jews and the Arabs. I pray for all the hatred to stop, and I pray for our children to grow up in safety and friendship."

"How do you feel after doing this for fifty years?"

"Like I'm talking to a fucking wall."

With toe-stubbing swearing, the actual expletive used is functionally immaterial. It's the act of letting off steam, emitting some pent-up emotion that speaks, if you like, independently of the words used. This semantic vacuum is highlighted by the secondary meaning of the word "expletive," that is, "any syllable, word or phrase conveying no independent meaning, especially one inserted in a line of verse for the sake of the meter," such as "tra-la" in "The flowers that bloom in the spring, tra-la / Have nothing to do with the case." That's one to remember next time you get called out for swearing.

In this kind of swearing, we've momentarily lost our cool—our *poise,* that state of tight control that each of us exerts over ourselves in the company of others so that our boundaries remain intact and our interpersonal contact nonabrasive. Most of the time, we're unaware of the amount of mental energy we expend in maintaining our poise. Occasionally—the frequency is a matter of individual variation—a crack appears in our cool.

The sociologist Erving Goffman wonderfully refers to such cracks, which for him typically are the breakdown in the intactness of the body's boundaries, as "flooding out." Crying is a beautiful example of flooding out, and so is swearing. The two acts are not unrelated, as we shall discover later, when we look at gender issues in foul-language usage. A famous *Punch* cartoon of 1913 has an old lady leaning down to talk to a little boy who is clearly distressed. She asks, "Why are you crying, little boy?" To which he responds, "Because I bea'nt old enough to swear."

Crying and swearing may be linked on more than one level. Cognitive scientist Steven Pinker compares human language with other animals' communication systems. He found that the vocal calls of primates are controlled not by the cerebral cortex, as in humans, but by older neural structures in the brain stem and limbic system, areas that are closely involved in emotion. (I once received a free-floating scrap from cyberspace that stated: "The hypothalamus is one of the most important parts of the brain, involved in many kinds of motivation, among other functions. The hypothalamus controls the Four Fs: fighting, fleeing, feeding and mating.")

For his part, Pinker bundles swearing with laughing, sobbing, moaning, and the sounds one makes when in pain. We might call these emissions more primitive or perhaps more essential—as close as we can get to the *ipsa ho-*

minis essentia. I'm not sure if anyone has ever used these findings as a legal defense against a charge of offensive language—"I was acting subcortically" or "My limbic system made me do it"—but it's a thought.

There's an element of the unexpected in toe-stubbing swearing. Our even progress has suddenly been interrupted. This is neither comfortable nor welcome, because we tend not to like nasty surprises. Our natural inclination is to go through life in a state of natural, naive optimism, expecting that our wants and desires will be fulfilled without impediment. It's the Pollyanna Hypothesis, the very antithesis of the more down-to-earth Murphy's Law. Ludicrous though it may seem, the Pollyanna Hypothesis is sustainable because without it, ordinary daily life would be intolerable.

So when our expectations are capriciously overturned, as they regularly are, we're massively, if momentarily, put out. Our psychosocial equilibrium is ruffled, but the expletive(s) we utter as a vehicle of our emotion—our relief valve for this untoward surge of energy—goes a long way toward righting things and restoring a healthy balance. Until the next time, anyway.

There is another well-known reaction to the unexpected—laughter. Someone once said that all laughter, to varying degrees of sophistication, is an instinctual reaction to a well-dressed person striding boldly along the street and slipping on a banana peel. I think it was Freud who claimed that we laugh at the banana-peel incident out of relief that the experience was someone else's. But whether the unexpected elicits laughter or an expletive depends on a constellation of variables. For example, are you alone or in company? If the latter, who are you with, and what is your relationship to them? Is pain involved and, if so, whose pain? Your own is more likely to elicit an expletive, someone else's a laugh. A sad comment, perhaps, on *Homo sapiens*.

Releasing an expletive is possibly beneficial to our health, by serving a relief-purifying-pacifying-purgative role and reducing stress levels. Expletives may be directed toward an inanimate target—some people go to town on the cupboard that bashed their head or the doorway that jammed their finger, investing the offending object with agency, volition, and malice. One notable characteristic of what is sometimes called "annoyance swearing" is that it doesn't require an audience, any more than a burp or any other, even less polite, bodily emission does. You could go so far as to say that the very absence of an audience affords the uninhibited expletive its maximum range of freedom.

The knowledge that the legendary maiden aunt (or some other self-confessed non- or anti-swearer) is within earshot may constrain even the sharp pain of a stubbed toe, perhaps converting a "Shit!" into a "Sugar!" In the richly complex way of language, the maiden aunt will know that it was respect for her ears, and hence for her, that affected the conversion, and she will be inwardly pleased, even if outwardly disapproving.

The second domain of swearing is abusive or vituperative swearing. It's as emotive as cathartic swearing, perhaps more so, because the verbal episode in which it occurs is likely to be of a longer duration than the simple expletive that emerges from a (mere) toe stub. As I was walking my dog this morning, I passed what appeared to be a family, a man, a woman, and a young child, all walking in the same direction but not abreast; they were quite spread out, with more than a dozen paces between them. The man was verbally abusing the woman, and she was giving as good as she was getting. As far as I could gather, in between the B's and the F's, the topic was swearing in the presence of a child. I conjectured that the altercation may have started out on a different topic, then degenerated into swearing, whereupon the topic moved to the fact of swearing, and doing so *devant l'enfant*. Their voices were so loud, I couldn't help eavesdropping. It seemed like a familiar script, and the main actors certainly knew their lines. I marveled at how elegantly it was crafted. The little girl traipsed along behind as if she'd heard it all before, and no doubt she had.

It was a beautiful example of abusive swearing. The part to which I was privy lasted about four minutes, but it surely began before me and continued after me, so there's no telling its full duration. It might even be this couple's default discourse style. After viewing *South Park: Bigger, Longer & Uncut* (for research purposes), I concluded that it's possible to insert a swear word into every utterance, much as an Orwell or a Conrad might insert a finite verb.

It's not for nothing that such verbal abuse has been called "fighting words." Cognitive psychologist Timothy Jay reminds us that the protection afforded by the U.S. Constitution to the individual's freedom of speech is withdrawn in the case of libel, slander, obscenity, fighting words, and words that provoke imminent danger. Just as with the wording of their constitutional right to bear arms, Americans have been struggling with these definitions ever since.

There seem to be two schools of thought about fighting words. The first, dubbed the words-can-wound camp, argues that fighting words, or personally provocative epithets spoken face-to-face to an individual, are linked to the notion of harm—either physical or psychological or both. The opposing camp argues that a distinction needs to be drawn between verbal and physical assault, as between physical and psychological harm. Some contend that verbal violence, as a substitute for physical violence, minimizes rather than increases physical aggression, and may even serve a stabilizing and protective role.

Attitudes toward swearing, as encoded in cultural constructs such as taboos, church rules, or secular legislation, have an underlying common denominator—the belief that certain words used in certain ways and under certain circumstances have a symbolic power, sometimes thought of as magic. It's such cultural attitudes that invest a culture's particular inventory of swear words with their perceived sense of danger. It is a reflexive relationship: the view that certain words have power invests these words with power; this manifest power then reinforces the view that these words have power.

This is a variation on "they'll only hurt you if you let them." The actual words might shift over time, as we will see when we discuss the currently fading power of FUCK, but this is incidental to the underlying belief in word magic. As one word goes, another replaces it. The taboo shifts a little, but the magic is enduring.

Abusive swearing not only differs from the toe-stub variety in its aggressive, albeit symbolic, intent, it also differs in its participation framework. This is Erving Goffman's term for who has an active (participating) and a passive (observing) role in an interaction; who is front stage (centrally involved) and backstage (peripherally involved); ratified (known to be a participant) and unratified (not known to be a participant). A defining feature of abusive swearing is the necessary participation of an other(s). While cathartic swearers can howl their words to an audience of none, abusive swearing requires a target, because the abusive swearer wants to wound, to rupture, to inflict harm—in short, to abuse.

Some writers, including the nineteenth-century poet Samuel Taylor Coleridge, have sought to distinguish two subcategories within the emotionally charged class of abusive swearing. The first is closer to the nature of cathartic swearing in that it's a venom-cleansing device for the swearer, but with the distinction of being aimed at someone as a target. Its core motivation is the need to discharge some emotion, and the target, poor thing, was in the wrong place at the wrong time. This kind of swearer may say some awful things in the heat of the moment but does not really mean them and, a little later, may well be over it.

The second subcategory identified by Coleridge is when the verbally violent swearer is genuinely malignant in intent, with motives as nasty as the language used. It would be unfair to lump the two together, because while they might sound similar and draw on the same reservoir of foul language, their intentions are different, as is the seriousness with which they are to be interpreted. One way of distinguishing the two is to consider some swearing as coming from the lips only, while the more serious comes from the heart.

Analyzing abusive and cathartic swearing separately is not to suggest that they cannot combine. It's very easy to imagine how an emotional release to an unwelcome impediment transforms, or upgrades, if you like, to a bout of vituperative swearing. That's why we have all these rages (from road to surf to air). Perhaps the presence of an animate target fuels the tank, so to speak, by turning what might have been a momentary expletive into a full-blown outburst. An abusive assault can achieve two ends for the swearer, a cathartic release as well as a venting of spleen on a chosen target.

If cathartic and abusive swearing are siblings, the third domain of swearing, social swearing, is—using the metaphor of family relations—not even a second cousin. Studies have affirmed what we know intuitively: in relaxed settings where people are comfortable with other in-group members, their language is characterized by a high degree of swearing. Australian linguist Kate Burridge writes, "Generally speaking, the more relaxed a group, the more swearing there is." Social variables such as class and gender impact on this claim. There is less swearing in mixed-gender groups than in single-sex groups of either sex, but there's a definite connection between easygoing and swearing.

These circumstances allow words that would otherwise be deemed nasty expletives to be a token of pleasant wonder or surprise. "Fuck, you sure have brought a lot of beer!" or "Put your shit over there and come and have a drink." (The presence of alcoholic beverages in both these spontaneous examples is probably significant). Swear intensives such as "bloody," "goddamn," "fucking," "a bitch of a," "a helluva," and so forth slip comfortably into relaxed discourse among in-group members, imbuing their language

with color and emotion and contributing to the general ca-
maraderie. This is a classic example of the two macrofunctions of language—the substantive or transactional, and the
interpersonal or relational—working congruently and co-
operatively. Indeed, more often than not in social swearing,
the substantive or transactional message is far less important than the interpersonal one.

As well as dipping into the collective reservoir of swear
words, social swearing has its own peculiarities. One is the
compounding of swear words, such as the alliterative
"bloody beauty," or "fuckin' fantastic," or nonalliterative but
common compounds such as "bloody awesome." There's
also the superlative intensifier that comes in the form of an
infix, where the swear word is inserted within an existing
word: "abso*fucking*lutely," "in*fucking*credible," "fan*bloody*tas-
tic," and "inde*goddam*pendent"; or the no-vowel version that
has appeared as a bumper sticker: "nfknblvbl."

This linguistic phenomenon is also known as the integrated adjective. In fact, a poem of that name by John
O'Grady (aka Nino Culotta) was published in the epony-
mously titled *A Book About Australia,* in which numerous examples of the integrated adjective appear: me-bloody-self,
kanga-bloody-roos, forty-bloody-seven, good e-bloody-
nough. No wonder "bloody" has been called the Great Australian Adjective. The man who brought the work to my
attention wrote, "I read the book because I was considering
emigrating to Australia at the time. It did not discourage
me."

Typically, a social swear word originates as one of the
"bad" words but becomes conventionalized in a recogniz-
ably social form. Using swear words as loose intensifiers

contributes to the easygoing, imprecise nature of informal talk among in-group members, a phenomenon explored by college English professor Connie Eble in a study of the relationship between slang and sociability on university campuses. While such swearing may be directed at others, it is not derogatory; it often takes the same form as abusive swearing but has the opposite function, intending playfulness rather than offense. In sum, this is jokey, cruisy, relaxing talk in which participants oil the wheels of their connection as much by how they talk as by what they talk about.

Social swearing is a great device for flattening the hierarchy. You can even see managers and workers talking like this at social get-togethers. This is not to say that there are no constraints on communication in such gatherings. Everyone involved knows that this is a social event that is hermetically sealed off from other workplace practices. Workers take their cue from managers, never vice versa. When the social event is over, it's back to business as usual, with no seepage or residue.

I have found, when lecturing an audience with whom I am not familiar and feeling uncomfortable about being unable to read their reactions, that the odd low-register word, inserted judiciously in a throwaway line ("bloody" or "hell" do the trick), can palpably soften an audience hitherto corseted in a rigidly tight-lipped, distant formality. At such moments I've sensed a visceral relaxing, an all-around lightening up, and what follows becomes easier for me and easier for them. A definite win-win. Initially, I must have employed this device subconsciously, intuitively. Later, when I noticed how a shift rippled through my audience, how they unbent and became more receptive, I deployed the strategy consciously. I have no doubt that regular speech-givers and comedians employ similar tactics.

Sometimes the truth of an assertion can be tested through looking at its converse. Here we're asserting that social swearing is a group lubricant, an indicator of in-group membership, a barometer of how relaxed a group is. The converse would be to use language to widen the social distance between people, not to narrow or bridge it. We all know the technique of withdrawing warmth or closeness through hyperformality, arguably more powerful than even a verbally abusive joust in its goal of widening social distance. I'm told the Japanese have refined this to a fine art, and their language, being so well endowed with respect markers, enables many subtle manipulations.

I've heard it said that a strategy used in relationship counseling is to get the quarreling pair to back off by having them change the language they conventionally use with each other. Instead of the intimate (albeit bickering) discourse of a married couple, they adopt a more distant and formal way of speaking, such as people might use on first acquaintance. Arguably (and I have no evidence to support the contention), this is intended to break the cycle of verbal bickering. Or maybe it just makes things more pleasant for the therapist.

I'm not sure whether Tom Cruise and Nicole Kidman tried such discourse-switching to save their ten-year union, but Cruise himself is known to use politeness as a barrier. An article in *Time* magazine featured Cruise on the cover, under the heading BEING TOM. The profile of Cruise and his spectacular success in Hollywood included this observation:

What [Cruise] seems to have perfected—on film and in life—is the ability to win you over, to be liked without really being known. He is solicitous. He laughs at your jokes. He is curious without being prying. He looks you in the eye. He even asks your advice . . . yet he can be as distant as he is pleasant, as guarded as he is engaged, *his very politeness a kind of barrier.* . . . Cruise remains someone about whom we have never quite been able to connect the dots. (italics added)

Politeness as a marker of social distance is the converse of swearing as a marker of social solidarity. It's not that Cruise can't do both. He can, as can almost everyone. He's only being judicious about the time, place, company, and circumstance, and in this sense, if few others, swearing is no different from other bits of language.

4

WHERE THE FUCK?

"You want what on the fucking ceiling?"

—MICHELANGELO

In approaching a new dictionary, I use FUCK as a litmus test. First thing I do is leaf my way to the F's, seek out FUCK, and see what they have to say. If the given definition fails to satisfy, if it doesn't align with my pragmatic knowledge of how the word works out there in the world in all sorts of contexts of action, then I put down the dictionary and move on.

After all, I know what FUCK means. You'd have to be hermetically deprived of contact with the real world not to know. So if a dictionary fails to satisfy me on this word, I take it as a cue that it's untrustworthy on any other.

A big leap? Too harsh a generalization? Perhaps, but as a short-order, rough-and-ready litmus test, I can assure you it works. And if you suggest that I plow my way through the dictionary and take a fairer sampling before making a reasoned, statistically driven decision, then my answer will point to the brevity of life and ask that we move on. Depending on my mood at the time, or how far up the irritability index I find myself, I might employ the word in question, to make my point, as it were.

Public discussions about FUCK simmer away on the back burner, bubbling up every now and again with a touch of outrage, less now than before. If anything, the most noteworthy thing about FUCK is its ubiquity. Some attribute its prevalence to the evil forces of loose-moral-dom and place it in the same basket as teen pregnancy, drug use, falling literacy, and gay marriage. Others argue that, given the degree of separation between the word and the act to which it once referred, the word's power has largely washed away.

It would seem that not only has FUCK lost its referential base but, as an intensifier, it no longer intensifies. In other words, nowadays it takes more FUCKs to achieve what one lone FUCK would have achieved ten years ago. But we'll return to these contentions later.

Back to my litmus test. It dates back to a naughty adolescent moment when I looked up the word (genuinely) and found "an act of sexual congress." I was stumped by "congress." At the time, I was studying nineteenth-century European history, the Congress of Vienna, in point of fact. I wondered how the one congress might relate to the other—was that what they did at the end of the day when they'd finished signing documents? I'd gone to the dictionary wide-eyed, trusting, and in need of illumination. I came away wider-eyed and more in need of illumination. A sad moment at a formative stage.

However, not all was lost. The legacy of that fruitless quest is this peculiar litmus test, which the *Oxford English*

Dictionary fails outright. Its entry begins with the date, 1503, and the caveat that a correspondence with the Middle English term "fuken" cannot be demonstrated. We're told it means "copulate" and, used transitively, takes a "with." We're told, too, that until recently, it was a taboo word, spoken rather than written, and a coarse equivalent of "damn." But I put it to you that in instances such as Dennis Hopper's character in *Blue Velvet* saying "You fucking fuck, fuck you," or Paul Lazzaro's famous exhortation in Kurt Vonnegut's *Slaughterhouse-Five* to "Go take a flying fuck at the moon!," the *Oxford* would be of little use.

The *Collins Australian Dictionary* is pretty good. It gives taboo, slang, and offensive tags to various uses, and provides a variety of derivatives, including "give a fuck," "fuck off," "fuck about," "fucker," "fucking," and "fuckwit." Now we've got both feet in the real world and we're talking. The *Collins* also has a nice little gray box headed "Language Note":

> The use and overuse of FUCK in the everyday speech of many people has led, to some extent, to a lessening of its impact as an expletive. However, the word still retains its shock value, although it is less now than it was when the critic Kenneth Tynan caused controversy by saying it on British television in 1965.

We'll come back to Mr. Tynan another time, because it's a great story.

The *Bloomsbury Dictionary of Contemporary Slang* attracts my interest because of its orientation, outlined in its introduction. In it, Tony Thorne says that putting together a dictionary requires one to read a word in its social context: who typically says it, in what circumstances, and with what intention. He's interested in how the word behaves in the language, in its overtones, nuances, associations, and "partly perceived influences affecting . . . sound or meaning." This is music to my ears, and I turn to the F's in great anticipation. There I find over four pages of various permutations of FUCK. The one that distinguishes this list from others is "fuck-a-duck" (exclamation) being defined as "a virtually meaningless expression of surprise or disbelief." And now the disappointment sets in. By "meaningless," I suppose Thorne wishes to indicate that the reference to fucking a duck is unconnected to anything literal or relevant. There is, however, a great deal of nonliteral meaning in "fuck-a-duck"; in its pragmatic function as an indicator of surprise or disbelief.

The *Macquarie Learners Dictionary* treats the user to a feast of grammatical opportunities:

"Oh you've gone and fucked it now!" (finite verb)
"Stop fucking around. We've got to get this job
   done!" (gerund)
"Try not to fuck up this time!" (infinitive)
"Don't fuck with me, mate!" (negative command)
"Get the fuck out of here!" (noun)
"That's fucking ridiculous!" (adverb)
"Fuck! That's a big dog!" (exclamation)

(They do, however, omit the nonstandard but very common conjunctive use: "Mary is beautiful, fuck, she's also stupid.") In this learner's resource, the emphasis is perhaps on the productive use of the word, although one might argue that there's wisdom in people who are new to English spending a year or so in the country before they try FUCK on anyone in a public place. That will have given them time to have been exposed to most of the variables that shape the word's meaning. You're less likely to fuck up with a year's apprenticeship behind you, but even then there are no guarantees.

It's not as if there's a contest among dirty words, with annual prizes and awards, but if CUNT wins credits for power and venom, FUCK is the hands-down winner in terms of morphological flexibility. In a later chapter we will see linguistic historian Geoffery Hughes's eight categories of use and test FUCK's extraordinary flexibility of usage, which Hughes explains as "in an emotional context, normal constraints of usage and grammatical function are relaxed." Such constraints are always in force, even if invisibly and unremarkably, preventing ordinary verbs from morphing uncontrollably into a widening range of grammatical classes and speech act functions.

Take the verb "to walk," for example. It's a regular verb and, as such, has the usual inflections ("walked," "walking"), as well as its infinitive form. It also works as a noun ("a walk"), an agent noun ("a walker"), and a gerund ("walking is healthy"). The present participle ("walking"), unsurprisingly, can function as an adjective ("a walking tour"), and the past participle, again unsurprisingly, can function as a passive form ("I'm all walked out"). There's nothing unexpected about this range of classes and functions, evidence that "walk" has been comfortably corralled into its usual English categories by the constraints that serve to keep a language from departing so far from its own rules as to risk becoming something else.

Swear words, however, seem to grow legs, to move about and fulfill amazing (im)possibilities and edicts, as evidenced in the terms "motherfucker" and "go fuck yourself," both relatively recent developments. The mass media, American culture, globalization, and the spread of English, especially as the language of pop culture, have all played their parts in the dissemination of FUCK and, ultimately, the weakening of its power. I'm told FUCK is used quite liberally by the youth of Nigeria, who picked it up directly from American hip-hop music. But this dilution of force is not peculiar to English. In the same period, for example, the Finnish word *perkele* moved from a high-shock loading (the equivalent of "bloody hell") to a minimal loading, if any at all (the equivalent of "oh boy!").

Hughes's categories, comprehensive though they are, still don't include variations of FUCK such as the incestuous improbability of "motherfucker" or the rather incomprehensible "fuck yourself." Nor do they include any of the seemingly limitless variations on the noun form in position of object:

- a fuckhead, implying stupid or not nice;
- a fucker, implying someone worthy of a wide range of emotions from contempt to pity;
- a fuckwit, an Australian contribution, a comment on a person's lack of brainpower rather than moral character; and
- a fuckup, suggesting a disastrous situation or a person in need of serious psychiatric help.

Angus Kidman offers an alternative and useful categorization of the semantics of FUCK in his *How to Do Things with Four-Letter Words,* in which he differentiates the functions that the use of FUCK can achieve for the user.

One is referential, where FUCK stands for the sexual act or, to return to my childhood dictionary experience, "an act of sexual congress." It is a precise and economical term for which, funnily enough, there is no replacement. "Making love," with its obvious emotional dimension, clearly is not coextensive in meaning; and "having sexual intercourse" is a whole different register. It's also rather odd that, although FUCK has no other exact synonym ("screw" and "bang" come closest), its referential sense is today one of its less frequent uses.

Kidman gives many examples of FUCK used by both males and females to describe sexual acts. Back in 1981, Germaine Greer claimed it was a lewd term used only by males about "acts performed on the passive female." Today it has comfortably entered female discourse, though perhaps not as fully and equally as the male (I discuss this in more detail in "Son of a Bitch").

Today FUCK is known and used more for its emotional meaning. From this perspective, it can achieve multiple functions, including displeasure ("What the fuck is going on here?"), intensification ("It's fucking hot in here!"), and abuse ("You fucker! Don't you fuck with me!"). But what's extraordinary is its migration pattern.

It started out as a taboo word because of its referential function. Then, as the word gravitated over time toward more emotional outlets, it lost its referential meaning. Now the taboo still lurks, though nowhere as strongly as even twenty years ago. There is barely a sexual glimmer of meaning in the word, as it often means something more like "go figure." There's the resigned "Oh fuck it!," the lost "Where the fuck are we?," the perplexed "I know fuck all about it," the suspicious "Who the fuck are you?," and the disbelieving "How the fuck did you manage that?"

What does the *NTC Forbidden American English* say about FUCK? (This, mind you, is a work that specializes in defining the perimeters of various taboo words.) It claims that FUCK is "taboo in all senses," and yet it admits that the word is rarely used referentially, being more commonly used in anger as an intensifier. Confused? In a nutshell, the sex has nearly gone, the emotion remains, and the taboo lingers, albeit unevenly.

Arnold Schwarzenegger once said, "I have a love interest in every one of my films—my gun." It may come as a surprise to a few that there is a long-standing and widespread association between sex and violence. Those who are surprised should consider the overlap in names for weaponry and names for genitals. For example, in Latin, *telum* means "weapon" or "tool" or "penis." Many other languages use their words for daggers and swords as names for the penis. English likens the male organ to instruments used for battering, chopping, and stabbing ("club," "rod," "stick," "shaft," "poker," "pole," "gear stick," "dagger," "sword," "bayonet"); others more specifically liken it to a firearm ("pistol," "cock," "gun," "bazooka"), with ejaculation serving a pretty obvious analogy ("shoot," "bang," "fire," "discharge").

That is not to say the terminology is exclusively violent. There are plenty of colorful expressions, too, such as the

Australianisms "wedding tackle" and, for coitus interruptus, "getting off at Redfern." (The Sydney suburb of Redfern is one station before Central, the end of the line. It would not surprise me to find out that other urban transit systems feature in a similar way.)

The *NTC Forbidden American English* lists "tool" for penis, "toolbag" for scrotum, "tool-check" for a VD appointment, and "toolshed" for vagina. With the last, a note is added: "a jocular match for the 'tool.' Not widely known but easily understood." A further note reminds the reader that women consider it offensive to have the subject of their bodies mocked or treated trivially.

Why include this latter note? Those in the habit of referring to the vagina as a "toolshed" know the pejorative association. They are not very likely to run to the dictionary to check on usage and propriety guidelines prior to, or even after, use. Likewise, no woman within earshot or, worse, directly referred to needs a dictionary to get a handle (sorry) on the user's intention or meaning in the context. All of this leads me to the rather obvious conclusion that the only people who use dictionaries of abusive language, taboos, and dysphemism are people like me—and maybe you, too, dear reader?

The point has been made that there is no other word for FUCK that means FUCK. British writer and politician Wayland Young contends that the supposed alternatives and euphemisms, such as "copulate," "fornicate," "have sexual intercourse," "sleep with," and "make love" are either incorrect or inappropriate. He argues that FUCK clearly and unequivocally says what it means.

Montagu also commends the word's referential function, describing it neatly as "a transitive verb for the most transitive of human actions." And Australian barrister, human rights activist, and self-declared "amateur philologist" Julian Burnside writes, "If only our social masters could reconcile themselves to the idea that sex is a legitimate part of human existence and is here to stay, it may be that *fuck* will eventually be accepted in polite use." However, as long as FUCK is so effective as a general intensifier, despite its increasingly diluted power, it's not likely to move into the drawing room anytime soon.

C. S. Lewis wrote that "[w]e lack a language to comfortably talk about sex." But this is no accident. The whole point of the original taboo was to make it difficult to raise such topics in public, and there's no better way to enforce a taboo than to remove any polite options. Nothing in the cornucopia of sexual slang and vulgar expressions, or the clinical terms reserved for clinical contexts, serves to resource the polite, public venue. In fact, any explicit reference to sexuality forces the selection of terms drawn from the gutter, the nursery, or the anatomy class, each unsatisfactory for the purpose. Hence the healthy supply of evasive terms. Euphemisms come in very handy when nothing else will do, but almost by definition, they're all beating around the bush in comparison to the simple FUCK, which, it's been argued, has the virtues of brevity, sturdiness, adaptability, expressiveness, and comprehensibility.

Research into sexual naming conventions has revealed that couples in intimate relationships create their own situation-specific, context-rich idiom to furnish their intimate talk. They give each other's body parts (and functions) names, even personalities and likes and dislikes. At http://www.mum.org/words.html, the Museum of Menstruation's collection of names that women (and their partners) give to their monthly cycle reinforces this research.

The same jocular use has filled another gap, namely in how couples get around or take advantage of the fact that English lacks a word for a live-with-but-not-married-to partner, other than the bureaucratic "de facto" or "designated spouse equivalent." Some research I did in this area discovered that de facto couples generally evolve their own ways to accommodate the absence of the word. Some terms bubble to the surface and become popular for a while. I was told by an Australian who lived in England circa 1980 of his encounter with the rather cute (at the time) POSSLQ (pronounced "posselkew") for "persons of opposite sex sharing living quarters." Another was "bunkmate," which was young-and-cool in the shared-accommodation sense, and easily interpreted as friendly-casual, ongoing, "but not seriously it."

One Australian woman told me that, after many years with her man, she finally arrived at the line of "This is my bloke, John." Sometimes it was "my fella." Her John, on the other hand, was not quite able to manage the corollary, "my girl" or "my woman." Over time he began to describe himself as "her children's de facto stepfather." These are conscious, studied choices by a caring and considerate couple. So it was a memorable moment when one of the children casually introduced John to his friends as "Mum's bonk."

"Bonk" is itself a recent addition, in British and to a

lesser extent Australian English, to the list of words that mean sexual activity but also have another, violent meaning. It is commonly used as a verb ("to bonk") and also as a noun. A bonk can be both the act of sex and the person with whom the act was shared ("Is he a good bonk?"). "Bonk" started life as a British colloquialism but became more generalized in the English-speaking world when it was gleefully used by tabloid headline writers to describe tennis star Boris Becker's allegedly vigorous sex life. The happy alliterative impact of "Bonking Becker" probably contributed to the word being catapulted off center court more firmly into the language.

Another coinage heard around the same time was the adjective "bonkable," which in theory, at least, could become a noun, "bonkability." Alan Ayto suggests that "bonk" is a metaphoric extension of the word that meant "to hit" (first recorded in 1931), modeled on "bang." Ayto gives numerous examples of "bonk" being used in newspapers between 1975 and 1987. Despite its physically violent etymology, the word (which remains more British than American or Australian) currently does not carry a violent overtone but has a somewhat jocular flavor, is used equally by males and females, and is more common among the cool young than among the thick-waisted mature.

A correspondent of mine looked back on his wild days with some wistfulness:

We didn't always have such a good-humored, affectionate term for the good-humored, affectionate deed. Leaving adolescence and attending university in the years of sexual revolution and counter-culture, it seems we appropriated and to some degree tamed the old four-letter lexicon but it remained at best blunt, coarse or mechanical. "Roots," "screws," "shags," etc. Or there was "making love" (not war), somehow always a little too earnest.

An Australian newspaper columnist has suggested that English tabloids invented "bonk" to cater to the national obsession with those raunchy sex scandals that regularly engulf the rich and famous. He attributes this to the "twitching lace curtain" syndrome—"the insatiable urge to see what them next door is up to, luv." So "bonk" means FUCK but, by being emollient, it serves the purpose of public discourse, from Boris Becker to David Beckham.

5

THE WILD THING

"Heads are going to fucking roll."

—HENRY VIII

To begin our word-by-word, in-depth analysis, we must start with the four-letter word FUCK. This term has had an interesting history, much of which, including its etymology, remains suffused in folk supposition. Though it is a major swear word, its origins are uncertain, having given rise to much speculation and mythologizing.

Getting to the bottom of the etymological mystery is hampered by the fact that, as we'll see with CUNT, taboo terms come with buried or suppressed evidence—just as the word was suppressed, so, too, was information about it. Even lexicographers have been shy about including and discussing FUCK in their lexicons. It is therefore not surprising that many theories exist about the word's origins.

Its most likely etymological roots are in English's Continental partners—the Latin *futuere* (or *pungere* or *battuere*), the French *foutre,* the German *ficken.* All these words follow the pattern of having two contextual meanings: the first, a physically violent one (to beat, bang, hit, or strike); the second, to engage in sexual activity for which a multitude of euphemisms exist. As linguistic historian Geoffery Hughes puts it, "[Although] some people might feel that beating, driving and love-making are quite distinct . . . these are clearly deep metaphorical matters."

For some writers on swearing, including Ashley Montagu, FUCK derives from the blending of the Latin (*fu*) and German (*ck*), "combining the vocalism of the one and the consonantism of the other." Neat, but is it correct? Richard Dooling says that FUCK is related to a widespread Germanic form (Middle Dutch *fokken,* Norwegian *fukka,* and Swiss *focka*), all of which have striking, thrusting, pushing-type meanings.

If etymology were a question of personal preference, we might be able to offer a different, more appealing explanation for those who are uncomfortable with, say, the violent alter ego of many sex taboo terms. They might be happier with the Sanskrit *ukshan* ("bull") or the Cantonese *fook* ("happiness").

Certainly, folk myths regarding the roots of FUCK abound. A common one is that FUCK, along with most of the other dirty words, is Anglo-Saxon in origin. It's an easy but erroneous assumption. Hughes points out that the Anglo-Saxon origins are limited to "shit," "turd," "ass," "bitch," and possibly "fart," showing a particularly scatological emphasis, while "piss" is claimed by Norman French. In the uncertain-origin category, we find FUCK, "CRAP," "CUNT," and "twat."

The erroneous equation of lewd with Anglo-Saxon has

strangely been perpetuated in a number of well-educated circles. In his judgment in the famous 1933 prosecution of Random House for obscenity—for publishing James Joyce's *Ulysses*—Judge John M. Woolsey observed that the so-termed dirty words were well-known "old Saxon words." The judge handing down the verdict in favor of *Lady Chatterley's Lover* in 1959 also referred to "four-letter Anglo-Saxon words." Erving Goffman gave credence to the myth in *Forms of Talk,* where he referred to the "Anglo-Saxon terms for bodily functions."

Another theory is that FUCK is an abbreviation, "for unlawful carnal knowledge," possibly coined by the police. Well, the police have codes for everything. On television they're always getting messages on their car radios—"Robbery in progress," "Officer down"—but each with its own *numerical* code, which makes FUCK as a police abbreviation highly unlikely. But there is more than one version of this theory.

One version suggests that naval commanders in the early nineteenth century were in the habit of abbreviating "for unlawful carnal knowledge" in their logbooks. Many years ago, I was told another version by a teenager older than I was. The gist was that in medieval times, girls found to have been involved in such acts were paraded through the streets, à la scarlet letters, while the town crier sounded a giant bell and slowly enunciated "F-U-C-K," which everyone standing around understood as "found under carnal knowledge." I don't remember questioning the strange use of the preposition "under," nor being stirred to want to know why only the girls, not their partners, were subjected to such treatment. But I was young then, and the information was passed to me in the hush-hush tones that discouraged the seeking of further morsels.

An earlier and more eminent, if not more plausible, theory dates back to a royal edict issued at the time of the Great Plague. Here the letters are taken to stand for "fornicate under command of the king." Geoffery Hughes gives his own evaluation of this by querying "why precisely procreation should ever become a Royal Command performance, and why the injunction should be issued in such arcane form." He goes on to speculate that "Charles II would have been more likely to echo King Lear's ferocious edict: 'Let copulation thrive!'"

In any case, the etymological jury remains out on the subject of FUCK, for which we can thank the centuries of word gestapos, who, by excluding the word from dictionaries, effectively deprived us of the list of citations that would have allowed a more thorough and systematic tracing of the word's history.

FUCK might be popular, but it's not alone as a choice four-letter word. The composition of the Big Six, as they're affectionately called by some, varies depending on which authority you're consulting, but generally includes FUCK, CUNT, COCK (or, if you prefer, DICK), ASS, SHIT, and PISS. They're all one-syllable, four-letter words; all, as we've seen, erroneously believed to be Anglo-Saxon in origin; and all concerned, at least nominally, with bodily functions of the nether regions—the first three sexual, the last three scatological.

If CUNT is generally agreed to be the most powerfully negative, without a doubt, FUCK is the most prolific. According to lexicographer Stuart Berg Flexner, the first widespread use of FUCK as an expletive began in the late 1800s. But it has been since the liberalizing 1960s, most especially, that FUCK has, as it were, taken off. As if to capitalize on this ubiquity, the clothing company FCUK (French Connection United Kingdom) shamelessly exploits the apparent serendipity of their initials to emblazon their brand across as many billboards as possible, contributing to the general anesthetizing effect.

However, FUCK had taken imaginative hold long before the 1960s. Some attribute its proliferation to the military. If the ideals of the French Revolution were spread on the bayonets of Napoleon's soldiers, then it might be said that the worldwide penchant for FUCK was spread by American soldiers on the battlefields of World War II, as evidenced at the very least by Norman Mailer's *The Naked and the Dead*. Ashley Montagu writes that for the American GI, all fouled up and far from home, "it was an incomparable benison to have such an expletive at his command, all the more so since he had very little else." And if the GIs started it, Hollywood and later the Internet continued it.

That the military and swearing go hand in hand is by no means an Anglo-only phenomenon. Finnish writer Ilkka Malmberg comments on the scandal caused by *The Unknown Soldier*, a book that first appeared in Finland in 1954:

> Its naturalism inflamed a nation recovering from the war. One of the book's most troublesome aspects was the soldiers' use of language. The cursing caused a scandal. Our heroes do not swear! Of course they swore, in their dug-outs and their foxholes.

Indeed, so widespread has FUCK become that it is now—at least in its adjectival form, "fucking"—less a swear word than "a statement of quality and color about the noun that is to follow." In his book *Eros Denied,* Wayland Young attributes the following to Australian origin:

"I was walking along on this fucking fine morning, fucking sun shining away, little country fucking lane, and I meets up with this fucking girl. Fucking lovely she was, so we gets into fucking conversation and I takes her over a fucking gate into a fucking field and we had sexual intercourse." One almost feels for the cheery lad: when it comes to the choice of a word to describe or denote the act itself, he is at a loss for one that is congruent with the register and circumstance established.

This old joke captures the same sense:

A man had just been told that his best friend had an affair with his wife. He got drunk that night and in the pub said, "I'll fucking kill the fucker. How dare that fucking bastard have sexual intercourse with my fucking wife?"

As we have already seen, if you look up FUCK in a few modern dictionaries, you'll find it there in all its glory. The *Collins,* the *Chambers,* the *Oxford,* the *Macquarie,* the *American Heritage Dictionary of the English Language,* to name but a few, all include it in many of its various forms. Yet from this array, you derive no sense of the colorful, sometimes volatile history the word has had over the last few hundred years. A hint of it remains, perhaps, in the censoring function achieved by Microsoft's spelling and grammar check. When I misspell "fucking," I'm given the following options: "tucking," "ducking," "bucking," "funking," "tuckering," "fluking." No "fucking."

Excited by the discovery that Microsoft might be indulging in some social engineering, I deliberately misspell CUNT, and yes, the alternative spellings are "cone," "cane," "cave," "cue," "cunje," and "cube." I then can't help myself and proceed to test the hypothesis on PISS, SHIT, and FART:

pies, pips, psi, pins, and pish (the last, coinciden-
    tally, being Yiddish for piss);
shott, shift, shirt, shot, and shut;
forte, fate, fare, farce, and farre.

My flurry of research activity left me wondering: Is this a Bill Gates version of washing out the world's English mouth with soap? (Weirdly, though, Headmaster Gates's spelling checker does not actually highlight any of the Dirty Dozen as misspellings, so they are part of his vocabulary—it is just that their correct spellings are simply not offered when you inadvertently or advertently misspell them?)

Going back five hundred years, we find the verb and noun FUCK, as well as the adjective "fucking" happily and uninhibitedly romping through Scottish poems and folk songs, for example, in this unashamedly raunchy poem by Alexander Scott:

Fairweill with chestetie
Fra [when] wenchis fall to chucking [fondling]
Their followis thingis three
To gar [cause] thame ga in gucking [fooling]
Brasing [embracing], graping [feeling] and plucking
    [pulling about]
Thir [these] foure the suth [truth] to sane [say]?
Enforsis thame to fucking

Montagu speculates, with some tongue-in-cheekery, that it may be Scottish frugality that caused them to opt for the one-word FUCK and eschew less economical euphemisms.

It's hard to know what happened, but by 1575 FUCK had largely ceased to appear in print. The relationship between FUCK and the print medium is no doubt of interest, but what's even more curious is the rather pained and strained history of the relationship between the word and early dictionary makers and their successors.

FUCK first appeared lexicographically in John Florio's Italian-English dictionary, *A Worlde of Wordes* (1598), where it was entered as one of five equivalents of the Italian *fottore*. I'm not going to speculate here on whether the red-blooded Italian connection is relevant to this early appearance. Nevertheless, nearly a hundred years had to pass before the word appeared in its proper alphabetical place in an English dictionary—in Stephen Skinner's *Etymologicon Linguae Anglicanae* (1671). But if things seemed to be settling in nicely, in 1755, Samuel Johnson turned them around by omitting the word from his *Dictionary of the English Language*. Dr. Johnson may be forgiven his prudery, if only for the rejoinder he reputedly offered a lady who congratulated him on omitting improper words from his dictionary: "So have you been looking for them, madam?"

Five years later, Marchant and Gordon followed Johnson's lead when they compiled their strangely titled *A New Complete English Dictionary,* taking "especial care to exclude all those Terms that carry any Indecency in their Meaning, or at least Tendency to corrupt the Minds of Youth." In 1775, John Ash chose to include FUCK in his *A New and Complete Dictionary,* giving several definitions, as well as the description "low" and "vulgar."

In 1785, in the *Classical Dictionary of the Vulgar Tongue,* written by the exceptionally well-named lexicographer Francis Grose, FUCK was included but in the form "f**k." This avoidance strategy was to be aped by many in the future as a way of having their cake and eating it, too—including the word but making it virtually unpronounceable, or rendering the pronunciation so far removed from the short, monosyllabic burst of the pure form that the taboo gets washed out in the process. Where would censors be without the asterisk?

In 1936, Eric Partridge was finally able to overcome what he calls "an instinctive repugnance" when he published his *Dictionary of Slang and Unconventional English,* which included FUCK as "f*ck." The inclusion did not pass without note. There were protests to the police, school authorities, and libraries, and until the late 1960s, the reference book was kept under lock and key and could be looked at only via special application. If what we're measuring here is progress, then note that the word was allowed to appear with only one asterisk. Still not pronounceable but getting closer.

In contrast, the editors of all editions of the *Oxford English Dictionary* issued between 1884 and 1928 declined to have anything to do with vulgarity, asterisks or not. The taboo was still being applied in the Supplement published in 1933. Oxford lifted the ban in the early 1970s, though the listing was still omitted from the *Oxford Etymological Dictionary of the English Language* in 1988.

Webster took a stand on FUCK, though not on the other four-letter words. The omission remains in the 1962 edition of *Webster's New International Dictionary* and was defended on practical rather than lexical or even moral grounds. The dictionary makers were fearful of the adverse economic effect that might result from the predictable outcry. Such commercial implications have been the driving force of decision making across the board.

Random House's *Dictionary of the English Language* (1966) omitted all the so-called four-letter words even while stating in the preface their commitment to including "an exact record" of the language any person sees or reads. The poor besieged editor can't be faulted for trying. Before deciding to omit the words, he met with a group of editorial workers and sales managers. They all agreed that bad words were words and should be included, but the editor noted that no one at the meeting was actually able to use the bad words, and any mention of "bad" words prompted a "shuffling of feet and a wave of embarrassment." On the basis of these attitudes, he arrived at the view that the public was not yet ready for an exact record of the language.

These bannings are more than minimally curious in the light of the fact that FUCK and SHIT are tagged as among the three thousand most frequently used words in English. Significantly, developments in lexicography—particularly the use of computerized data in the compilation of dictionaries—have brought a major change in policy on foul language. Now that dictionary makers can determine precisely the frequency with which words are used, defining has changed to reflect a greater emphasis on currency than on history. The shift comprises both the "now" factor and the spoken factor, and both take precedence over the historical and the written.

The career of BASTARD, over a period of a mere thirteen years, may serve to illustrate the shift from written/historical to spoken/contemporary. In 1982 the *Concise Oxford English Dictionary* provided the primary meaning of "bastard" as "one born out of wedlock." In 1995 the *Longman Dictionary of Contemporary English* gave four meanings. The first, tagged "slang," was "an offensive word for someone, especially a man, who you think is unpleasant." The second, tagged "spoken," was "an insulting or joking word for a man." The third, tagged "British," was "something that causes difficulties or problems"; and the fourth, tagged "old-fashioned," was "someone whose parents were not married when they were born."

Such computerized data and their frequency listings create a dilemma. Should the newly available data be taken to indicate a slide toward linguistic permissiveness? After all, in the same time frame, swimmers have gone from neck-to-knees to one-pieces to bikinis—is linguistic permissiveness nothing more than a verbal corollary of sexual mores? An alternative view is that such data simply furnish lexicographers with statistical grounds on which they can formalize generalizations about language. These general-

izations have always been present but were hitherto un-
available for recording because of earlier attitudes toward
what constituted proper and polite behaviors.

Computerized data is drawn from such a broad sampling that dictionary makers can no longer assert, as they
did freely in the past, that "improper" words were the ef-
fluent of the lowest classes. In 1887 the *Oxford English Dictionary,* for example, included a reference to "bloody" as
a "horrid word" frowned upon by respectable people.
Around the same time, J. S. Farmer and W. E. Henley, in
their seven-volume study *Slang and Its Analogues,* bemoaned
the "wearisome reiteration" with which "bloody" fell
"from the mouths of London roughs," and felt unable to
give the term any meaning, not even "a sanguinary one."

These days we no longer see the shameless elitism that
once permeated dictionaries' descriptions of who says what
to whom. This is not to say that we have lost our biases
against the ways in which others speak, many of which are
grounded in class affiliations. Peter Trudgill famously said
way back when that if you don't like their vowels, it's probably a case of not liking their values, attributing linguistic
prejudices as irremediably classist in nature. Language and
identity are closely linked, and class, gender, ethnicity, and
age are primary sociolinguistic variables that impact on language. This hasn't changed—it's only how we express our
prejudice that has been affected by the politically correct
movement.

If FUCK is pretty well uniformly included in most modern dictionaries (I say "most," as Webster still has a hole between "fuchsia" and "fuddle"), its tags are in no way
uniform. The range is staggering: "taboo," "colloquial,"

"slang," "informal," "coarse," for starters. The *Chambers* is my favorite. It seems to want to cover all the bases and describes FUCK as: "old word, long taboo, all words, meanings still vulgar."

Like the human appendix, which has very little purpose but is apparently a clue to our evolution, this variety of tags may be the only remaining indicator of the colorful history of lexicographers' attitudes toward the inclusion of impropriety in the books they publish. Certainly the time has passed when shock-and-horror reactions were to be expected.

Richard Dooling writes slyly:

> Warning! usu. considered obscene. Do not try to use *fuck* at home. . . . Do not remove this tag! Risk of shock! Do not open or attempt to service this word unit unless you are a qualified linguistic technician. . . . If use of this word persists for more than 48 hours consult your physician!

And just as there are folks who call up dictionary publishers and urge that "cancer" be left out of the next edition, people's attitudes to the presence of FUCK in the formal, hallowed pages of the dictionary provide testimony to the remaining embers of power in the old taboo. But for how much longer? We can predict, perhaps, that its power is on its way out, in large part because of its ubiquity. Not only is its referential meaning largely ignored, its emotive force is nearing exhaustion.

Writer Robert Dessaix suggests that "perhaps the face of public taste has grown numb with slapping." The sense I get from examples like "the fucking fucker just fucking won't fuck" is that four rather tired FUCKs are needed today to achieve a fraction of what one bright-eyed and saucy FUCK might have achieved some time ago.

Before anyone gets too teary, however, we have to concede that FUCK has had a good run. Its only power is in the underlying taboo, and that's not going anywhere. It's re-morphing, changing the way it operates. Over time, FUCK will probably be replaced by something more immediately potent.

The result? Even more FUCK for your buck.

6

A CUNT OF A WORD

"Workers of the world unite! You have nothing to
lose but your fucking chains."

—KARL MARX

The word CUNT has never been innocent, at least not for a good number of centuries.

Of all the four-letter words, CUNT is easily the most offensive. Germaine Greer called it "the worse name anyone can be called." The 1811 edition of the *Dictionary of the Vulgar Tongue* was unashamedly misogynist. It said the word was "a nasty name for a nasty thing." I trust I'll be forgiven for suggesting that there is something refreshingly non-PC about an editor who was able to be totally sexist without feeling the obligation to euphemize or obfuscate.

As with other swear words, tracing the history of CUNT is rendered more difficult than a less problematic word simply because its taboo suppresses evidence of usage. The first instance of the word cited by the *Oxford English Dictionary* is in Middle English, in the name of a London street, Gropecuntlane, dated 1230. You have to wonder who named the street, and why, and what went on there—although you could probably hazard a guess. It's been very logically suggested that, given the public nature of a street name, CUNT at that time may have been a publicly acceptable term. This would seem to fit in with the notion that, prior to the Middle Ages, parts of the body and bodily functions were accepted as commonplace and referred to quite freely. To support this, one might consult Lanfranc's *Science of Chirurgie,* written early in the fifteenth century: "In women the neck of the bladder is short and is made fast to the cunte."

Etymologists are unlikely to come to an agreement about the origins of CUNT anytime soon. One nominated source is the Old English *cwithe* ("a womb"). Another possible candidate is the Anglo-Saxon *-cynd* ("nature or essence"). Both these words seem to have cousins in Old Norse, Old Frisian, and Middle Dutch. Given that these languages are considered offshoots of the much older Proto-Indo-European language, which probably existed four to six thousand years ago, opinion is generally agreed that the various C words all somehow relate to the Icelandic *kunta.* Eric Partridge interprets *ku* as "the quintessential physical femininity . . . [which] . . . partly explains why in India the cow is a sacred animal."

The jury is still out regarding "the likely but problematic link" with the Latin *cunnus* ("vulva"). Some prefer to link CUNT to the Latin *cuneus,* meaning "wedge," which probably supplied the Romance relatives of English with their *con* (French) and *conno* (Italian). These latter, incidentally, while low, are mild compared to their offensive English cousin.

A variant of CUNT, "queynte," considered a deliberate substitution, appears in Chaucer's *The Miller's Tale* and *The Wife of Bath.* Geoffery Hughes takes this to mean that the word had begun to lose its pre–Middle English public acceptance. Shakespeare also avoided the word directly, although it is contained within his many puns. "*Constable*" (*All's Well That Ends Well,* II, ii, 29–34) and "*count*ry matters" (*Hamlet,* III, ii, 116–22) are thinly disguised allusions to the C word that gave rise to many an adolescent snicker in the days when Shakespeare was a compulsory and substantial presence in the school curriculum.

CUNT has been held as obscene from the start of the eighteenth century. Printing it in full was deemed an offense except in the reprinting of old classics. The original edition of the *Oxford English Dictionary* avoided the word altogether, although later supplements included it after the *Penguin English Dictionary*'s first inclusion in 1965. We have to appreciate that lexicographers were themselves subject to the taboos that made swear words too hot to handle.

The word received a great deal of mileage during the scandal surrounding the censorship of D. H. Lawrence's *Lady Chatterley's Lover.* In 1960, Penguin was charged with obscenity in the United Kingdom for attempting to publish the full text. First published privately in Florence in 1928, the book had been available only in an expurgated edition. It's hard to believe, these days, that the book outraged to the extent that it did, necessitating a trial full of overearnest, po-faced academics intent on determining the precise nature of obscenity. Doubtless, though, it brought CUNT to attention in the written word.

Here is the gardener and lover, Mellors, giving Lady Chatterley a lesson in lexicography:

> "What is a cunt?" she said.
> "An' doesn't ter know? Cunt! It's thee down theer, an what I get when i'side the, it's a'as it is, all on't."
> "All on't," she teased. "Cunt! It's like fuck then."
> "Nay, nay! Fuck's only what you do. Animals fuck. But cunt's more than that . . ."

Mellors was neither the first nor the last to have trouble with this most troublesome of words. The particular difficulty he encountered in the quotation above arose because of his attempt to use a taboo word in a denotative or descriptive way. By this I mean he tried to define CUNT as one might, say, "chair" or "physics" or "collective consciousness." It just doesn't work. This is because taboo words—the nuts and bolts, if you like, of the discourse of swearing—are overly invested in connotative or emotional associations rather than descriptive or dictionary meanings. A dictionary will tell you the meaning of such a word and may also indicate that it's an offensive term. But the actual felt quality of connotation can be derived only from the situation or context of use.

Cognitive scientist Timothy Jay draws attention to the difference between descriptive and emotional meanings. He recalls a piece of graffiti he encountered on a bathroom wall: "You are all a bunch of fucking nymphomaniacs." The adjective was circled, and another hand had added, "There ain't no other kind." The second graffitist was deliberately choosing to interpret "fucking" in descriptive, not connotative, terms.

The tension between these two senses or meanings is a rich source of humor that has long been plumbed and exploited by comedians, as in the following joke:

> A middle-aged woman comes back from the gynecologist after her annual checkup and announces to her husband what the doctor had said to her. "He told me I still have firm, uplifted breasts like a twenty-year-old, the blood pressure of a thirty-year-old, and the figure of a forty-year-old." Whereupon the husband replied, "Oh yeah, and what did he have to say about your fifty-year-old cunt?" "Oh," she replied offhandedly, "we didn't have time to talk about you."

Like other taboo words, CUNT is used mostly for intense emotional effect. A woman is no more likely to hear her gynecologist refer to the relevant part of her anatomy as her CUNT than to be asked, "Any burning down there when you go wee-wee?" Contexts or venues come equipped or endowed or constrained with their almost prefabricated scripts, and a large part of being a socialized member of a speech community is knowing when and with whom to use what script. Comedians, of course, often step outside the boundaries, and in giving them permission to break the rules, we are rewarded with the gift of laughter.

An interesting aspect of swearing is what I'd like to term the "numbing" effect. The first time you hear CUNT in a context, there's an element of shock value. This will vary depending on where you are, who you are, what is happening, etc., etc. If the word continues to be used in that context, the shock value wears off. I am told that during the performance of the stage play *The Vagina Monologues,* the audience was asked to chant the word CUNT repeatedly as a desensitizing strategy (although you'd expect that most people who showed up to see a play of this name would do so with some expectations as to what they might hear and therefore be less shockable).

In a similar vein, I was told that some years ago, an artwork by the name of *My Cunt* was being discussed on Australian radio. As you can imagine, it is very hard to talk about an artwork without at some point mentioning its name. However, it's difficult for the listener to sense quotation marks, italics, or capital letters, so the people being interviewed were painfully aware that they might come across acoustically as "my cunt." However, something interesting happened. During the discussion, the word was used so many times—hundreds, in fact—that by the end, the participants were quite inured to its power and effect. CUNT had assumed—through overexposure, if you like—the character and timbre of an ordinary word. In fact, one of the many influential literary figures brought in to testify at the trial on *Lady Chatterley's Lover* remarked that he had found in reading the book that the allegedly obscene words "were being progressively purified as they were used."

One of the readers of an early draft of this manuscript wrote the following comment:

I've read your essay three times now. It occurs to me that each time I've read it, I've felt shocked and uncomfortable at the beginning, reading the word. The first encounter is like a shock to the eyeballs. But by halfway through, its shock value has lessened and by the end, I was reading cunt like any other word.

You, my reader, may be thinking the same thing, now that you've had a few dozen exposures to CUNT. You, too, may have been shocked at the start, though you really can't complain about unexpected trauma (or sue for damages), since, after all, you knew pretty well what you were in for when you bought the book! Still, you're in the best position to pass judgment on my theory of diminishing shock, or the numbing effect.

The taboo of a word must be maintained for the word to have shock value. The more people hear a word, the weaker its taboo and, therefore, its shock value become. We saw, when we discussed FUCK, what happens when overuse so dilutes a word that nearly all its shock power has been bled out of it.

The few linguists who specialize in swearing have identified a correlation between intensity of meaning and flexibility of use. In other words, as a term becomes more highly charged, the grammatical range that it can achieve grows. Geoffery Hughes has done a detailed study of swearing force and flexibility. With great taxonomic precision, he has created eight categories of use to which he has applied the following swear terms—DAMN, FUCK, CUNT, SHIT, FART, PISS, BUGGER, BASTARD, ASS, and ASSHOLE. Without digressing too far away from our central topic, it will be useful to illustrate Hughes's eight categories with reference to FUCK.

The first category is, simply, personal and involves direct address: "you" + swear word = "You fuck!" This is most prevalent in American English. The second category is personal by reference, and here the swearer is referring to something or someone else who may or may not be present—"The fuck!" Variations on this category include exclamatory questions, "What the fuck?" or "Who the fuck?" The third category is called, quite cutely, destination and refers to the swearer's desire for the object of the abuse to be taken or to take themselves somewhere else—"Fuck off!" The fourth category is called cursing and is direct and unambiguous—"Fuck you!"

The fifth category is the use of the word as a "general expletive of anger, annoyance, frustration"—simply, "Fuck!" as in the stubbed-toe circumstance. The sixth is "explicit expletive for anger, annoyance, and frustration"—"Fuck it!" In more circumstances, this would be interchangeable with the fifth category, although it's clear that including the object ("it") brings the matter closer to the here and now of action, and we know that immediacy, at least in swearing, always heightens force. The seventh category is reserved for those words that can be expressed through a phrasal verb: we can quite comfortably FUCK about and PISS about (though, because CUNT is not a verb, we cannot CUNT about).

The eighth and last category relates to the word's "capacity for adjectival extension," primarily through the affix "-ing" (as in "fucking") or "-y" (as in "shitty"). FUCK is unable at the present time to affix the "-y," though this is not to say it never will. (Things change in the land of swearing, as in every other aspect of language. I recall my surprise at first hearing "It sucks.")

CUNT seems to be one important exception to the general rule that links intensity with flexibility. It is the most emotionally laden taboo term of English, and yet it has not moved into a verb category. For example, we can't say, "Cunt off," "Cunt you," "Get cunted," or "Go cunt yourself." Nor is CUNT commonly capable of adjectival status in the sense of describing something as "a cunting X" or "a cunty Y," although an adjectival function can be achieved through the phrase "a cunt of a" as used, for instance, in the title of this discussion.

Despite this slight adjectival foray, CUNT is largely confined to a noun class, and even there, some limitations apply. It can take the plural form, "You bunch of cunts," but this is nowhere near as frequent as the singular. Confined to noun status, CUNT is therefore restricted to Hughes's first two test categories—personal/direct ("You cunt!") and personal by reference ("The cunt!"). It could be that CUNT has retained its level of venom by remaining largely as a noun. In a sense, there's a reflexive relationship between the limitations, grammatically speaking, of CUNT, and the emotional intensity it has retained. Perhaps there's an "I dissipate, therefore I lose venom" principle quietly in operation here.

Again, we can use FUCK to illustrate the point. It would seem that as words jump into new classes and become increasingly commonplace, moving from the taboo category to the slang category, a concomitant process of bleaching out happens. We become inured to them through overexposure. The shock-and-horror reaction is no longer valid. After all, if you hear a word everywhere, in all sorts of situations, it's unlikely to shock anymore, even with those whom competent swearers have always known it's good to draw the line and curb their tongue—the elderly grand-mother, the maiden aunt, and the school principal.

I recently overheard one side of a telephone conversa-tion between two sixteen-year-old girls. I wrote down the side I was able to hear and subsequently reconstructed the other side by interviewing the girl who was in my earshot. B was the voice I could hear:

1A: Did you hear that Rod dumped Kim at the party on Saturday?

2B: Fuck! You're kidding me. Really?

3A: Yeah, that's what I heard.

4B: Oh-my-God. Fuck! Who told you?

5A: Cynthia. She was there.

6B: Fuck! How bad is that! Fuck!

7A: Yeah, Kim's really upset.

8B: Fuck, yeah! Who wouldn't be!

9A: Yeah.

10B: Oh-my-God. Oh-my-God. Fuck. That's so awful.

For B, FUCK serves a few functions. It's an exclamation marker, allowing her to express surprise. It's also a filler—a pause-creating device by which she gives herself a moment to encode her next utterance, without risking the loss of her turn. Its frequency (and virtual interchangeability with "Oh-my-God") turns it into a point of punctuation, a de-vice that signals her turn in the conversation. In Turn 6, it serves to mark the end as well as the start of a turn. Clearly, for these girls, the original meaning of FUCK and its taboo has long been lost. It simply serves now as an in-group marker, a way for them to solidify their individual sense of belonging within their adolescent-girl collective.

Yet CUNT has retained its shock-and-horror capacity. A good test of this is how a word is treated in the media. Most print media still balk at printing CUNT, resorting to the rather quaint convention of asterisk substitution (c★★★). This, many will recall, was how FUCK used to be treated.

In aural contexts, the form is "the C-word," which itself is rather anomalous. The C, of course, stands for CUNT, but its sound is the soft one we associate with S (as in "silly"), while CUNT starts with the hard form of C (as in "cat," "car," "crazy," and "cunnilingus"). This confusion adds a slightly weird flavor to the equation. These days the phrase "the C-word" is sometimes deliberately used to mean something else, while exploiting the intertextuality of the original meaning. For example, a newspaper feature in the Spectrum section of *The Sydney Morning Herald* was called "The C Word," but here the C was for "competition," duly labeled women's "final hurdle."

Women seem to have largely accepted "their" word becoming a term used most often by males, and mostly in all-male company. This gives the term even greater provocative power on the rare occasion when it is used by a woman. In such instances, there's the sense that it's an import sourced directly from a restricted male discourse. It's as if it comes from beyond the feminine and, in so doing, breaks an additional taboo.

Occasionally, there's evidence of women trying to reclaim their word. In such instances, it's not used in anger or hurled as abuse. It's denotatively, descriptively, deliberately

stripped of its emotional connotations. Here, CUNT signi-
fies something of mystery, the quintessential feminine
space that doesn't need to be explained, defended, justified,
or even rendered rational for those who would equate the
feminine with the irrational.

If women can reclaim the word as part of womenspeak,
they can subvert the male-endowed perniciousness of the
word. Some feminists argue that "the way to change some
of the false and undermining messages is to change the usage of the word. . . . Defuse it, and in doing so we subvert
the culture that prescribes negative meanings to words that
don't deserve or need them."

The denotative use of CUNT is part of a broader libera-
tionist-linguistic strategy by which conventional targets of
-ist behaviors (whether sexist, racist, or colonialist, etc.)
seek to neutralize the power of the oppressor's language by
using it liberally themselves. "Queer," for example, once
homophobic, has been taken up by homosexuals of both
sexes and for many of them now replaces "gay" as a preferred word for self-identification (though I am not suggesting that "gay" and "queer" are interchangeable). In the
film *Training Day*, the character played by the black actor
Denzel Washington claims "nigger" as one of "his" words.
He uses the term abusively ("my nigger") on a white
rookie cop who has been assigned as his partner for the day.
The reversal of power manifested in the reversal of the
direction of the abuse is a powerful example of this libera-
tionist strategy.

Some women actively cultivate a use of CUNT that they
hope will shift usage and attitudes, most especially so that
girls don't grow up "believing they possess something dis-

gusting in their bodies and young boys [don't grow up] . . . believing that what they were born from is the most offensive thing they can call another person." Germaine Greer, for example, has sprinkled her conversations and writings with the word since the 1970s. She railed in *The Female Eunuch* against penetration as the definition of sexual intercourse ("foreplay" is only foreplay, as linguist and feminist Dale Spender has famously said, if you're focused on what comes after it). Later, in *The Whole Woman,* Greer spoke out against oppression by the medical patriarchy, which oppresses through poking and probing the patient who has been positioned into passivity. Greer sees a woman's body as "the battlefield where she fights for liberation," and part of that liberation is in the removal of the mystery (read "ignorance") generated by having internal or concealed genitalia.

The way to win this battle is to use the word denotatively and so, over time, defuse its connotative message. We are urged by Australian writer Jen Saunders to "begin to like the word. It's a good word. . . . It doesn't have to describe people you don't like, jobs you hate, cars that won't go. . . . Use it gladly, rather than shamefully." Some women, however, seem not to need any political reframing of the word. Consider this Finnish woman's comments on the Finnish for CUNT:

> *Vittu* is . . . an ancient word, familiar from Finnish folklore [and] the harshest of all our swearwords. . . . It is particularly popular with young people. It punctuates speech like a comma and irritates older people exceedingly. To let a *vittu* out when

speaking with one's own parents would be as if a frog had jumped out of one's mouth, a terrible blunder. A group of derivatives has developed around [the] word. It has been made into a verb meaning "to be annoyed," and an adjective attribute, meaning "un-friendliness." It has been made into countless vivid idioms. The most poetic of them is probably the ex-clamation *vittujen kevät!* ("spring of the cunts!").

This writer goes on to claim that telling the target of your abuse to go ski in a *vittu* "is a Finnish speciality. Not even the Norwegians have that." So there.

However, we're still a long way from a widespread de-notative usage of CUNT by women as part of a larger anti-sexist movement. It remains an extreme term of abuse, carrying the meanings of evil, unfair, devious, and of the lowest nature. We still can't quite get our heads around the fact that so few of men's terms for the vagina are other than nasty (one rare, affectionate one a friend shared with me is "artichoke," with a variation, "Jerusalem artichoke," for the vagina of a Jewish woman). Nor is it any less than troubling that "women still find themselves bereft of vocabulary for their own parts and inhibited by the implications of cunt."

The really interesting question is why a word for female genitalia should have such power. One traditional argu-ment is that female genitalia, being hidden, have connota-tions of cunning (linked to CUNT?) and deviousness. From there, so the argument goes, it's a slippery slope to "bad" and then to "evil." After all, it was Eve who tempted Adam to eat the apple.

The suggestion, while logical, seems to put the cart before the horse, to seek a literal explanation for something that is actually far more symbolic. After all, if it were all about not being seen, the middle ear is also hidden, but few would cast aspersions in its direction, even under heavy provocation.

The notion of the hidden also points to men's fear of women. The suggestion is that, from the Middle Ages through to the nineteenth century and perhaps beyond, men have feared the unknown quality of a woman's sexuality, most specifically her ability to deceive when it comes to conception. The CUNT is the place where deception and betrayal transpire, and this fear goes hand in hand with the twin fears of entrapment through marriage and the loss of a man's property (his wife!) through her infidelity. Taking these two together, the male ego would feel sufficiently threatened to need to deride and denigrate the female quintessence.

Too far-fetched, you think? A simpler, perhaps more plausible explanation is to be found in the locus of power in patriarchal societies. Given that it is held by males, and given that it falls within their capacity to adopt as their most abusive term the word that denotatively refers to the most intimate female place, this is what they have done.

In the spirit of the old joke: Why does a dog lick his balls? Because he can.

7

SHIT HAPPENS

"Where the fuck is all this water coming from?"

—Edward John Smith, captain of the *Titanic*

SHIT happens. We all know this, but let's face it, we'd rather not think about it, and fair enough. Some bodily functions are not to be spoken of in proper company: topics that generate reactions such as "offensive," "revolting," and "disgusting." Shit is something to be avoided, at best, and if avoidance is not an option, then it should be camouflaged discreetly.

But young children, bless them, are fascinated by things that make adults blanch. I recall being at the Boston Children's Museum, which really should be called the Boston Museum for the Age-Irrelevant Curious, when my son was about six years old. We were there all afternoon, and at some point, a visit to the facilities was deemed necessary. This room—the toilet—turned out to be as educational as any other in the museum. A chart was mounted on the wall, and on it was a three-dimensional display of many different animal feces.

Under each cluster of facsimile fecal matter (or "poo")—I remember wondering if they had used the same art materials as the makers of the displays of food outside Japanese restaurants—was a description of, say, squirrel poo or beaver poo. The chart was positioned in such a way that the kid sitting on the toilet could be visually absorbed in it while otherwise, uh, bodily occupied. It created a nice congruence between the two activities. I recall thinking how this approach to poo was able to step outside the conventional taboo and use language that was neither negative nor condemnatory. Without the taboo overlay, the curiosity was nourished and fostered.

Recently, I was told about another chart, used in hospitals with mostly older patients. It also has pictures of feces, but human this time, and only two-dimensional. The purpose of the chart is to allow the patient to describe his or her bowel movements—something I fear the elderly have more occasion to do—without having to find the language to do so (in fact, hardly a word need be uttered). The patient can simply point to the illustration that most closely resembles the bowel movement under discussion. A little like a multiple-choice question. I've been told most people cope quite well with the chart, except for gastroenterologists, who have been known to describe it as disgusting.

Yes, SHIT happens, but it's hard to talk about it, because by the time you're old enough to have the illnesses that take you to the hospital where you'll be faced with a chart like this, you'll be so completely socialized into the taboo that it's almost impossible to discuss bodily functions with equanimity. Having to dwell on the subject by describing color, shape, consistency, etc., may be quite beyond the realm of possibility. Doctors and nurses, of course, have developed a clinical and euphemistic lexicon to facilitate these exchanges ("bowel movement," "stool," "waste product," "pass water," "pass wind"), as well as a paralinguistic demeanor—a wonderful ability not to display shock or disgust—which helps them manage such talk.

Parents typically manage these topics by resorting to baby talk, which couches the items in childish terms, a process that presumably takes the edge off the disgust factor. Cognitive scientist Timothy Jay alludes to this in his joking counterpoint:

Grandmother: Kitty went poo-poos in the litter box.
Four-year-old: Gran, you mean feces, don't you?

The Greek word for SHIT (*skat*) gives us our "scatology." Greek distinguishes between human and animal excrement ("dung"), with *skat* covering the human variety. Many languages—Latin, English, Japanese, and Italian among them—make this same distinction. English uses "scatology" as a formal word for the processes and products of human elimination. At first glance, it may seem unnecessary to have such a word. I mean, it's not one of your two thousand most used, is it? But when you consider that there is no shortage of people with a professional interest in excrement, the need for the term becomes more evident.

Pathologists, regular and forensic, poke around in excrement for diagnostic purposes, as do medical researchers. Paleontologists love the fossilized versions, because they open up (sorry) windows on the past. Psychiatrists are always revisiting the basic bodily functions (remember Freud's "anal phase"?) and have identified particular perversions where excrement and sexuality become overlaid. Consider here the Woody Allen film in which a woman's boyfriend ties her naked to the bed and then defecates on her stomach. Apparently, it is a metaphor for relationship abuse (something that had to be pointed out to me), but whatever the reason, it remains a graphic image long after the final credits have rolled.

Child-care workers know all about defecation because of the number of little accidents that befall the under-fives and because of the (not unconnected) scatological orientation of taboo language in the same age group. And at the other end of the life span, as we have seen earlier, the very basics of body functioning reassume an unwelcome centrality (this time).

Let's not forget the horticulturalists, who have their own specific perspective on animal excreta. This is predicated on a core respect for the nitrogen cycle, by which new vegetable life is forged. It follows that they would use a different term ("manure"), one unhindered by the negativity associated with words like "excreta" or "feces." "Manure" is a much happier word, serving both as a noun (the substance) and a verb ("to manure") for the process of spreading the substance on the land. (The word comes from the Latin *manus* ["hand"] because of the way in which manure was conventionally spread.)

Finally, linguists are into it for something called the semantics of disgust, by which we mean the language conventionally used to express the psychological state of disgust. Disgust, incidentally, is a form of rejection (and there are many forms) based on where the offending object comes from or has been. Because of the associated taboos, disgust items such as excreta and vomit are considered outside the province of normal conversational practice, which is why we have such a rich reservoir of euphemisms (for instance, an upset stomach may have us going to the bathroom) to get us through the odd hairy moment where spillage may inadvertently and reluctantly bring the taboo topic to center stage.

Swearers come from a different place. They approach the scatological terms for disgust items, particularly shit-related, from the opposite direction. They are looking for a dysphemism to express the emotion of the moment—typically anger, frustration, surprise, or some element of being put out. The word SHIT is the verbal equivalent of stamping your foot—when you just miss the bus, when you find a parking ticket under the windshield wiper, when you're stuck behind a slow driver.

SHIT is handy, expressive, monosyllabically quick and easy, and not over-the-top offensive. It's versatile in both solitary and social situations. The latter do need to be calibrated, however, which is why "sh . . . ugar" or "sh . . . oot" sometimes pop out as a substitute. South Africans often say "shame" to express commiseration for misfortune, however petty. I have a hunch that if you did a thorough etymological and pragmatic search, you'd find that their "shame" may well have started life as a redirectioned and suitably calibrated SHIT.

Disgust might feel natural, innate, normal, and universal, but it isn't. It's an acquired response. Children are taught that feces and vomit are disgusting and offensive.

Richard Dooling writes, "Shitting is pure, aimless bliss—until our parents intervene with their own hostile opinions."

The lessons begin at a very early age. Children start getting salient messages from the velocity with which dirty diapers are removed, to the immediacy of the flush, the "Yuck! Don't touch!," the post-toilet washing of "dirty" hands, the fact that they're socially excluded from kindergarten until they're toilet-trained. Heaven help the little ones who soil (any connection to manure?) themselves in elementary school. This is a shame from which it's hard to recover. Timothy Jay asks, with reason, "How could a child not be fascinated with feces when he or she is made well aware of the power of being 'dirty'?"

Early childhood scatological interest also manifests itself in a preoccupation with feces along with food. One American linguistic study looked at speech play in a Boy Scout camp—undoubtedly a golden opportunity to collect instances of peer talk of the boy type. The researchers recorded the boys' inventiveness in their scatological naming habits, in particular their association of food and feces. Gravy on boiled rice became "shit on lice." Instant pudding became "scoots," a term for brown stains in underwear. Conversely, their term for diarrhea was "Hershey squirts." As they grow older, boys add sexuality to their scatology and use both as a resource for swearing.

The fact that disgust is a learned response leads inevitably to the influence of cultural values. Different cultures have distinct and very different beliefs about what constitutes disgusting behavior. In some places, you can with impunity expectorate or evacuate the nasal cavities in public, sometimes aiming your missile from bus window to pavement. In others, you may loudly blow the contents of your nasal cavities into a small square of folded material, which you then return to your pocket or bag and carry around with you all day.

A universal disgust theme is human excreta. However, in some cities' crowded streets, where there are many homeless people, one can become almost inured to the presence of human poo, just as the canine variety lurks with relative impunity around more affluent pavements and mocks local council edicts about owner responsibility. Central to the rejection of excreta is the notion of contamination. "Yuck! Don't touch!" says it all, really. There's a drawing-back, a retreat, a keep-awayness. It's a psychological aversion manifested in an actual physical withdrawal.

It carries from the thing reviled to the words that represent it. The fear of contamination from dirty things becomes the fear of contamination from dirty language. Feces are dirty; therefore, their associated thoughts or words are also dirty—as if exposure to them could contaminate as much as exposure to the thing to which they refer. It's considered ugly or unpleasant, foul, gross, impure, or just plain off. As Kate Burridge says in her highly entertaining *Blooming English,* "poor little words, they can't help it!" So we have "dirty mind," "dirty thoughts," "dirty words," "dirty jokes." "Toilet humor" is the umbrella term, used as much for the stand-up comic's quick line for a surefire laugh as for the character of a lot of children's talk.

It's not that long since little children who uttered so-called dirty words had their mouths washed out with soap, often in a public display, à la Baghdadi public hangings or hand amputations in downtown Riyadh. The setting is important if the message is going to reach a wide audience. It happened once to my son—the mouth-washing-out, not the amputation. More correctly, he was among the forced spectatorship of a mouth-washing-out event at a kindergarten.

When I subsequently complained to the director, both as a parent and as a linguist, she shrugged nonchalantly and said, "It works, that's all that matters." Apparently, the public spectacle of forcible mouth cleansing is followed (for a while) by a diminution in audible foul language. Machiavelli has a lot to answer for. The kindergarten director apparently believed that a biannual mouth-washing, not unlike an annual pest check, would act as an effective deterrent.

It's probably not surprising that, what with all the socializing energies that go into toilet training and learning what's clean, dirty, and appropriate, children emerge from this stage of life with a scatological bent to their talk. It's impressive, too, how quickly they learn about register—choosing your language to suit your audience. Without a doubt, taboo language comes into its own in their peer talk.

In fact, swear words can appear as early as twelve months. In *Why We Curse,* Timothy Jay says that child swearing follows a predictable pattern. The active lexicon grows from three or four words in the first two years of life to about twenty by the end of preschool. Growth continues until it reaches about thirty words at preadolescence. During the teen years, cursing rates peak, especially in boys. What happens afterward tends to follow socioeconomic lines. The adult cursing lexicon ranges from twenty to sixty words used publicly, not necessarily all on the same occasion.

The very young child, not unlike some stand-up comics, thinks it's funny to use words such as "pee-pee" or "poo-poo" for bodily functions or sexual organs. Scatology will remain a major source of swear words ("butt," "asshole," "piss"). However, when they start mixing with others, children become aware of differences among themselves, and they supplant their earlier "poo-poo" with offensive labels such as "four eyes," "fatso," or "retarded." It can make you wonder which kind you prefer.

Offensive labeling, often with a scatological bent ("butt-face") is an effective weapon in the race for popularity and dominance. Name-calling is a tactic in the construction of in-group and out-group membership, effectively creating solidarity among the in-group and ostracism for the out-group. To my lasting shame, I remember being, at about fourteen, part of the clique that used the label "bella" (I've no idea how we knew it meant "beautiful") to mock and alienate a class member whose crime was being overly tall, greasy-haired, sullen, and flat-chested. There are probably few more sadistic agents of torment than a gang of pubertal girls.

Parents like to blame their child's foul language on bad influences in the child's peer group. It's a fairly sure bet that the parents of those bad influences are probably at home identifying your child as the bad influence. The fact is that kids swear because they copy the modeled behaviors around them, usually in the home. You stub a toe, you swear. Your child overhears and learns how to react in similar circumstances. It doesn't matter what the phrase is, it becomes the language associated with the emotion of anger or frustration.

The doyen of scatological swear words is of course SHIT, perhaps because it's been around for such a long time. A very early sighting ("shit-breech") showed up around 1202, followed by "shit worde" in about 1250. Over a hundred years later, we find "shitten" (1386), then, two centuries on, "shit-fire" (1508). Another century on and "shitabed" is used (1690), and in 1769 the rather quaint "shit-sack" is defined as "a dastardly fellow."

The lexicographer Eric Partridge lists over sixty word combinations involving SHIT, from the archaic to the current. Indeed, SHIT has shown itself to be a particularly generative word, with new coinings arising all the time. Take, for instance, "shitcan," which started out as U.S. Army slang for trash can. It continues this meaning but has since acquired a verb form with the meaning of "to discard in a speedy and permanent way."

From a structural point of view, SHIT is conjugated along the lines of "sit," so its past tense is "shat." The base adjective is "shitty," and there are also compounds such as "shithouse" that work adjectivally. The noun is singular mostly when the word is used alone as an expletive ("Shit!") and usually works without a preceding determiner ("a," "the," "some," etc.)—"Shit happens." There are exceptions—"the shit hits the fan," and the determiner is usually present when it's used as a plural noun—"get the shits with," which in Australia is a rough equivalent of "get pissed off at." As a verb, it can work alone ("he shits me") or join forces with others to create particular meanings, as in "shit-stir," for making trouble.

The semantics depend on context, and although SHIT is a four-letter word, its meaning is by no means exclusively negative. "Holy shit!" (or "Shit, eh?" in Australia) is a common marker of surprise, a more extreme and perhaps somewhat eccentric version being "Shit a brick!" SHIT can be added to an adjective to intensify its meaning ("shit-scared"), but here it isn't really functioning as a swear word. When used as an intensifier, SHIT can have positive associations: A "shit-hot party" means one not to be missed. The Australian "shit-hot" can be reduced simply to SHIT, or in the United States, "that was the shit."

In a study of American college students' casual talk, Connie Eble argues that a major function of this talk is to cement group identity, part of which is achieved by opposing authority. Discussing the fact that the same word can have either a positive or a negative meaning, she cites SHIT as a prime example, contrasting "I have all this shit to do for my English class" with "I know my shit for that class" and the even more positive "Michael's new BMW is the shit." In a similar way, the verb "bitch" is mostly negative, but the adjectival form can be positive ("a bitchin' chick" is a serious commendation) or negative ("what a bitchin' exam!"). We've seen comparable trends in teenage slang: for example, "sick" for excellent.

Foul-language researchers each seem to have a preferred swear word. Richard Dooling's hands-down winner is SHIT. "It's 'shit's double-charge that makes it such a friendly epithet. If 'fuck' is a warlike word, if it sounds like two stags banging antlers, then 'shit' is a happy and comradely word. Saying 'shit' forces the lips into a grin. . . . It's a buddy word, you say it to somebody . . . who has their shit together."

However, SHIT most frequently carries a negative association even if it's merely mild exasperation ("Oh shit") when things don't go exactly the way you would have liked. Various combinations such as the adjectival compounds "shit-ass" and "shitface" allow a more expressive vent. An abundance of nouns provides a bank of nasty things to call people: "shit-head," "shit-for-brains," "shit-kicker." We have verb-based catchphrases ("shit on your own doorstep") as well as whole-clause expressions ("they think their shit doesn't stink," "shit or get off the pot"). The rhetorical question "Do bears shit in the woods?" serves as a long-winded alternative to "yes." There's also "'Shit!' said the king," which is a shortened version of the more elaborate "and all his loyal subjects strained in unison" or "and ten thousand loyal subjects shat."

Shortened versions of prefabricated utterances, such as "you can lead a horse to water" (but you can't make him drink) and "up shit creek" (in a canoe without a paddle) build solidarity because they rely on assumed inferences for their meaning, and shared assumptions can make people feel like chums.

But wait, there's more. You can "get the shits," "give someone the shits," or "have the shits with" someone. You can be "shit out of luck," "not worth a pinch of shit," or find yourself "in deep shit." You can "know your shit," "get your shit together," or, either way, "not give a shit." There are "lucky," "dumb," "crazy," and "sweet" shits; "heavy," "deep," or "nasty" shit; "bull," "horse," and "chicken" shit. You can be "hot shit," "in the shitter," or "in the shithouse." Oh, and before I forget, you can also "throw," "sling," "catch," or "cop" shit.

The drug connection has always been very shit-generative: You can "smoke," "buy," "sell," "lose," or "find" shit. You can be philosophical and shrug and comfort yourself with "shit happens." Or you can be much less forgiving and curse your enemy with "eat shit and die."

Different varieties of English develop their own preferences when it comes to foul words, as they do for everything else in language. For example, though in Australia, you hear both "bonk" and "bang," the former is undeniably British in origin, while the latter is American. I suspect, too, that SHIT is American in origin, especially phrases like "holy shit," though it has traveled far and wide. I was tempted to do a cross-dictionary comparison (British, American, and Australian) for the number of "shitty" words, but the selection criteria for dictionaries vary so widely that any tally would have questionable validity. Suffice to say, for those who believe SHIT is a predominantly American favorite, *The Macquarie Dictionary of Australian Colloquialisms* cites twenty-four entries for SHIT and nine for compounds involving SHIT. Of the thirty-three entries, only one ("shit out of luck") is flagged as American in origin.

A classic Australianism is "deadshit," which, when I was growing up, was the word you'd use for the kind of nice boy your mother would prefer you to date. Another is "shitless": an intensifying adverb that attaches itself after a negative adjective—"scared shitless," "bored shitless"—to great graphic effect, but doesn't work with positive adjectives: you can't be "happy shitless" or "rich shitless." This in itself raises the philosophical question, for which we don't have the contemplative time, of why the state of being sans SHIT is associated with negative experience, unless it's an allusion to the humiliation of soiling, a childhood legacy that never goes away.

Many of these terms have more than one function. Take "bullshit," for instance. It can have a referentially vague meaning, rather like "shit" as in "They're teaching us a whole lot of bullshit in this course"; or it can be used in an exclamatory way, "Bullshit!," where it works syntactically as a rejoinder to a preceding remark. It functions as a denial of a truth being proposed. A: "I put the check in the mail yesterday." B: "Bullshit!"

As for the etymology of "bullshit"—it remains a mystery. Most people make an automatic bovine connection (something about bulls must suggest this), but some link it to "boule," which itself offers connections to notions as disparate as balls, legislative councils, decorative woodwork, and white bread. Take your pick.

SHIT has some scatological cousins—terms that have an associated meaning but omit the "shit" reference. The best-known is "brownnose" (both as a noun and adjective), for a yes-man or what Hughes calls a "toadying parasite." British and Australian English cut to the source of the shit with "arse-creeper" and "arse-licker"; American English uses "ass-kisser" and "ass-wipe."

If horticulturalists like to spread it, and paleontologists like to date it (in time, not out on the town), and forensic pathologists like to look at it under a microscope, linguists have their own foibles to indulge. Typically, they will collect a database of authentic occurrences of the word, having taken precautions not to influence (or contaminate) the incidence by the presence of either a researcher or any recording device. Then, working with identified contextual factors such as where, when, what, and who, they strive to classify the uses and functions of the word. Those with a particularly taxonomic bent will work toward some spectacular display of their findings. When they've achieved this, they are usually satisfied that they have come to understand the pragmatics of the word—how it works in its contexts of use. If the linguist is also a lexicographer, then this information will help to flesh out the various senses or definitions provided in dictionaries.

Angus Kidman collected a database of "shitty" utterances and emerged with three distinct senses for the word. He classified these into "shit (referential)," "shit! (expletive)," and "shit (stuff)."

The first category is where SHIT conveys the sense of "feces," with the only distinction being one of register or suitability to social situation. (Competent language users know that the use of SHIT is more appropriate in a pub than in a bank.) We might say that the words "shit" and "feces" are semantically similar but pragmatically distinct, in that the social context determines whether the technical term ("feces," "excrement"), the euphemism ("waste"), or the taboo ("shit") is used. These are different ways of depicting the same circumstance.

While the referential use of SHIT is a low-register version of "feces," this is probably its least frequent usage. SHIT really comes into its own when deployed to convey emotion. Indeed, as the word became conventionalized and formulaic, which is what happens to words on the way to expletive-dom, the literal meaning is shed and a metaphorical one substituted. For example, remarking that the university lecturer "bores me shitless" will cause none of your listeners to infer that you are suffering from constipation.

SHIT lends itself more readily to metaphoric usage and wordplay than FUCK. Kidman has an interesting theory for this: "Metaphorical uses need a common ground for the metaphor to succeed." He suggests that "'fucking' is a highly personal experience which is not universally accessible, while 'shitting' is (presumably) much the same experience for everyone, and a necessary part of continued existence."

The second of Kidman's categories is the expletive SHIT! Linguists generally agree that the word serves a cathartic function in expressing a range of emotions from irritation to annoyance, frustration, anger, disappointment, surprise, disgust, or dismay. Academic linguists Keith Allan and Kate Burridge include anguish, though personally I would be looking for something stronger for any of my own anguishes.

Language instructors who are brave enough to try teaching swear words to students of English as a second or foreign language might be tempted to place SHIT! on a sloping incline, perhaps with FUCK! farther up the incline and DAMN! some distance below it. Such an approach aims to convey diagrammatically the relative intensity of various expletives but ignores the fact that particular swear words may have comparable intensities but be used in different circumstances. In addition, we have to bear in mind that one person's "goddammit" is another's "fuck it!," and it would be an interesting piece of research to investigate the degree of correlation between biographical variables such as religious upbringing and swearing preferences.

When teaching foreign students, I used to find it much simpler, if perhaps somewhat cowardly, to lump together such terms in one group (conventionally called "bad" or "foul" language) and recommend their judicious avoidance. It's good advice, since native speakers tend to have an adverse reaction to foreigners swearing with an accent in the target language. Because it's difficult to feel the intensity of a swear word in a language not your own, foreign speakers' errors seem, more often than not, to err on the side of overintensity. Which is why, all things considered, avoidance might be the safest path.

You have to admire the versatility of SHIT! as an expletive. You can use it when:

> you accidentally spill a drink ("Oh shit! sorry");
> you're in pain ("Shit! that really hurt!");
> you suddenly encounter a beautiful sunset ("Shit! that's so beautiful");
> you dial the wrong number ("Shit! stupid me");
> you're dismayed ("Shit! that's awful news");
> you're shocked ("Shit! you're kidding, right?");
> you're regretful ("Shit! I wish it were different"); or,
> to use one of Kidman's authentic examples,
> when you're on the point of an orgasm ("He shouted, 'Holy shit, oh my God, I'm coming'").

How can it be that a language as rich as English allows its users to employ the same expletive to cover such a range of diverse circumstances? Kidman tries to solve this puzzle by suggesting that all these scenarios are underpinned by a core element of the unexpected happening at the moment of utterance. Clearly, the man on the brink of ejaculation can't be too surprised that it happened, only at its precise timing, if it was somewhat sooner than he anticipated. It's handy that SHIT! is monosyllabic, perfectly suited for such an instantaneous reaction, but it's not alone in this. And while SHIT! serves mostly to convey a negative tone, it is by no means limited to this, as the sunset and the orgasm demonstrate.

Why do we tolerate the spoken expletive "shit" far more than we do the printed version? Perhaps because the spoken expletive is a spontaneous outburst, more an involuntary reflex, and therefore its sudden appearance may well be forgivable. Then there's the fact that, like other four-letter expletives, it's ephemeral, gone the moment it's uttered, almost not worth making a fuss about. Recalling that Mark Twain is reputed to have said that Wagner's music "is better than it sounds," Richard Dooling claims that the written "shit" means much, much more than the spoken form, presumably because it has lost these spontaneous, involuntary, and ephemeral qualities.

Kidman calls his third, very large category of SHIT uses "shit (stuff)." If we thought that the expletive "shit!" served many masters, so elusive and diluted is the meaning of SHIT in this category that, as the denotation "stuff" suggests, its most basic core meaning is simply that of a nominal. In other words, it is not much more than a *name* of something, a stand-in for another noun, a kind of pronoun.

"What's all your shit doing here?," "I'm too old for this

kind of shit," "I don't want to hear any more shit"—in each of these cases, SHIT refers loosely to something familiar to both speaker and hearer. The thing it represents is either there, in front of them, in the here and now, or it's present in their shared understanding, their previous conversations, what they know about each other through some degree of blended biographies. Either way, it doesn't need spelling out. One reason you don't use SHIT in the "stuff" sense with total strangers is that they might not be able to infer what the SHIT refers to in the way a friend, acquaintance, or intimate could.

And if you're trying to connect the SHIT of "stuff" with the SHIT of "referential," the link may be that referential SHIT is waste—something the body has finished with, what's left over and (composting aside) serves no use. In the two prototypical utterances "There's shit [feces] on the pavement" and "Your shit [possessions] is all over my living room," we can drill down to a common core. Both identify a useless thing as being present, and express a wish for it to be made absent.

Kidman's tripartite division of how SHIT works is only one of the ways, albeit a neat and easily digestible one, in which SHIT has been carved up, so to speak, by linguists interested in foul language. David Crystal comes at it from a slightly different angle. First, he separates positively associated uses of SHIT (such as the general emotive responses of wonder, sympathy, or embarrassment) and SHIT as referential within slang usage (where SHIT stands for, say, cannabis) from negatively associated uses. In the latter category, he offers:

personal abuse ("you shitface")
dirty activities ("the shit work")
negation ("ain't got shit")
trouble ("go through shit")
fear ("shit-scared")
deception ("don't shit me")
nastiness ("a shitty thing to say")
rubbish ("load of shit")

Once again, the word is serving a multitude of masters. In addition, the euphemisms that can replace SHIT ("sugar," "shoot," "shucks," etc.) serve both the general positive use and the negative ones. If ever we needed an example of how meaning is achieved through particular circumstance, SHIT is it.

SHIT happens, we've said, and it can be pretty disgusting. You might think that disgust is disgust is disgust, but people who study these things have shown that it's more complicated than that. For example, Allan and Burridge asked a large number of students and university staff to provide revoltingness ratings for body products, by which I mean things that the body produces (pus, snot, urine, etc.). The body products or, to employ the more mellifluous euphemism, "effluvia" were to be rated on a five-point revoltingness scale from "very revolting" down to "not revolting," with a central value of "revolting (R)." The researchers conceded that revoltingness ratings vary from society to society, but the notion of effluvia as a taboo topic is almost universal.

The highest scores went to shit and vomit, for which 84 percent of respondents gave a revoltingness rating greater than R. Fast on their heels were menstrual blood (80 percent rating for men, 47 percent women), belched breath (78 percent), snot and farts (70 percent), pus (67 percent), sperm and urine (58 percent), and spit (50 percent). Items rated as not revolting were, from least to most innocuous: nail parings, non-belched breath, blood from a wound, hair clippings, breast milk, and tears. Apparently, tears scored least in the revoltingness stakes because they are not waste products, do not stain, and the flow does not (usually) lead to death.

Revoltingness is inextricably linked to taboo, which in turn is governed by the twin concerns of procreation (and its concomitant protectiveness about genealogy) and waste contamination. Taboo, in terms of mentionability of body parts and effluvia, is also more stringent for men than for women, as demonstrated by the fact that menstrual blood and words for "vagina" are more revolting/taboo than semen and "penis." The fact that urine is rated much lower than shit is also borne out by cultural habits—in a public restroom, men don't need privacy to urinate, but they do retire, one hopes, to a closed place to defecate. Even toddlers know that poo is more serious than pee.

These revoltingness responses are not fixed in concrete. Attitudes to breast milk vary depending on whether we're talking about the milk as nourishment for the infant or the leakage that stains clothes. It also depends, as does all effluvia, on whose body it originates from and your connection with that person. The wet nurse is no longer common in Western societies, but in neonatal wards, where mothers of premature babies often experience lactation difficulties, excess milk from other mothers can be used, and revoltingness does not even enter into the picture. Perhaps it's a woman thing.

Your state of mind, and hence your response to effluvia as revolting, also depends partly on your circumstances. You won't be revolted by a blood transfusion if your life depends on it. If the semen or sweat is from an intimate, it may be welcomed or its repulsiveness tempered. If the shit or vomit is from a child or a sick person, it is tolerated differently—though taxi drivers have a blanket dread of the stuff.

A cousin to revoltingness is the Mentionability Index, or what people are comfortable talking about. This is mediated by the contextual variables of whom you're talking to, where the conversation occurs, and to what purpose. It's no accident that genitalia are euphemized as "private parts," but it's a function of context as to which term is actually used. In general, formal or technical terms are more mentionable, so "feces" rates higher than "shit," and "semen" higher than "come."

So, SHIT not only happens, it happens when you say "shit happens" in the wrong place. As Kate Burridge says:

Never doubt the potency of dirt in language. . . . As with most things forbidden, dirty words have a special fascination. What is taboo is revolting, untouchable, filthy, unmentionable, dangerous, disturbing, thrilling—but above all powerful.

8

IN THE NAME OF GOD

"Any fucking idiot could understand that."
—ALBERT EINSTEIN

An old dictum tells us that cleanliness is next to godliness. We've gone along with this belief for centuries—encouraged by the odd plague or two—and aren't about to change now. On the contrary, if clean gets you close to God, we in the Western world using hospital-strength Lysol must be up close and personal. Ecclesiastical power might have waned, but we continue to overpay our tacit dues to the clean-godly equation. Indulge me as I explore this connection a little, because as you'll see, it opens a door on the connection between swearing and religion.

Let's start with our obsession with clean. Our homes—especially their countertops and toilet seats—have never been so clean, our skin so squeaky. Who among us hasn't used industrial-strength germ fighters? So over-the-top are we in our dread of bacteria and contamination that we spend billions annually on unnecessarily thorough cleaning agents that are as ecologically unsound as they are, presumably, psychologically reassuring. Closer to the body proper, we invest comparable amounts on products to clean, wash, condition, moisturize, tone, deodorize, sanitize, soak, and camouflage—the list truly is almost endless. God help us if we ever smell less like honey, mint, lavender, or aloe vera and start to smell like, um, ourselves. If indeed we can remember what we once smelled like.

I won't pry into the ins and outs of our obsessive psychological drives; that's well beyond the parameters of our topic. Instead, let's make our point of departure the fact that cleanliness today is so built into the fabric of our lives that we rarely question it. Children of various ages often need some additional encouragement to get into the bath, but bear in mind that they're not yet fully socialized. By late adolescence, we may begin to have hope for them; and by the time they're off our hands, they'll be as clean-livin' and lovin' as we could wish for. Indeed, the ultimate measure of maturity and right-to-vote entitlement may one day be more in the nature of a sniff test than an actual coming-of-age.

We're expected to be pristinely clean of body when we have contact with the world, particularly with the religious world as contained in a church or temple or mosque. And not just our physical selves but also our apparel. We dress differently—more conservatively, properly, respectfully. We assume that our outer selves will represent us, stand for the regard that we want to display. It wasn't so long ago that people's Sunday best came out of the wardrobe only for wearing to church (Saturday or Friday best for those with alternative Sabbaths). Moslems wash before entering a

mosque and leave their shoes outside as acts of religious respect. Jews are enjoined to wash their hands ritually before
breaking bread, and even those who are generally non-
observant will participate in this ritual hand washing before
joining in the meal known as the Pesach seder.

Cleanliness of body has most to do with the borderlines
between our body and the outside world. This includes
everything that leaves the body at different sites and in different ways—things that are private, secret, and a potential
source of shame. To participate fully as social beings, we're
expected to keep all bodily functions to ourselves, in the
backstage of our lives. They're not to be seen, heard,
smelled, touched, or talked about. Failure to abide by these
expectations suggests the antisocial, even the disturbed.
When someone is falling apart, one of the first things to go
is personal hygiene.

An old joke asserts that Frenchmen don't wash their
hands after they urinate but *before*. They wash before because they are going to handle something sacred, and of
course they don't wash afterward because it would be profane to imagine that something sacred was dirty. The male
friend who shared this joke with me assured me that in
truth there is no logical reason why men should wash their
hands after urination. According to him, the familiar little
ritual indicates either that they do not understand the very
different hygiene consequences of urinating versus defe-
cating or, as is more likely, they are acting on a subconscious belief, perhaps acquired in early childhood, that
handling your penis is a dirty deed. The cleanliness-
godliness doctrine must surely contribute to the compulsive vigor with which (some) men wash their hands after

simply urinating. That's his view. Moi? I'd just like them to keep on washing, thanks very much—before is optional, after's a must.

When it comes to religion, clean of body is matched with clean of soul. The spiritual equivalent of dirt or bodily effluvia is sin, or any act that brings one into conflict with certain cardinal moral precepts. Living our lives according to preset rules or moral principles—or, for the more secular, by one's conscience or according to the rule of law—are ways by which we keep clean on the inside. These constraints keep us well scrubbed internally; our souls as squeaky clean as our soles. If you get dirty, you can always clean yourself up. To this end, different religions have different ways of offering absolution and scouring away those grubby marks of sin.

Just as we pay our respect to the house of God in our attire and demeanor, so, too, do we honor it linguistically. The Arabic of the Koran is not the same language spoken domestically or commercially. Ultra-devout Israeli Jews distinguish between the Hebrew of prayer book and religious service, and the daily vernacular they use for other mundane purposes, if they use Hebrew at all. The Latin of the Roman service marks the venue and occasion as different and worthy of particular reverence. Even the language of Protestant services, which insist on a common understanding by the congregation, is of an archaic register and thus marked as different. New translations of religious texts, which are generally more ordinary, accessible, and user-friendly to the average worshipper, tend to provoke strong negative reactions from those who wish to conserve the sacrosanctity of apartness.

Over time, the special language associated with a particular place, such as a house of God, will develop its own mystique, the more so if it is intermeshed with power and privilege. Throw in a bit of awe, fear, or dread, and the mystique increases accordingly. A more cynical interpretation would see the chicken and egg differently and argue that these special languages are intended from the very outset to create the mystique that in turn creates a suitably religious awe, for in the wake of awe come obedience and conformity. After all, even magicians and shamans indulge in a certain amount of mumbo jumbo to render an audience suitably receptive to the performance.

People come to the language associated with religion with strong views about what is good and bad, hygienic and unhygienic, right and wrong. Reactions to the violation of the good, the hygienic, and the right tend to be remarkably similar. There's a particular, near-universal facial expression denoting disapproval or disgust, and it's as handy for displays of immodesty, dishevelment, and immorality as it is for so-called bad language. You could put the expression on in the morning, and it would cover you for any mishaps in the disgust department that you might encounter during the next twelve hours or so.

Folk-linguistic notions exist about swearing much as they do about other aspects of language. And probably for the same reason—because they appear to make some sense of what otherwise might seem senseless. One such notion is that bad language is generally unruly, rather like the speaker. If someone is violent and overemotional, it's easy to leap to the conclusion that his language will also be out of control. Emotional mood is being made to equate with linguistic system or order. I call this a folk-linguistic view because, despite an appealing surface logic, it doesn't stand up.

Swear words have their own rules, and competent swearers abide by these rules, even without knowing that is what they are doing, in much the same way as we abide by grammar rules without necessarily knowing that we do, or even what the rules are. Such rules for swear words can be syntactic (like what goes with what), lexical (such as the possibilities and limitations of the word "fucking"), grammatical (such as the fact that while both DAMN and HELL are expletives, both roughly appropriate at the stubbing of the toe, you can't substitute DAMN for HELL to make "bloody damn" or "go to damn"), and pragmatic or context-driven (for example, DAMN and HELL may have an approximately equivalent taboo-loading, but they are not fully interchangeable).

The invisibility and complexity of the rules that govern swearing are evident from Deborah Hill's research into the contextual constraints that need to be considered over and beyond taboo-loading. Working with a database of Australian English drawn from contemporary Australian drama (it's much easier to research words written down, as in a script, than it is to catch the spoken data, which are so much more ephemeral and unpredictable), Hill focused on three seemingly interchangeable "imprecatory interjections"—"goodness knows," "God knows," and "Christ knows"—in an effort to identify the underlying rules. She made two findings. The first was that "goodness knows," "God knows," and "Christ knows" reflect an ascending order of emotional intensity.

The second was that the different interjections carry

particular attitudes. "Goodness knows" tends to be used when the speaker does know something, or at least may have an idea of what it may be. Hill's example is: "They're always crying out for what they haven't got, which isn't much, I can tell you. Goodness knows they've got enough toys to keep them out of mischief."

"God knows" and "Christ knows" are similar expressions, and both suggest that the speaker doesn't know. However, "God knows" differs from "Christ knows" in suggesting that it wouldn't make any difference if the speaker did know, while "Christ knows" suggests that the speaker believes things would be different if he did know. Her examples are:

A: How did the press find out?
B: God knows. It doesn't matter now anyway.

A: We said goodbye at Central. I told her I'd always love her.
B: Was it true?
A: Christ knows. . . . Next time we met, we sat in a car in French's Forest for hours, while she begged me to let her be my mistress.

Hill concludes that while there is some interchangeability among the three interjections, any of which can be substituted by the much milder "Who knows?," the nuances of meaning change depending on which one is chosen. Further, these nuances are not accidental but are systematic and orderly, deliberately deployed by speakers and understood by hearers.

But back to the taboo. It would be fascinating to know whether those raised within a Christian culture are more likely to swear using profanities or blasphemies than those raised outside the culture. Being an insider might give a Christian-raised swearer a more meaningful taboo to break. Conversely, the non-Christian swearer may be less inhibited about using "Christ knows," in the same way as people swearing in a language that is not their first language usually fail to feel the words' intensity or taboo-loading. Research in this area has tended to focus on receptive rather than productive tendencies—that is, offendedness (the individual's capacity to take offense) rather than offensiveness (the word's capacity to cause offense)—and has confirmed that religious background is a highly likely correlate of offendedness. No surprises there.

Apropos offendedness, Robert Dessaix writes that he is still affronted by the use of one or two religious expletives, particularly when they're used by people who aren't Christian. "I suppose I sense an added layer of contempt for the culture in which I was brought up. I'd be less offended . . . if a vicar cried 'Jesus' as he fell over the cat, than if a rabbi or imam did."

A few centuries ago, church power was more real than symbolic. Until the Reformation started the process of denting the power, influence, and prestige of the Catholic church, all things religious had obligingly provided swearers with a fertile reservoir of taboo language.

Studies of the history of swearing tend to identify the church-dominated Middle Ages as the time when swearing was most frowned upon. But, as is the way with many prohibitions, what is openly banned tends also to flourish, albeit covertly or obliquely. By the end of the thirteenth century, swearing in England and France had become so pervasive a pastime that church authorities were seriously put out.

Ecclesiastical distress was evident in the mid-fourteenth-century English translation, by the monk Dan Michael, of a French work written in 1279. The work went by the rather odd name of *The Again-Biting of the Inner Wit, or The Remorse of Conscience,* which may say more about the limits of translation than about its content. Its title notwithstanding, the work made it very clear, for anyone who doubted it, that the clerical attitude toward swearing was condemnatory and disapproving.

To this end, the original author painstakingly categorized "the seven modes of swearing." These were: bold swearing, needful swearing, light swearing, habitual swearing, foolish swearing, swearing by God and his saints, and false swearing. No need to delve further into these categories—how they were formulated, defined, and illustrated. Let's just say that the analysis is sufficient to convey quite unambiguously the church's position on swearing.

The powers-that-were invested the language associated with religion with a sacrosanctity that made violation a taboo punishable by pain of death or just by pain. Given the techniques used, the latter was bad enough to function as a deterrent. The "holy" fathers of the church deployed the notions of blasphemy and profanity to great advantage to achieve their ends of control and suppression. As Timothy Jay puts it, "the church banned profanity because it had the power to do so at the time." He also points out that "how seriously one treats blasphemy depends chiefly on one's view of God." No surprise, then, that as faith has waned, so, too, has the power of blasphemy.

So arcane is the distinction between blasphemy and profanity that even the *Oxford English Dictionary* defines each in terms of the other. As I indicated in my glossary, blasphemy is *necessarily* profane, while much profanity is likely to involve blasphemy. But in the Middle Ages, it would have been hard to prove one's lack of blasphemous intent in order to save oneself from being burned at the stake. The distinction, dare I suggest, would have gone up with the smoke.

It is not surprising, perhaps, that some institutional religions—Judaism, Islam, and Brahmanism—have tried to enforce a ban on any use of the name of God. Think of it as a trust thing or, properly, a distrust thing. So sure are the founding fathers that the use of the deity's name will lead to profanity of some kind that they impose a blanket ban on the holiest-of-holy words. It's an insurance policy of sorts.

The Jewish case is an interesting one. The name of God in the Bible was written without vowels (as YHVH) and spoken as Yahweh or Jehova, alternative ways of reading the four Hebrew letters—*yud-hey-vav-hey*. Since the Hebrew Bible was written originally without vocalization, no one knows precisely how the name of God is to be pronounced. A tradition exists that the high priest uttered God's name once a year, when he entered the holy of holies on Yom Kippur. He would have learned it orally, from his predecessor.

The loss of the word's pronunciation, and the danger of uttering God's name indiscriminately, inspired priests to replace the four-letter name in Bible readings with the Hebrew word *Adonai* ("my Lord"). When vowels were added to the Hebrew text, the vowels in *Adonai* were added to the four-letter name of God. Christian Hebraists (which may appear to be, but isn't, an oxymoron), were not conversant with the Jewish practice and read the four letters with the assigned vowels as the hybrid "Ya-ho-vah."

Some believe that the four Hebrew letters of God's name are based on a combination of the past, present, and future tenses of the verbal root *hey-yud-hey,* "to be," indicating that God is the One Who was-is-will-be simultaneously. This view is supported by a passage in the Book of Exodus in which God identifies Himself to Moses as *ehyeh asher ehyeh* ("I shall be as I shall be") using the future form of the verb "to be."

The Jewish *Adonai* carried over to Christianity, where "Lord" stands for God or Jesus. Today devout Jews refer to their God as *Ha Shem* ("the name") and in English write the word as "G-d," once again encouraging nonutterance with vowel deprivation. Whoever invented vowels probably had no inkling of how handy they (or their omission) would be.

The old Semitic prohibition on naming the name found its way into the Ten Commandments, and from there into Christianity. In the Anglican holy communion service, for example, the minister quotes from the *Book of Common Prayer* with the same exhortation as the biblical commandment: "Thou shalt not take the name of the Lord thy God in vain." Some Christian churches use "I H S" for Jesus, and multiple interpretations of the letters exist, including "In His Service" or *In Hoc Signo,* Latin for "in this sign."

It's powerful stuff—simple and supremely clever. If you

can't say the name, you're less likely to take it in vain, either profanely or blasphemously. And by not saying it, for fear of what its utterance might do, you invest it with almost magical significance. The trouble with blasphemy, however, is that it's all about intention and, as such, is subject to interpretation. If you're unlucky, your alleged blasphemy may be more serious in the eyes of others than in your own—as Salman Rushdie found when the Ayatollah Khomeini of Iran deemed Rushdie's novel *The Satanic Verses* a blasphemy against Mohammed and his wives. Khomeini invoked a fatwa on Rushdie's head, sending him into many years' effective exile.

Of course, just because one's faith says you can't doesn't mean you won't. Total blind obedience isn't in human nature, and this is where euphemism comes in. You could argue that this is euphemism's whole purpose—to let you have your cake and eat it, too. You can appear to respect the prohibition on using deitic names profanely while swearing your head off, if that's what you like doing, by using stand-in words for the prohibited ones.

Between 1350 and 1909, no fewer than, and probably many more than, thirty-six euphemistic expletive versions of "God" were recorded. Here are some of them, in order of evolution:

gog	od
cokk	odso
cod	ounds
Jove	odsbodikins
'sblood ("God's blood")	agad
'slid ("God's eyelid")	ecod

'slight ("God's light")
'snails ("God's nails")
zounds ("God's wounds")
'sbody ("God's body")
'sfoot ("God's foot")
gods bodykins
   ("God's little body")
gad
odsbobs
gadzooks ("God's hooks")
godsookers
egad

goles
gosh
golly
gracious
Ye gods!
by George
s'elpe me Bob
drat! ("God rot!")
doggone ("God damn")
great Scott
good grief
by Godfrey!

It might be argued that some of these are less euphemisms than merely variant and creative blasphemies. This, however, fails to account for what I like to think of as the euphemistic career. Euphemisms have a short shelf life—once the stigma of the original catches up to them, the battery that runs the euphemistic device goes flat. The only way forward is to invent a new euphemism.

The range of linguistic inventiveness is staggering. "God" can be clipped ("odso"), distorted ("egad"), omitted ("snails"), or substituted ("s'elpe me Bob"). A part can be made to stand for the whole ("'sblood"), or sometimes blends are involved ("gosh" from "God"+"sh"), or full semantic substitutions ("gracious," "heavens to Betsy!"). We see similar permutations of "Lord": "lordy," "lawdy," "la," "land's sake"; and "Jesus": "jis," "jeeze," "jove," "gee," "gee whiz," "by jingo," "jeepers creepers," "jiminy cricket," "Christmas," "cripes," "crust," "crumbs," "crikey," "for crying out loud."

So far removed from the original are some of the re-modelings that we can assume most people using them would not be aware of either their etymology or the original euphemistic intent. We know that over time, euphemisms tend to become clipped and conventionalized. The passage of centuries sees them disengage from their origins and eventually morph into their own ritualizations. A further few centuries down the track, we're merrily saying "what the devil" (or "what the dickens" or "what the deuce"), completely unaware of the reformulations that have occurred on the Norman French oath of *Deus!* ("God").

It's hard to know exactly when the original religious connections washed out. We do know that Shakespeare had Ophelia utter a wealth of profanities of which she was much more blissfully unaware than her audience would have been—"la," "Lord," "by Gis," "by Saint Charity," "fie," "by God." This state of blissful unawareness is not so difficult to grasp. When today we politely say "bless you," apparently to prevent the devil from entering the body, which has been momentarily emptied of its soul by virtue of a sneeze, we are no more conscious of the phrase's original superstitiously religious significance than we are of the fact that we have omitted "God" for reasons of blasphemy—or profanity—avoidance. Similarly, when we say "speak of the devil," we are echoing a belief that if you spoke Satan's name, he would promptly answer the summons.

Centuries of development and semantic shifts, together with the ongoing secularization of society, have left us with a great reservoir of religion-based swear words whose religiosity, and hence much of their tabooness, has largely been bleached out. We're left with a barrage of words that have lost, well, their shtick.

Robert Dessaix suggests that "the Christian panoply of sacred beings" is heading in the same general direction as the old Norse gods of Thor and Odin. The British essayist G. K. Chesterton once remarked that no one these days can take Odin's name in vain. None of this is a problem to swear-word aficionados, because as "hell" and "damnation" became less relevant, they were replaced by secular alternatives such as FUCK, which were more appropriate to "an age of unfaith."

Nonetheless, the sheer quantity of religious terms and epithets is impressive. Consider the breadth of Christian terminology that is available for invocation. There are names of deities (God, Lord, Christ, Jesus, Jesus Christ, Jesus H. Christ, Merciful Father, Gracious God, Jehovah, Gabriel) or sources of infernal power (Devil, Satan, Lucifer, Beelzebub). There are also the names of sacred paraphernalia associated with the church (the holy cross, the sacrament, the holy mass, God's wounds, God's flesh and blood). Then there are the names of those on the A list—Mary, Moses, Job, Judas, the pope, and the various saints, but particularly Peter, Patrick, Mark, and Thomas. Similarly, certain tourist sites are popular points of invocation (Jerusalem, Jericho, Damascus, Nazareth, Bethlehem, the holy grave, the abbey). Lastly, there are all the words associated with future life (heaven, hell, purgatory, damn, bless, save).

Very few people would use "gracious" to avoid a direct reference to God or the charge of profanity or blasphemy. Indeed, God (in His various guises) is constantly being appealed to for a wide variety of services and in a wide variety of circumstances, from momentary inconvenience and minor frustration to serious emotional angst. These days, if religion vies in any way with sexuality as a source of taboo words, it's in the sheer number of words generated and still in circulation, rather than in their force. The thunderbolt is missing.

A term like "holy shit" might be thought of as an attempt to derive more bang for your buck through the combination of taboo elements—giving the taboo of excretion along with that of religion, plus the taboo that comes with the act of combining. Some traditionally Catholic countries make a veritable feast of their combinations, as seen, for example, in the Italian *porca Madonna* ("the Madonna is a pig"), *porca Dio* ("God is a pig"), and *putana Madonna* ("the Madonna is a whore").

One way to measure their effect is through the notion of taboo-loading. This could be defined as a measure of the shock value contained in a swear word used in a particular situational context. Swear words can be graded on a scale of increasing vehemence, with a taboo-loading from 0 to 6. As the influence of the church has waned, so, too, has the taboo-loading of swear words, once powerful because of their sacrilegiousness. Where once the word "God" had to be avoided or camouflaged, now it can be used freely and with impunity among most communities, save the most observant.

When calculating taboo-loading, the context is pivotal to the equation. This is because meanings are not absolute; they are language- and culture-specific. If you're having Christmas lunch with a community of Catholic nuns, you'll avoid dropping loose references to God through your meal, no matter what frustrations you might encounter. In this context, considering the variables of setting, participants, and calendar day/occasion, the taboo-loading on "God" or "Jesus" will be predictably very high.

Given the punitive resources available to the church, it's hardly surprising that words such as "hell" and "damnation" have been so fertile a domain for bad language. Perhaps because they were for so long held up as possible destinations or outcomes for the sinful life, these terms have served the Christian church well. "Damn you," "God damn it," "go to hell" are rather tame curses in today's secular world, but once possibly made the heavens shudder. Most studies of the changing patterns of swearing over time show that, for the general populace, religious terms have lost their clout. "God is dead," declares Timothy Jay, and words such as "hell," "damn," and "the devil" are but "garlic in the stew of good conversation."

That's not to lessen the dread with which hell was perceived in earlier times. Unlike other swear words, which relate to body function or effluvia, "hell" stands out as being the only swear word that is a place. In *The History of Hell,* Alice Turner writes, "the landscape of Hell is the largest shared construction project in imaginative history, and its chief architects have been creative giants." She's referring here to, among others, Homer, Virgil, Plato, Augustine, Dante, Michelangelo, Milton, Goethe, and Blake. In our much less imaginative secular lifestyle, we may be disdainful of former beliefs about the place called hell, but we cannot ignore the fact that "entire civilizations . . . have lived in terror of it, sworn by it; endured lifetimes of self-sacrifice and died slow, painful deaths in the hope of avoiding it."

Indeed, Montagu suggests that cursing may have evolved as a less antisocial alternative to killing. The hypothesis works like this:

> If we assume that all human groups will at some moments fail to live in total blissful harmony, then acts of violence are inevitable. But unchecked killing is antithetical to group cohesion and, ultimately, to group survival.

So it is plausible that early societies condemned killing not so much on moral grounds (the sanctity of human life and all that) but on the grounds that the deaths of productive members of the society would interfere with the economic well-being of the group and, ultimately, with its physical survival. Call it the Marxist take on the origins of swearing.

But where does that leave anger? If you no longer have the option of bashing your neighbor when he gets in your face, what's left? Enter the curse—anger management at its most elegant. The beauty of the curse is that it allows you to be symbolically violent, to achieve your purpose without breaking the prohibition on actual bodily harm. In fact, if you're really lucky, the curse might work, as the bumper sticker proclaims: MAGIC HAPPENS! In the meantime, if you simply feel better for having uttered the curse, and your target feels worse, then that's good enough. The curse is an economical win-win strategy.

In its earliest form, cursing existed alongside a strong

belief in the supernatural. It didn't matter which deity was being invoked, whether pagan or Christian, the curse was grounded in the faith of the curser (and the cursed). If you didn't believe that the energy you were investing in your enemy's downfall had some chance of bearing fruit, your motivation would surely start to drop off.

And quite a degree of energy was involved in cursing. The ancient Greeks and Romans employed the cursing tablet. The baths at Bath were full of these tablets at one time, and versions of the practice are still known in parts of modern-day Tuscany and Ireland. The stone tablet was inscribed with the tailor-made curse of one's choice and then buried or, more commonly, thrown into deep water.

The Romans favored throwing the curse-inscribed tablet into a sacred place—note the interface of the sacred and the profane—but the backyard well or the nearest river or ocean were also favored spots. Generally, where you flung your tablet probably depended on how far you had to lug it.

Many of these tablets have been recovered and restored, and one of the best-known now resides in the Archaeological Museum at Johns Hopkins University. This particular specimen, from around 50 B.C., contains a most grisly curse made against an allegedly villainous man with the rather ominous name of Plotius. I say "allegedly" because, as we haven't heard Plotius's version of the circumstances, we shouldn't leap to conclusions.

Good and beautiful Proserpina (or Salvia, shouldst thou prefer), mayest thou wrest away the health, body complexion, strength and faculties of Plotius and consign him to thy husband, Pluto. Grant that

by his own devices he may not escape this penalty.
Mayest thou consign him to the quartian, tertian and
daily fevers of war and wrestle with him until they
snatch away at his very soul.

From this point, the curse itemizes poor Plotius's entire
anatomy:

I give thee the head of Plotius . . . his brow and eye-
brows, eyelids and pupils . . . his ears, nose, nostrils,
tongue, lips, and teeth, so he may not speak his pain;
his neck, shoulders, arms and fingers, so that he may
not aid himself; his breast, liver, heart and lungs, so
that he may not sleep the sleep of health; his thighs,
legs, knees, shanks, feet, ankles, heels, toes and toe-
nails, so that he may not stand of his own strength.
May he most miserably perish and depart this life.

This might be a touch labored, but for thoroughness, you
can't fault it. It's also preemptive. In the full text, the curser
reveals that she fears Plotius has organized his own cursing
tablet, so she wants her curse to be visited by the end of
February. Payment is promised on delivery: "as soon as
thou has made good my vow."

An iron spike was driven through this tablet before it
was cast into the river, a symbol of the longed-for piercing
of the enemy's soul. Clearly, a physical demise was insuffi-
cient: The soul had to be targeted, too. Such embellish-
ments gave this type of behavior its definitive name of
"defixive" cursing.

Stone cursing, in common with other, more conventional rites, had its own formula that any would-be curser was advised to follow rigorously, for maximum effect. The first step was a formal, respectful term of address to the deity being invoked. This was followed by a detailed description of the tribulations to be visited upon the victim. The next item was some promise of material reward (after all, deities have to make a living, too). Last of all was a stipulated date for the curse to eventuate. Not so removed from a tax invoice, really.

In case you think that stone cursing was one of those peculiar, quaint, but essentially localized, ancient customs like chariot racing and hemlock tasting, it is sobering to learn that the most recent public instance of cursing along the lines of the ancients' tablet style was the 1910 publication of a curse in a French provincial daily newspaper. The target was a woman living in Paris, and the curse invoked "great Saint Exterminus" to "go and torment the soul and spirit of Madame Fernande X . . . [her Paris address was given], through the avenue of her five natural senses." It continued, "May she be tormented, besieged, by the desire to leave her husband." Saint Exterminus is then invoked to torment the spirit of the curser's husband, also through his five senses.

We could hypothesize that the curser had discovered an illicit liaison between her husband and the said Madame Fernande X, but it would be pure conjecture, because the curser goes on to wish "May he [that is, said husband] have only one idea—to give me money." It may have been a case of multiple motivations. As for Madame X, one wonders if she read provincial newspapers, because if not, she'd have had as little warning of her impending doom as an ancient victim.

It's not hard to mount a cogent argument in favor of cursing. Three benefits spring to mind. First, it encourages you to articulate and externalize your emotion; to demarcate it, focus on it, and channel it quite specifically. This has to be good for you. Life coaches at motivational seminars are big on these strategies. Second, by targeting another person, you are attributing responsibility for your own grief, whatever it may be, to an external agent. It's much easier to pass the buck. Third, demarcating the cause of contention limits its impact on you, prevents you from being overwhelmed by its negativity.

Psychologists are quick to tell us that external attribution is a much more healthy response option, mentally, than its alternative. Indeed, internal attribution is reputed to be the stuff and soul of pessimism. Furthermore, cursing is grounded in strong faith, and as any researcher on happiness will tell you, believers have it over nonbelievers, hands down. In other words, formal cursing, even if not of the inscribe-your-own-tablet variety, would seriously cut down on the nation's mental-health bill and reduce our growing dependence on antidepressants, psycho-professionals, and alternative healers. The pharmaceutical and naturopathic industries may not be pleased, but that's too bad.

Some argue that there is a link between religious faith and cursing and, concomitantly, between lack of religious faith and swearing—the cursing-stops-then-swearing-starts school of thought. It argues that the Greeks and Romans of yore had no need of run-of-the-mill bad language—also known as vituperative swearing—because they had complete faith in their defixive cursing, itself codified in the earliest body of Roman law, which put limits on who, where, and why you could curse. It wasn't a free-for-all; it was taken very seriously because, at its core, it was built on faith. A curse therefore was more than words—it was a tangible weapon that was expected to have tangible results.

If cursing rests on faith, then it follows that the absence of faith will surely wreak its effect on cursing. If you no longer believe in the power of the deities previously beseeched, you're not likely to ask them many favors. However, life being what it is, you'll still have the odd ratty moment, and you'll still have the odd enemy. This is where vituperative swearing steps up to the plate, giving its user immediate cathartic release, if nothing else, by using the verbal formulae previously available for cursing. "It is when a people can no longer curse with any assurance of success that swearing undergoes a luxuriant growth."

It's clear why swearing and cursing (or the more regional "cussing") are now almost interchangeable. It is also clear why Richard Dooling, among others, makes impassioned pleas against the laws limiting freedom of speech, both for obscenity and vilification, arguing that the need to swear "erupts from our intact, primate unconscious," which is the part of us that links our speech to "the vocal calls of primates." He's talking about a need-fulfillment dating back to the beginning of time. "Swearing has been with us since the first caveperson bumped her or his head on her or his way out to take a piss—probably before words, wars, words of war, and wars of words were invented."

It's tempting to think of a curse as a primitive and undifferentiated speech act, something almost instinctual. Without contesting the role of instinct, however, the record shows that it's not the case that a curse is a curse is a curse. Curses are highly differentiated, both over time and through space. For starters, there are two broad types, depending on the sought-for direction and, ultimately, the intention. If it's the neighbor who needs a good whack, then the curse is other-directed: "Turn off that loud music or go to hell!," "May God punish you for ogling my wife!" But the curse can also be turned on the self: "May God blast my soul if I don't do as you say!," "God damn me if I didn't just forget your birthday!"

The self-directed curse is even more symbolic than the other-directed curse. Indeed, the self-directed curse is another term for "adjurative" swearing or, simply, promising. Consider this oath: "I swear to tell the truth, the whole truth, and nothing but the truth, so help me God." Invoking the wrath of a higher being is widely accepted as a serious indicator of sincerity in the promise stakes. Even today we call them oaths (in court) or vows (in marriage) or legal contracts (for almost everything else).

There's a whole swath of oaths based on religious terminology. "By God," "by the Lord," "by the cross," "by the Holy Ghost," "by the Holy Mother of God," "by the saints above," to name just a few Christian invocations created for solemn occasions. This particular version of swearing has always been seen by the mainstream church as distinct from profane or blasphemous swearing, with the difference lying in the intention.

Interestingly, some Christian sects, such the Puritans and the Quakers, frown on such oaths in the same way as the church frowns on more overt kinds of profanity. I asked a strict Seventh Day Adventist neighbor of mine if Adventists could swear on a Bible or by God. He replied that this rule, like others, isn't written down as such, though "Jesus said we were not to swear nor to judge." That would seem to rule out not just oaths and curses but swearing per se. So today we have the interesting situation in which two people—one a dedicated atheist and the other an observant member of a minority Christian sect—may refuse to swear in court on the Bible or by God, and their refusals are based on entirely different lines of reasoning.

Thus curses and oaths both have their origins in purposeful, if distinct, behaviors, and each has served its cause well. Still, most people would agree today that they have largely outlived their usefulness. Their modern-day descendants—generalized swearing—are all that remain of what was once a rich, some might say noble, set of highly differentiated verbal behaviors. Some might even mourn it as a lost language.

The evolution of one of its stalwarts—DAMN—is a good illustration of the semantic career of a swear word. Like much else in the religious-based lexicon of swearing, DAMN has moved from its central punitive position, as a purely ecclesiastic word with an infernal sense, to a modern secular term for mild exasperation or disapproval. As we shall see, along the way, it has taken on the different shades and hues of the camouflages that have served it eu-phemistically.

The English DAMN dates back to 1280. Derived from the Latin *damnum* ("damage," "loss," and "hurt"), it means to inflict harm or damage or loss upon; to condemn or doom to punishment. "Doom," incidentally, in its modern sense of fate, ruin, or destruction, dates back to the early seventeenth century and is linked to the finality of the Christian Judgment Day. In its earliest form, to damn was to pronounce judgment upon, but from about 1325, the church could resist no longer, and the earliest theological use is recorded that year.

To appreciate the church's opposition to ordinary peo-ple using DAMN as a curse, we have to understand the es-sential territoriality of the issue. It's as simple as "you can't have this word because it's ours." The church regarded damnation or, more correctly, the function of condemning a person to eternal hell, as the sole prerogative of the church. As my Adventist neighbor said, judgment is not something for man [*sic*] to do. To presume to usurp this function would bring ordinary people into mortal danger, in terms of the fate of their own souls.

If nothing else, this shows a nice congruence between act and punishment: Should you presume to curse by damning another, you yourself will be damned. And it's not hard to understand why the church would jealously guard its jurisdiction. After all, having the clout to pun-ish—which, at the end of the day, let's face it, is what damning is all about—goes right to the heart of power. You might argue that it's a much more economical option than a billion-dollar defense budget. And you can't blame them for the belief that relinquishing the keys to punity would signal the beginning of the end. Maybe they were right.

If you can see that, however, you can also see why ordinary people would want to have the power to damn. After all, damners don't need any formal qualifications, special props, or paraphernalia. It's a simple verbal act. Like others in the linguistic class of performatives, DAMN achieves its intention simply through the act of utterance. Other such verbs are those associated with formal pronouncements such as declaring a couple to be married, baptizing or naming a baby, launching a ship or a book, or opening a restaurant. You say it, it happens. Damning is this easy, which makes it so seductive. One economical monosyllable gets you there.

> The power to damn has had an irresistible appeal. The fire and brimstone, the smoke and sulfur, and all the tormenting devils that populate the nether regions provide the conditions most fitting to that realm to which one may satisfyingly consign one's enemies.

You don't even need to know what brimstone is to sense its power. Given the appeal and the ease, it's little wonder that the church's protestations were consistently ignored. By the early fifteenth century, "Goddam" was so pervasive a word in the English language that it was the slang term by which Englishmen were known in France. In the latter half of the eighteenth century, the French satirist Voltaire spent some time living in England, where he came across "Goddam" and used it with relish. One of the characters in

Beaumarchais's play *Le Mariage de Figaro* (1784) asserts that "Goddam" is the basis of the English language.

When the German philosopher Georg Lichtenberg visited England in the 1770s, he caustically suggested that if towns were named after the first words that greeted a traveler, then London would be known as "damn it." And when Captain Basil Hall visited the islands that were to become Hawaii, some forty years after Cook landed there, he was officially greeted by an islander with the words: "Very glad see you! Damn your eyes! Me like English very much. Devilish hot, sir! Goddam!" Across the centuries, then, and across the map, DAMN was traveling lightly.

Although neither the Puritans nor the Quakers were given to oaths or cursing, DAMN somehow managed the transatlantic journey and arrived on the east coast of America, from where it enthusiastically took off. *The Linguistic Atlas of New England* gives a long list of euphemisms for DAMN. Most start with the "d" sound—"dem," "dum," "dim," "deam," "dan," "dang," "ding," "dash," "dast," "dag," "dad," "drat"—and are transparently euphemistic. They allow "the speaker to begin as if he were going to say the prohibited word, and then turn off into more innocent channels," which nonetheless hearers would well understand. However, with time, "d" evolved to include "blame," "blast," "bust," "burn," "botherm," "bugger," "butter," "confound," "condemn," "consarn," "condarn," "curse," "cuss," "crump," "gast," "gum," "hang," "rat," "ram," rabbit," "shuck," "torment," "plague," "dunder," "tarn."

By the time of the American Revolution, the word "tarnal" was widely used. It's not as much of a leap as you might think. Over time, "eternal damnation" had dropped the weak initial syllable of its first word, spawning "darn," "darned," "darnation," and "tarnal." An unconfirmed report states that in 2001 the expletive "go darn your socks" was still considered the ladylike alternative in some parts of New England. At the same time, "God dammit" had evolved into the euphemistic "dog on it," which, in turn, would become the popular expletive "doggone." The surface canine connection seems so far removed from its forbidden religious origins that almost all taboo has been bleached out.

We have seen that the primary function of euphemism is to ameliorate the taboo-loading of a word. "Doggone," for instance, has a much lower loading than "goddammit." Of course, these loadings are not totally fixed. As Justice Oliver Wendell Holmes observed, "a word is not a crystal, transparent and unchanged; it is the skin of a living thought and may vary greatly in color and content according to the circumstances and the time in which it is used."

So there's no easy, one-size-fits-all manual, like those guides in which you look up an offending stain (oil? wine? blood?) and are told how to remove it. The rules about swearing are much more context-dependent, a fact that makes them appear more rubbery and changeable. For one thing, a word's actual taboo-loading depends on subjective interpretations of its acceptability as well as the relationship between speaker and hearer(s) and the social context in which the word is used. Rather like that earlier example of having Christmas lunch with a group of nuns in their convent.

Just as we need appropriate guidelines for swearing, so, too, we need to know the appropriate responses. It would be ludicrous, for example, to interrupt a colleague's fluent bout of swearing by pointing out his or her "taboo-loading of five." In normal circumstances, normal people don't talk about how they talk. Hence the very practical idea beloved of the anti-cussers, the swearing jar, a simple punitive device that funds a night out but also sidesteps the issue of talking *about* the swearing *during* the actual swearing.

Finally, it should never be forgotten that there may well be an aesthetic element in social swearing. A wonderful story is told about Mark Twain, who was much given to swearing. His wife was so put out by the habit that one day she treated him to a stunning display of swearing, in the hope of showing him what she had to put up with. He listened politely before remarking dryly, "The words are there, my dear, but the music is wanting."

9

SON OF A BITCH

"It's a fucking good deal."

—FDR

Consider this. While the semantic field of "man" yields a huge number of terms that are by and large positive or neutral in connotation ("guy," "bloke," "chap," "fellow," "dude," to name a few), those for "woman" are primarily negative, sexually infused, and very often carry a condemnatory moral overtone. Here's a sampling: "bird," "broad," "bitch," "chick," "whore," "slut," "cunt," "cow," "mistress," "crumpet," "hag," "shrew," "strumpet," "filly," "battle-ax," "dish," "vamp," "tramp." Even "femme fatale" is, at root, an insult.

This is one of two extraordinary semantic imbalances between the sexes and concerns emotional or connotative associations. There are differences here depending on which variety of English is being referred to. In Australian English, for example, the word "woman" slips into abuse with greater facility than "man." There's a different feel to "bloody woman driver" compared to "bloody man driver" or "bloody driver." Somehow, the "woman" gives the abuse just that extra edge. The distaste that many women feel when they're referred to as "ladies" derives from the unarticulated assumption that "lady" is being used euphemistically because "woman" is somehow not nice.

This underlying stigma does not attach to "man" and "gentleman" since "man" is capable of standing alone as a strong neutral or positive word. Let's face it, it had to be strong and upright—until very recently, when feminists pointed out that "man" effectively excluded 50 percent of the population, it happily stood for the whole human race!

The second imbalance has to do with the pattern of meaning changing over time. Linguistic historian Geoffery Hughes maps over a hundred terms for women (a list he claims is far from inexhaustible), from the start of the thirteenth century to the twentieth. What he finds is that many of the negative words currently applied just to women once had broader meanings and were applied to both males and females. More important is his finding that it is only when a word started to narrow in application to women exclusively that its negative connotations emerged. Though it may now seem improbable, "harlot" and "wench" were once not gender-specific nor, at that time, pejorative. The linguistic process by which this happens goes by the lovely name of "the semantics of deterioration."

Sometimes the negativity is in place prior to the narrowing of application. Imagine a *This Is Your Life* episode with the spotlight on the personal history of the word "shrew." This what the presenter might say:

You began life as the name for a rodent, and later, with the passing of time, you gradually developed monstrous metaphorical extensions that built on the malignancy associated with rats. Poor hygiene habits among crowded unsanitary living arrangements, as well as the odd plague, helped these developments. You continue your career by moving into a new area where you develop a satanic sense of evil. At this time you still only apply to males. But, as your semantics continue to degenerate, you find that by the early thirteenth century, you have begun to feminize. For example, Chaucer mentions you in his Prologue, using you the way we today might angrily say "bitch." And then, before you know it, your use has narrowed to be applicable only to females. "Shrew," congratulations! This is your life!

This phenomenon is not peculiar to gender issues in language. If we look at the stigma associated with old age, we find that words originally introduced as euphemisms to camouflage the stigma of age quickly attract the stigma to themselves and therefore lose their euphemistic quality. It seems amazing that the word "senile" was originally a euphemism for "old." The same applies to taboos such as death. The word "undertaker" once had a much wider, more generalized meaning (someone who undertakes a task), but as it became euphemistically associated with funerals and death, its semantic range narrowed accordingly. Stigma and taboo so easily, contagiously, and perfidiously attach themselves that their euphemisms tend to have a very short shelf life. For this reason, sexuality, bodily functions, and death have enormous semantic fields.

Simply put, every time a stigma or taboo reattaches itself, the current euphemism drops out of active duty, and a new one is needed. I used the word "disabled" recently in conversation and was admonished for not coming up with a better term, a comment that suggests that "disabled" is going the way of "handicapped" and that we're in the market for a new one. Not surprising that we have an extraordinary twenty-five hundred words for male and female genitalia!

Linguists, especially lexicographers, are taxonomic in inclination, which means they love to classify words into sets and subsets, and then to stand back and admire how neatly they all work out. Hughes does this with "women words" and comes up with nine categories. There's the diabolical woman in the witch/hag group, which overlaps somewhat with the unnatural, aggressive, manlike woman of the virago/shrew group. There's the woman seen as the superhuman, spiritual creature of salvation in the angel/goddess group. And the others: woman as endearing pet (mouse/lamb and other small cuddly creatures, as seen in Valentine's Day ads); woman cursed in bestial terms (bitch/cow); woman as available object of delight (dish/tart); woman as object of revulsion (filth/slut); and the largest category by far, woman as sexually perverse (whore/harlot), which tails off into the hussy/broad group. The spread is as diverse as the menu of a New York deli.

The semantic imbalance across the genders can also be seen when comparing terms of abuse. There's a limited range of words that women can use in swearing at a male, and most of them—"bastard," "prick," "dickhead," and "asshole"—make statements about the target's irritating personality or, at worst, absence of moral fiber. (An Australian male informant disagrees with me, arguing that "creep," "boofhead," and "limpcock" are much worse.) None of these, however, compares with the evil that emanates from an abusive CUNT, hurled male to female.

We have explored CUNT's permutations in her own essay, but there is more to be added in the context of gender imbalance. While medieval superstitions about Satan and the supernatural have largely passed, CUNT remains the closest synonym for "evil" in the modern world. It is part of a long-standing tradition of what Hughes rather beautifully calls "the feminization of the monstrous." "Shrew," as we have seen, had monstrous evil connotations long before it was feminized. "Hag" was once an evil spirit in female form. "Dragon" was satanic before it humanized, then feminized. "Termagant," dating from the thirteenth century, is an archaic term for a nastily shrewish woman who was originally a violent deity said to be worshipped by Moslems. Nice one—this allows misogyny to join forces with xenophobia.

"Harpy" was a part-woman, part-bird-of-prey that was both filthy and rapacious. "Siren" was originally a serpent that evolved to another part-woman, part-bird that lured mariners to their doom with its seductive call—rather mermaidish, but without the tail. "Harridan," a French broken-down old horse, developed the English meaning of a most unappetizing, vixenlike, haggard old woman (as if "old woman" weren't enough). "Tramp" was (and still is in some places) a male vagrant before it was a sexually promiscuous female. And so it goes on.

The pattern continues. The *Collins Dictionary* includes the new term "bunny burner," a term for a psychologically unstable woman who stalks her male victim. The term originated in the 1987 sexual politics thriller *Fatal Attraction,* in which the Glenn Close character boils up a pet rabbit. It's a film that can turn you off bunnies as well as one-night stands.

It has been postulated that underpinning the dominant archetypes of "whore" and "angel" are the deeply embedded and religiously endowed role models of Eve and Mary. These two women (or should I say "ladies"?) offer "the opposed exemplars of the feminine character." On one side we have Eve—disobedient, earthbound, carnal, and seductive, with the associations of sin, suffering, guilt, and shame— and on the other, there's Mary: submissive, ethereal, and immaculate, the vehicle and symbol of redemption.

Eve, the stained-mistress figure for whom conception is a sorrowful curse, is tied to the myth of the Fall. Mary, the pure mother figure for whom conception is the source of blessing, is the potentially limitless instrument of grace. Hughes suggests that the twin archetypes coalesce at the scene of the crucifixion in the figure of the fallen Mary, or Magdalene, the maudlin prostitute, where "maudlin," itself a variation of "magdalene," comes to be associated with tearful penance. The dichotomy is one that has been observed in many other settings.

The decline in the power of the Christian church and its primordial notions of sin, guilt, suffering, confession, and redemption has lessened the degree of tension between the virgin/whore polarities. Consciousness-raising by feminists such as Germaine Greer no doubt has played its part.

As if the verbal abuse heaped on women through the language of swearing were not enough, men seem to dip into the misogyny arsenal not only when they're directly cursing a woman or speaking about a woman, but also when their target is a fellow male. "Son of a bitch" and "motherfucker" both offer circuitously female pathways toward verbal violence. Why, one wonders, is it not offensive to curse a man via his father or brother or son? But "son of a prick" or "fatherfucker" just don't cut it, do they? They lack that je ne sais quoi of the effective swear word.

Sometimes the effort to include the female takes the swearer into rather strange places. Consider the "yo' mama" jokes and the substantial range of mother insults available in black culture (for example, at www.pimp-daddy.com). Linguists who study graffiti are generously rewarded. The line "Your mother sucks the cum from dead dogs' dicks" was spotted in the 1960s on a bus shelter in Melbourne by a woman friend of mine whom I'd describe as sophisticated, worldly-wise, and unshockable. She assured me that she wasn't offended at the time of reading; yet the sentence has stayed with her for some forty years. She doesn't vouch for the accuracy of the original punctuation, rather doubting that the "dogs' dicks" phrase would have sported its plural possessive apostrophe.

Women might be forgiven for wondering why men direct so much venom at them. Where did the misogyny come from? One notion I'm drawn to is that males are essentially ambivalent toward females. On the one hand, there's the centrifugal energy that fuels their wish to escape the clutches of controlling woman (mothers, wives, schoolteachers). On the other, there's the testosterone-fueled, rarely abating, centripetal quest for sexual satisfaction.

This thinking-through-one's-dick mind-set, if glossy magazines are to be believed, claims young men have a sexual thought about every five seconds. It's perhaps no surprise that sexuality seems to infuse men's thoughts about women, both negative and positive. Margaret Atwood has pointed out that men use sexually based words as both insult and praise. Work by a male writer is often spoken of admiringly as having balls; work by a female writer can also be admired as having balls. But has anyone anywhere ever spoken admiringly of a work by a woman (or man) as having tits?

D. H. Lawrence contended that the syphilis rampant in Renaissance England left men with an awful horror of sexually transmitted disease, which could conveniently be scapegoated in a detestation of women. That it takes two to tango seems to have been forgotten. Another suggestion to account for the fear + loathing/attraction bind is the hidden nature of the vagina. Concealment fosters mystery. But if it's a mere step from hidden to mystery, then it's also a mere step from mystery to marginal, from marginal to evil, and from evil to fear.

It would seem more likely, in the context of other social and political inequities, that misogyny is part of the mind-set. Indeed, after extensive research into the historical semantics of sexuality, Hughes comes to the reluctant conclusion that the abiding and massive preponderance of unfavorable terms used by men to and about women is at heart a "mass psycholinguistic phenomenon" unaffected by, and unresponsive to, wider social developments. The statement that "women should be obscene and not heard" is attributed to Groucho Marx. Joking aside, this seems to say more about men than women.

In the study of swearing and gender, two issues dominate both empirical research inquiry and folk linguistics. One is quantitative, the other qualitative. The first has to do with the amount of swearing that males and females do, relative to each other. The second has to do with the actual language used by men and by women.

Let's start with quantity. Historically, there is ample evidence that men swore more than women. Regarding swearing in ancient Greece, Montagu says the heroes of Homer's *Iliad* must have sworn "for they were mere troopers and troopers have always sworn." This rings true if only for the expression "swear like a trooper," which has various forms, such as "swear like a sailor." But Montagu adopts the Marxist view that soldiers and sailors through history have excelled at the art of swearing by virtue of their oppression. In other words, swearing was "an easement to the much besieged spirit."

The massive and senseless slaughter of soldiers in World War I not surprisingly yielded an enormous quantity of swearing. The physical and psychological stresses, the pain and deprivation, the male-only environment, the pent-up anger and frustration released in battle together created ideal conditions for swearing to flourish. One report claims that "*fucking* was used as an adjective to qualify almost every noun in the soldier's vocabulary." In any light, this would seem appropriate. Allan Walker Read, an early writer on obscene language, remarked that a nation capable of sending forth its young men to slaughter and be slaughtered was unlikely to be squeamish about a few words.

It has been noted, too, that in such circumstances, swearing is akin to prayer. Both words of prayer and swear words appeal to a greater being, whether for increased firepower or for salvation in the form of physical survival. A soldier going over the top of a trench into enemy fire would shout as loudly as he could. According to one veteran, half of them would be praying, the other half swearing.

Research into gender variation in swearing is facilitated by the public nature of male swearing. However, even allowing for the fact that Homer and his ilk were more likely to record male-dominated activities (such as fighting wars) than female-dominated activities (such as holding body, soul, kingdom, and offspring together), there is nothing inherent in the female condition to prevent women from achieving equality with men in swearing. Neurologically, anatomically, physiologically, the equipment is the same.

The same applies to men when it comes to crying. There is nothing innate in the male to make crying more onerous or less spontaneous. Richard Dooling may differ here, or he may simply be exaggerating, when he claims that "because men are congenitally incapable of indulging in good, long cries, swearing provides them with a handy compromise when presented with the . . . alternatives of running away, crying or fighting." I haven't come across any direct or indirect link connecting estrogen and lacrimation, yet it seems that, cross-cultural differences aside, men seem always to have cried less than women. Swearing (for women) and crying (for men) are similar in that the genders are socialized into socially appropriate behaviors.

A female overcome by annoyance or frustration can, with relative impunity, burst into tears in most circumstances. Female tears carry two benefits: From the perspective solely of she-who-cries, tears provide immediate physical and psychological relief from pent-up emotion. It is plausibly claimed that crying releases a kind of natural narcotic, which accounts for the postcry feel-good state.

A second benefit is more socially tuned. Tears signal the crier's psychological state to whatever company or audience is present. Insofar as that audience's reaction will be shaped by the evidence of tears, we can say that nonsolitary crying has the character of a social event. Certainly, there are occasions when female crying is expected, and when that expectation is not met, the woman encounters suspicion and aggression. When Lindy Chamberlain was tried for the murder of her baby daughter, Azaria, and subsequently exonerated, she may have done irretrievable damage to her cause by failing to cry in public about the loss of her child.

Now consider the function and benefits of male swearing. From the swearer's perspective, there's the immediate cathartic release of emotion. In the context of anger—road rage is a good example, though any kind of rage works—swearing allows a dissipation of violent energy that might otherwise be vented through physical assault. But, as with female crying, it also has the social function of cueing the swearer's state to other participants/onlookers in the vicinity so they can select appropriate responses. These may be linguistic, such as placatory, conciliatory remarks aimed at defusing the situation; or nonverbal and escapist, such as closing the car windows and hitting the gas pedal. Alternatively, the symbolic violence may be matched with a return blast of the same, or it may escalate into physical assault.

I betray my gender, I know, when I say I can't help feeling that if both parties—road rager and road ragee—would burst into tears, then the energy dissipation and reconciliation might be easier and swifter all around. Ditto for international conflict. But then that wouldn't at all suit the munitions industries.

We know from social history and from literature that women were socially propelled into swooning or weeping when confronted with negative emotion in a public place. Ashley Montagu contends that the resource of weeping effectively rendered swearing unnecessary, an argument supported by a comment on a converse circumstance—the fact that prostitutes allegedly are accomplished swearers and also noncriers, or so claims Hamlet in one of his impassioned soliloquies (Act II, scene ii). Does permission to swear remove the need for crying?

There's a nice symmetry in this argument: High swearing goes with low crying. Personally, I'm a little more circumspect when it comes to making broad generalizations about prostitutes' (or anyone's) behaviors without a database of authentic utterances to draw on. If women of the night do have a well-developed penchant for swearing, might this not be because of the rough male company they keep in an industry where being perceived as tough is closely linked to staying alive?

Perhaps it is simply another aspect of being resilient. Resilience, or acquired life skills, is how some female research participants chose to interpret instances of female swearing. Furthermore, I'd warrant that few men would be well positioned to venture a guess on the nature and extent of prostitutes' tears when the women are either in female-only company or alone.

On the other hand, Montagu's point may be substantiated by the twin facts that contemporary women swear more and cry less in public. There's no question that female public swooning is long gone. Both the noun ("she fell in a swoon") meaning an instance of fainting, and the verb "to swoon" are flagged by dictionaries as "literary" or "archaic." When a word moves into these categories of usage, it means that the only place you'll find it is in a period novel.

Most of us would readily accept that in the first decade of the new millennium, women swoon less and swear more. However, do they swear as much as men? People *believe* that men swear more. Indeed, widespread folk-linguistic beliefs abound: Men swear more, in quantity and severity, than women; men are more comfortable with swearing than women; social expectation is more permissive of male swearing; female swearers are judged more negatively than equivalent male swearers.

Over the last three decades, these beliefs have been subjected to a range of empirical tests. We now know that while men show a statistical tendency to swear more than women, the issue of gender variation is nowhere near as clear-cut as folk linguistics would have us believe. The only solid evidence to emerge from a recent study of men, women, and language is the abiding belief, handed down over the centuries, that women *ought* to speak differently from men. But "ought" tells us more about prescriptive beliefs than actual speech patterns.

Research is hampered by the difficulties of data collection. Swearing happens mostly in informal settings, where access is inhibited, or spontaneous circumstances such as road rage, which are (as yet) difficult to predict. One finding consistently emerges, and this is that swearing is no longer a largely male prerogative.

Some forty years ago, Elizabeth Ross conducted a fascinating experiment on the relationship between stress and swearing. Its importance goes far beyond its limited circumstances. A university expedition to arctic Norway consisted of eight people—five men and three women, seven zoologists and a psychologist. Three of the group were considered nonswearers. The others' swearing tended to be blasphemous rather than obscene, a fact that could be attributed partly to their middle-class background and partly to the mixed-gender company. The experiment's findings highlight the social nature of one type of swearing.

Two kinds of swearing were identified and labeled "social" and "annoyance." Under conditions of low or no stress, when the subjects were relaxed and happy, the swearing was of a social nature and exhibited "one of the gang" solidarity-oriented behavior. Most of the swearing that took place on the expedition was social swearing, which—by definition being contagious and mutually reinforcing—requires the presence of a sympathetic audience of other swearers in order to thrive.

At one point in the expedition, half the group, including the three nonswearers, left on a separate trip. The swearing rate among those who remained immediately doubled and remained consistently high. The increased swearing activity boosted solidarity and apparently compensated for the loss of half the team. Maybe they realized intuitively that they had to swear harder to make up for their loss of numbers. Perhaps, also, they had been restraining themselves in the presence of the nonswearers.

Social swearing can be inhibited by a number of factors other than the presence of nonswearers. The presence of strangers, the absence of an appreciative audience, or a mixed-gender group individually and collectively can constrain social swearing. The men on the expedition arrived a week earlier than the women, and during that week, swearing had been common and friendly. However, this dropped off when the women arrived, not only because the men felt they had to watch their tongues in the presence of women but also because of the introduction of unknowns into a group that had already bonded. The issue of gender was not as much a factor in this study, however, as whether or not a person was a swearer.

Annoyance swearing was classified as a different kind altogether. It occurred under conditions of low to medium stress and functioned irrespective of audience. As stress and annoyance swearing increased, social swearing decreased. As the stress continued to rise, social swearing ceased altogether, while annoyance swearing continued to a certain point and then began to drop. In high-stress situations, swearing stopped, as did most talk. One inference to be drawn here is that annoyance swearing in a moderately stressful circumstance is a sign that a disagreeable situation is bearable.

Granted, it may not be necessary to go all the way to arctic Norway in a cold leaky boat (okay, I added the leaks, just for effect) to find out that swearing is a stress-coping and stress-relieving strategy. The bottom line is: If you're worried about which laid-off employee is likely to return with a semiautomatic and shoot up the office, it's the quiet non-swearer you should be wary of. On one level, I think we all know that.

Ross's research investigated the variable of gender within an enclosed social milieu where the variable of stress was also an issue. Studies in gender and language in the decades that followed pursued particular areas. Timothy Jay's investigation of gender differentiation produced a short dictionary of gender-specific insults. He divides swear words into those that insult males and those that insult females; then he semantically analyzes the patterns of use. Simply put, the genders do it differently, but what they have in common is that their insults target the behaviors or traits that deviate from cultural expectations or norms.

Men insult women using five different categories of words. "Slut" and "whore" target perceived sexual promiscuity or looseness. "Tease," "pricktease," "dicktease," and "cocktease" are based on the nonfulfillment of the perceived promise of sexual intimacy. "Hag," "dog," and "witch" are words that men call women they perceive to be sexually unattractive or socially inept. "Bitch" and "cunt" are terms used for a woman that, on their own, do not target sexual behavior—they're reserved for women perceived as socially deviant, mean, or overly demanding or smothering. When used woman-to-woman, they target personal or social problems rather than sexual identity.

Words that insult men can also be logically subdivided. "Motherfucker" remains the most offensive American man-to-man insult. As Jay puts it, "this word offends against sex, society and family. What more could a speaker want in an insult?" Apart from being told he fucks his mother, the man in Jay's research is most offended by having his heterosexual adequacy questioned. Terms like "cocksucker," "queer," "fag," "homo," "wimp," and "pussy" all achieve this goal and, like "motherfucker," are mostly man-to-man insults.

A third category of words includes "bastard," "prick," "asshole," "son of a bitch," and "cock" and targets social ineptness, noncaring, self-centeredness, and meanness. They are used man-to-man and woman-to-man. A fourth group contains terms such as "nerd" and "jerk" and highlights social ineptness or social unattractiveness. The last group— "macho," "wolf," and "playboy"—is used by women to characterize exploitative men who may be physically and socially attractive but are selfish, deceitful, oversexed, and lack compassion, intimacy, and the big C: commitment.

Jay concludes with the rather sweeping generalization that "men and women have different definitions of love and . . . a loving relationship. The male values qualities of physical attractiveness and sexual intimacy. The female is looking for the sense of commitment and caring or personal friendship."

Common sense suggests that men would swear more than women, as swearing has to do with power, and men generally have more power. Women are expected to have the capacity for self-restraint, while men can lose control with greater impunity. If you doubt that gender, power, and swearing are intertwined, consider for a moment a context where they co-occur. Sexual harassment is, by and large, a by-product of power and is usually perpetrated by a "powerful" man harassing a "subordinate" woman. Yes, some powerful women harass men (or other women), but the number of women in superordinate positions is far lower than vice versa, and fewer women harass than men.

The male preponderance toward violence is clear in the male/female statistics for violent crime. But as society changes, and females move into areas of employment that were previously male-only or male-dominated preserves, the rules are changing. Women are allowed to swear more— so much more that critic Rosalind Coward claims "Women are now talking seriously dirty." Women are showing less restraint, while men are required to show more, as women find their voice in workplace legislation.

Certain all-boy contexts are cordoned off and have their own rules. In the pub and the locker room, dirty talk is the lubricant for social bonding, flowing freely, especially when reinforced by alcoholic consumption. Such venues also signal a symbolic escape from the constraints of those who criticize, condemn, or control such language—predominantly mothers, girlfriends, wives, and schoolteachers. Then again, the door to this boys-only haven is being closed, as groups of girls now comfortably go out together.

Restraint is lifted on the playing fields of various sports— "trash talk" in basketball, "sledging" in cricket. The deliberate intention here is to offend and intimidate the opposing side; the game then becomes a ritual context for the displacement of violent feelings. Better that than going to war.

If men have a greater propensity for violence, it follows by extension that they are likely to experience more impotent rage, which they often discharge by turning on those they consider weaker—that is, less able to retaliate. This is why male swearing tends to target women and ethnic groups: because they're safer. If that suggests a certain cowardly contour to the violent, swearing, rampaging, out-of-control behavior of some men, I should be thankful that few of them would be likely to read this book.

Such views are folk linguistic in the sense that they are not empirically based. But the research scene is much foggier. Researchers come to vastly different conclusions, influenced no doubt by the constraints of their sampling, the context of research, and, dare I say it, their own beliefs and assumptions. Angus Kidman concludes that swearing usage in Australia is equal across the genders, that men and women make the same meanings out of the same words, and that social developments leading to greater gender equality have made swearing equally available to both genders.

A viewing of the Australian film *Teesh and Trude* provides ample evidence that gender is not standing in the way of swearing, or at least not within the categories of age (twenty-something) and class (low) to which the two lead female characters, Teesh and Trude, belong. The film is a day in the life of two unemployed, down-and-out young women living in a run-down place "at the lower end of the suburban experience." The apathy is as pervasive as the filth, and the language is a congruent fit. In what might at a stretch be called conversation between friends, the foul language serves as punctuation amid grunts, growls, and despair. In fact, so pervasive and rampant is their swearing that nothing, it could fairly be stated, is standing in its way.

In the first twenty minutes of the film, I counted some seventy-six incidents of swearing. Nearly all of these were female-to-female, and mostly in the presence of a child, Teesh's son, Kenny. The child was the direct target of swearing on fourteen occasions, where FUCK featured less than "shut up" and "bugger." In the female-to-female incidents, the choice of swear words fell into the following pattern:

20 FUCKs (including variations, like "fucking" and
   "fuck you")
9 SHITs (including "crap")
5 ARSEs (including variations, like "pig's arse")
plus a few each of PISS, BLOODY, JESUS, BITCH,
   NUTS, COW, and BASTARD

The small bank of key swear words served a range of speech functions, mostly the expression of irritation and anger. There were a few moments of social swearing, and, in regard to the child, swearing featured as (unsuccessful) attempts at control. One reviewer described the script as "a flavourless diet of four-letter words. It's as if being poor has starved them of the means to put a sentence together."

In this sampling of *Teesh and Trude,* the very noticeable absence of CUNT suggests an inequality of use. Unless it was absented to abide by film classification criteria, it would seem to remain a word that men use mostly to or about women. Anecdotal evidence suggests that women do use it to and about other women, but rarely to or about men. In other words, "feminization of the monstrous" continues to some extent, notwithstanding advances on other fronts—for example, the number of child-care facilities or women on corporate boards.

But Timothy Jay, investigating in America, concludes that men swear more than women, using different and more offensive swear words. They start swearing at a younger age, and the habit persists into old age. They are socially freer to exhibit hostile and aggressive speech habits. Further, the gendered differences in sexual semantics affect every aspect of sexual talk, from banter to joke-telling, to verbal dueling, verbal harassment, and aggression. He writes, "As with the case of love, men and women do [swearing] differently....They view the world differently....The language of insults and name calling supports the view that we are operating on different assumptions about what makes our hearts and minds tick."

In an interesting piece of comparative research, Jay studied swearing in public places over the span of a decade, and he came to the conclusion that patterns of swearing— based on geography, gender, mixed, or nonmixed company—were surprisingly stable, the only change being that women in 1996 were swearing more in public than they did in 1986. Part of his research involved graffiti in male and female bathrooms. He found men's graffiti more sexually suggestive, less socially acceptable, more racist, more homophobic, and less romantic than women's. No surprises there. He came to the overall conclusion that "humans come in two sexes, male and female, but gender identity is more elaborate than merely acknowledging genitalia."

In Australia, Amy Cooper observed male-to-male swearing within earshot of female company and notes that when girls pass young men sitting, for example, on a public bench, "the boys spread their limbs over the widest possible area and insult each other loudly"; while in Britain, Jennifer Coates claims that men in own-sex groups swear three times more than women, but that both groups dramatically lower their swearing in mixed company.

South African findings are closer to the Australian research. Vivian de Klerk finds little to support the widespread assumption that women's talk differs from men's, especially in the area of nonstandard speech. She argues that the stereotypes about nonswearing women break down with age. More significantly, the traditional bias in the lexicon (more English words for insulting women than men) is not matched within the mental lexicon of individual speakers. The female swearers in her sample knew more derogatory terms for males than for females. Further, in regard to the historical semantic imbalances, de Klerk points out that many of the abusive terms for women are in fact obsolete. She has a point there—when was the last time you heard a female called a harlot?

While the jury is still out on gender and swearing, and we lack conclusive empirical data, some writers on the subject have few doubts. Richard Dooling, for instance, points to what he considers an important gender difference in America: A man harassed by someone using foul language in the workplace will turn to the swearer "and forthrightly advise him to fuck himself and keep the baby," while a woman in the same position is more likely to file a formal complaint.

Despite the attraction of Dooling's deliberately hyperbolic, cut-and-dried, black-and-white propositions, I am, in the final analysis, more drawn toward interpretations that acknowledge the messy complexities of swearing, gender, and life. One was a research paper based on the interactions that took place on the Linguist List (a Listserv where linguists raise and explore online topics of professional interest). One topic was "rude negators"—"bollocks"/"the hell"/"my ass she did"—terms used to show strong disagreement with a point of view.

Susan Herring noticed that, in the ensuing discussion, many more men than women contributed opinions. In a follow-up survey of the contributors, she found that women were no more averse to the topic than men, which made her more curious about the gender pattern in the number of contributions. She puts forward two hypotheses. The first is the "quick response" hypothesis, which indicates that for various reasons, men are faster to respond to and by e-mail. This has to do with both access to the technology and a male desire to share first impressions in a public mode. There was also a correlation along status lines: Men's response rate resembled the high-status group, women's the low-status group.

Herring's second hypothesis is the "gendered discourse" view, which suggests that participation on Internet discussion lists favors the more transactional male communication style; discussing matters face-to-face with friends, family, and other nonlinguists is more the female discourse style. Also, the fact that the body parts used in rude negators favor the male (there just aren't female equivalents, like "ovaries" or "my tits he did") contributes to women's somewhat alienated response to the juvenile-male-bonding tenor of the discussions. Clearly, the issue of gender and swearing is more complex than counting CUNTS and FUCKS.

Do men swear more than women? Do they use different swear words? Are the genders still subject to different social constraints? The view from the folk-linguistics camp is satisfyingly simple but not hugely credible. The view from the research camp offers a picture that is so complex it sends us back, yearning, to our intuitions. Eventually, the influence of postmodernity, in its tolerance of ambiguity and blurry edges, may ameliorate some of the discomfort of inconclusiveness.

Understanding swearing in the context of gender issues is not as simplistic as counting up the words that females use in comparison to men, or contrasting female-to-male terms with male-to-female. It's a matter of understanding that our sense of gender is less something innate than something achieved, and it isn't set in concrete but is constructed moment by moment, interaction by interaction, unfolding individually and collectively over time.

Language choices also shape the sexual identity we present to the world. A teenage girl dabbling in swearing is making decisions, both conscious and subconscious, about her own stylistic practice, within which the use of swearing will be only one among many other aspects of the persona she will present to society.

> With each choice to swear or not to swear, the next choice is weighted by one's experience with the previous one—how was it received? How did one feel afterwards? . . . Such decisions are not made within a vacuum, but always with reference to and collaboratively within our communities of practice.

Our budding adolescent female swearer who is inserting the odd swear word into her discourse may simultaneously be achieving a range of goals: asserting autonomy from the norm-enforcing adults in her world; or deliberately distinguishing herself from those she sees as nerds or goody-goodies. She may be modeling herself on someone older whom she admires, perhaps a media personality or a pop star. She may see swearing as cool, independent, tough, different. She may be pushing the envelope.

And each modification of self that she makes will be delicately calibrated against the social landscape in which she operates. In turn, her own moves will shape the larger landscape against which she and others will continue to gauge their behaviors. Thus, in the feminist view, one small step for one teenage girl could become a large step for the sisterhood.

Women were once excluded from the company of men, presumably to protect their supposedly finer sensibilities from the taint of swearing. This practice was exquisitely conveyed in the paternalistic line "We'd like to hire you, but we use too much foul language on the job." Over the past hundred years, as more and more women have entered formerly male enclaves, this attitude has had to change.

For example, in World War II, women in the Allied nations were employed in large numbers in the war industries. An aircraft factory in Philadelphia boasted a sign that read: NO SWEARING. THERE MAY BE GENTLEMEN ABOUT.

10

BORN TO BE FOUL

"So where the fuck are we?"

—AMELIA EARHART

The culture-specificity of swearing should come as no surprise. Babies arrive in the world equipped to learn language, which will be the single most important learning they will undertake and achieve in their lifetime. Nothing else they do, from a holiday barista coffee-training course to a Ph.D. in rocket science, will approximate the importance of learning their mother tongue. Language is what makes nearly every other learning possible. It's what makes us human.

The equipment that makes a baby receptive to language works equally well for the infant of a Manhattan banker as for the infant of an Inuit fisherman. Indeed, learning conditions may favor the latter because the air might be fresher—that is, it may contain more oxygen. What the infants learn, however, will depend on what words are operating in their environment, and this applies as much to the "bad" words as to the ordinary "good" ones. The banker's kid hears "shit" (maybe on a bad trading day); the French child hears *merde;* the Japanese child hears *kusobaba.* I don't have an Inuit dictionary handy, but you surely see my point.

What they hear, they learn. Along with words, they will acquire the grammar that enables them to use those words to achieve their various objectives. These objectives start out as reasonably straightforward and predictable—food, sleep, clean diaper, comfort, watching *The Wiggles* on TV—but they progress rapidly. Within a remarkably short time, the child is able to mount a sophisticated argument for staying up beyond the mandated bedtime.

Along with grammar comes an understanding of a child's culture, a big part of which is pragmatic linguistic knowledge. These are the rules about what is said, how, with whom, and where. A by-product of this immense amount of learning in an average child is the ability to swear. Immersed as they are in the context of action, children quickly acquire pragmatic knowledge. Example: Mom says *merde* at home with Dad, and she says it more quietly if she thinks the kids are within earshot, but not at all with business clients, dinner-party guests, or the extended family, especially if *grand-mère* is present.

In learning about their language's underbelly, children learn about the forbidden. And it is this well of the forbidden that they will draw from when the need to swear arises, which it will. Initially, they may be cautious in mouthing words that they intuit are dangerous, but they soon find out that life goes on just as effectively post–swear word—sometimes more so. It's a simple case of action followed by reaction, which reinforces action. In this way, children begin to build up their swearing competence. Dirty words, to the child, are just words until they are labeled dirty and invested with magical powers.

As I hope will by now be apparent, my approach to swearing is to see it as one very interesting, albeit ordinary aspect of human verbal behavior, as normal and human as asking someone to pass the salt or calling the IRS for some information. Well, perhaps not quite as ordinary as the salt and the telephone, if only because of the taboo aspect, and because of the folk notions and prejudices that exist regarding swearing. So I'm arguing from the regular-common-and-human corner, not the shock-horror-and-corruption-reigns corner.

One argument (of many) for constructing swearing as normal is that it enables us to compare it with the abnormal. This gives us access to a useful linguistic tool: allowing the pathological to be our teacher. In this case, I use "pathological" to refer specifically to a person suffering from a neurological disorder called Tourette's syndrome (TS). This is described as "a rare and puzzling neurological disorder characterized by controllable muscular twitches, facial tics, vocalizations, repetitive movements, compulsive touching and uncontrollable cursing."

It's only the cursing that concerns us here. So specific is this swearing behavior to TS that it has its own name—coprolalia, from the Greek *kopros* ("dung") and *lalia* ("chat" or "babble"). In the 1994 documentary *Twist and Shout,* a number of TS sufferers are filmed talking about their experience of the disorder, and many scenes give examples of TS coprolalia. One young woman calls out, "Fuck me up the asshole!"; another says, "Dirty miserable motherfucking son of a bitch"; another can't help blurting out "Purple nigger" when standing in line behind a black man in a purple jogging suit—to the dismay of her mortified caretaker, who did what she could to manage the fallout from such outbursts, which unfortunately wasn't much.

Most of the examples were taken from a convention about TS, a context that might be considered a protected public space. One of the tragedies of TS is that public places seem to trigger coprolalia, while at the same time being the context in which the least understanding or allowance will be given. It doesn't require a lot of imagination to recognize that TS sufferers can quickly, if unintentionally, get themselves into hot water.

But TS has a lot to teach us, even though it is itself to some degree shrouded in mystery. Apparently, cursing is produced by the same neurolinguistic mechanisms in a speaker, whether he or she suffers from TS. The difference between the two is that, while both speakers have learned so-called bad words within a specific sociocultural context, the non-TS speaker has an inhibitory mechanism that suppresses the thought before it converts to cursing. The TS speaker's mechanism is faulty, out of order. The forbidden thought cannot be suppressed and comes out as swearing. Timothy Jay writes:

> What is intriguing about TS coprolalia is what it reveals about normal cursing. Children learn offensive words and then spend the rest of their lives inhibiting them in public. The Touretter [lacks the ability] to inhibit curse words that normal children can inhibit in "polite" situations. . . . The child who develops TS

reveals forbidden psychological and cultural anxieties
in [his or her] episodes of coprolalia.

Using TS as a point of departure for theory building, in
Why We Curse, Jay constructs swearing as the nexus of the
neurological, the sociocultural (what is forbidden in any
particular culture), and the individual psychological (biographical) factors that differentiate, for example, between a
self-deprecatory swearer ("fuck me up the asshole!") and
an other-abusive swearer ("dirty miserable motherfucking
son of a bitch"). Jay's "NPS" theory is the lens through
which he examines evidence of swearing in regular, non-
TS swearers.

It is the S (sociocultural) in Jay's NPS theory that is of
most relevance here. Cross-cultural evidence of swearing
reveals a set of nearly universal human preoccupations, the
specifics of which are shaped and constrained by the local
taboos particular to every collective. This is not to say that
the taboos are always respected, but rather to suggest that
they generously furnish a people with their own contextu-
ally powerful set of forbidden notions, which come in
handy for swearing purposes. After all, if everything were
allowable, it would be very hard to swear. It's no coinci-
dence that the taboo quality of FUCK began to fade in the
wake of the sexual revolution of the 1960s and 1970s. Perhaps the underlying principle might be: If it's okay to do it,
it's okay to say it.

Swearing is culturally and linguistically shaped in other
ways. For example, it has its own grammar, dependent on
the language in which the swearing takes place. Take, for
instance, the English sentence "Who *the hell* has been

here?," which is probably derived from "Who *in the hell* has been here?," just as "What *the fuck* are you doing?" may be derived from "What *in the fuck* are you doing?" Here the ordinary rules of English grammar combine with swearing-specific grammatical constraints, such as the use of "the" before "hell" and before FUCK, to give us a grammatically well-formed utterance.

Here we have to distinguish between grammatical correctness and social correctness. It is possible for a grammatically correct utterance to be socially incorrect. But as a general rule of thumb, swearing ungrammatically is contraindicated even without considerations of social correctness. There's not much that sounds worse than an abusive piece of swearing that is marked out as nonnative product. Perhaps the bottom line should be if you're unsure, swear in your own language. Your message will be carried by tone and voice quality, and it should at least be grammatical—if it isn't, chances are no one around you will be able to tell.

So the grammatical rules of the language and the embedded sociocultural features of the society together determine the form, shape, and feel of an act of swearing in any language. Swedes say, "Who *in hell* has been here?"; Poles, "Who *for cholera here* was?"; Hungarians, "Who *the sickness* was here?" The universal element is the insertion of a swearing phrase midposition in the utterance. The individual, unique flavor of the different utterances is a combination of the grammar (*in, for, the*) and the vocabulary (*hell, cholera, sickness*).

So we can discount the folk notion that swearing is the behavior of a lazy mouth. It takes just as much rigorous lexico-grammatical know-how to produce a socially incorrect, grammatically correct utterance as it does to produce a socially correct, grammatically correct one. (I could also put forward an argument, if there were space, that even the swearer who uses an ungrammatical, socially incorrect utterance has put in considerable effort. Errors are rarely the result of laziness—even if believing so relieves everyone other than the speaker of responsibility.)

It's significant that websites such as www.insultmonger and its "swearsaurus" contain swear words in umpteen languages, some of which you've likely never heard of, but they provide only vertical lists, with no cross-lingual comparisons. Significant though not surprising. It is extremely difficult to produce an accurate and definitive cross-language comparison of swearing. For one thing, few people have a complete knowledge of swearing in their own language/culture, because the conventions within a single language/culture are as variegated as the culture itself. They are distributed differently among the many strata of a society, being impacted on, to different degrees, by macrovariables such as age, gender, class, ethnicity, level of education, and social values. There's another important variable, a feature that for want of a better term I'm calling "embeddedness," borrowing from its use in the 2003 Iraq war for embedded journalists. Embeddedness is taken to mean the degree to which a person can be thought of as being mainstream or marginal in their society.

Compiling a list of marginal elements is challenging and will depend on the extent to which you are embedded. Lars-Gunnar Andersson and Peter Trudgill's list of peripherals or people on the edge includes criminals (the furthest out from the center), alcoholics, unemployed, and young people. I presume the last are in the marginal list because they haven't yet found their place in the world. No doubt the moment they enroll in first-year law, they shift to mainstream status.

The well-established difficulty in comparing swearing across cultures makes it valuable to provide valid and reliable modes of describing differences. I want to discuss three such modes—cultural, grammatical, and structural—that I believe can provide interpretative frames from which we can perhaps gain some comparative insight. At the very least, these offer a point of departure for comparing swearing across languages.

The first of these frames is the cultural. While acknowledging that swearing across cultures has some near-universal features, we must also note that such broad themes do have a local and particular manifestation. We might expect a Latvian speaker to swear differently from his Cantonese counterpart. The surface features of a language tend to be among the most colorful, largely because of their emotional accompaniments, and they give the superficial impression that languages vary dramatically in their patterns of swearing. My approach, however, tends to look for the commonalities. Put it this way: Whether you're advising the target of your abuse to tell his mother to go do it with a donkey or a mountain goat, the end choice of creature is less important as a point of cultural contrast than the larger commonalities (leitmotifs, if you will) of sexuality, mother abuse, and bestiality.

Nonetheless, some idiosyncratic styles of swearing have been associated with particular groups and cultures. A good example of this is what's been called "ritualized swearing" or "ritual insults," of which there are many examples over both time and space. Historically, this was called "flyting," from the Old English word meaning "contend" or "strive," with strong verbal associations of scolding or wrangling. Flyting was a feature of ancient Germanic societies as well as early Anglo-Saxon times. It lasted in England until around the fifteenth century, and even longer in the north, presumably because of the more tenacious Norse influence there.

Flyting is a verbal slanging match. Players engage in baiting and teasing, using grotesquely sexual and scatological references and trying to out-insult each other as they goad and egg on their opponents toward an imagined outlet of physical violence. It's as if a verbal space has been cordoned off, within which a sanctioned kind of swearing can take place and where taboos are knowingly and legitimately flouted, providing a linguistic and psychological safety valve for a public letting off of steam. From the immediate local perspective, it's almost a performing art, requiring a high level of spontaneous verbal prowess. From the wider perspective of social order, the metaphor of the pressure cooker applies, letting out a little steam under controlled conditions to avert an explosive catastrophe later. It's the circuses part of the bread-and-circuses dictum for political and social control.

In Scotland, flyting became a form of entertainment, designed for a sophisticated audience rather than a spontaneous street crowd. Not surprising, given what we know about taboos and swearing in Scotland, where the traditional authoritarian attitude toward swearing was severely punitive. Once again, we see the pattern of proliferation as the underbelly of prohibition.

The tradition of ritualized swearing, much like flyting, continues in a number of places in the modern world. It is perhaps most notable in black American communities, where it is called "sounding" or "signifying" or "playing the dozens." Variations of this kind of flyting provide social distinctions between in-group and out-group members. But they also act as lyrical cornerstones for much of the anthemic rap (particularly gangsta rap) that defines gang neighborhoods, including communities of young people from other ethnic backgrounds who admire gang values.

Here are two examples:

> *I don't play the dozens, the dozens ain't my game*
> *But the way I fucked your mama is a goddamn shame*

> *I hate to talk about your mother, she's a good old soul*
> *She got a ten-ton pussy and a rubber asshole.*

This style is also called "capping" and "cracking on" and is found as well in urban Aboriginal English in Australia. While players know that the taboos have been dropped for the occasion, some boundaries remain, and participants know not to cross them unless they are prepared for the ritualized verbal violence to escalate into the real thing.

There is an argument that this ritualized behavior is not so much swearing as insulting because the abuse is embedded in the literal rather than the symbolic meaning of taboo words. Much the same observation could be made about the common discourse routine where a member of an audience interrupts a stand-up comic's monologue by yelling out a provocative comment. The comic has to respond to

the heckler or lose face, and the response is typically blatantly aggressive.

In her book *Language: The Social Mirror,* Elaine Chaika
shows how the closed communities of Eastern European
Jews had their own version of ritual cursing long before
their emigration to the New World. Just as the verbal rituals of black urban youth are revealing of the social conditions and attitudes within which they live, so, too, do the
curses of Old World Jews.

> May you marry a raving beauty, live next door to the
> officers' club, and travel ten months of the year.

> May you back into a pitchfork and grab a hot stove
> for support.

> May your daughters' hair grow thick, black, and
> abundant—all over their faces.

Perhaps an easier frame within which to compare
swearing across language and cultures is the grammatical
mode. To do this, we have to put aside nuances of meaning
for the moment and concentrate on the building blocks of
sentence or utterance construction. (I prefer "utterance"
when what's at issue is spoken language, and most—
though not all—swearing is orally delivered.) Again, we're
looking for patterns by which we can compare and contrast
the ways different languages employ their swear words.

One theory uses a hierarchical frame to map the level of
interruption—a notion also called "intrusion" or "penetra-

tion"—achieved by a swearing expression in its relation to the rest of the utterance. At the lowest level of interruption, a swear word might be thought of as being comfortably embedded in its grammatical surrounds, for example, "absofuckinglutely." At the highest level, the swear word operates alone, without the cushioning of a verbal surrounding ("God damn you!"). There are five levels in this hierarchy:

1. Where the swear word is incorporated into a word; as a prefix ("shithead") or an infix ("absofuckinglutely").

2. Where the swear word operates as a minor constituent of an utterance, typically an adjective ("this fucking school") or adverb ("a bloody long way away").

3. Where the swear word serves as a major constituent of the utterance, typically as a noun ("that stupid bastard") or verb ("he fucks everything up").

4. Where the swear word operates as an adsentence—a bit loosely tied to the utterance—either before ("fuck, I forgot all about it") or after ("what's the matter, for God's sake?"), and is not grammatically essential in the sense that the utterance would not founder without it.

5. Where the swear word operates on its own, perhaps in addition to other utterances, or replacing them entirely: "Shit!," "Jesus Christ!," "Fucking hell!"

Using these five levels, we can examine the grammatical operational rules of any language's swearing repertoire and, if we like, compare it to another language or other languages. Precisely why one might want to get into the grammatical knickers of cross-cultural swearing is anyone's bet, but linguists do things like that. Investigating the grammar of swearing will not seem weird to people who happily spend three years exploring inflections in a little known African language, or comparing the level of directness across languages in asking someone to please move his or her car, or mapping the use of "ah," "eh," and "um" in university lectures.

It's claimed that the above hierarchy supports two interesting and quantifiable implications: The first is that if a language has swearing possibilities on one level, it will have them on all levels above; and the second is that if a language has swearing possibilities on one level, it will have a greater number of possibilities on all levels above.

Now, I confess I haven't tried this out on a range of languages, largely because I am not a competent swearer in a range of languages. Yet, applying it only to English, I sense an intuitively comfortable fit. Consider, for example, the imagined frequency (rare) of infixes like "abso-bloody-lutely" with that of stand-alone expletives and abusives such as "shit!" or "fuck off!" (very common).

Then again, the hierarchy might have been created with English in mind, thereby ensuring an intuitive fit. In any case, readers are invited to dip into their swearing competence in any other language and test the hypothesis for themselves (please send any interesting findings to me c/o the publisher).

The third mode for comparing swearing across languages is predicated on a view of the structure of society and is called, unsurprisingly, "structural." The underlying assumption is that swearing is intimately connected to social restrictions, and that these restrictions reflect social values. Two points of relevance should be noted. The first is that the social values reflected in swearing are not accidental or random but deeply embedded in the structure of a society, being the product of a long-standing interplay of multiple elements in the society's historico-cultural biography. The second, which we'll explore in greater depth shortly, is that societies are not monolithic or homogeneous but in fact display multiple layers of differentiation—you only have to look at the way students at private schools wear uniforms to know that uniforms can actually differentiate, not mask, the individual.

According to anthropologist Mary Douglas, social behavior or "style," including the presence or degree of swearing, can be linked to social structure and values. She argues that "a social structure which requires a high degree of conscious control will find its style at a high level of formality." This formality will be accompanied by a "stern application of the purity rule, denigration of organic process and wariness towards experiences in which control of consciousness is lost." In brief, high social structure equals strict constraints on swearing.

Before we look further into Douglas's theory, I need to introduce a quality I want to call "kemptness." This is a noun I've coined from "unkempt," a little word whose potential utility is grossly hampered by its limited grammatical flexibility. At the very least, "unkempt" needs a counterpart—

"kempt"—since unless we live in a uniformly disheveled universe (as those of us living with teenagers might think is the case), we do need to be able to describe both styles: those who tuck in their shirt and those who let it hang out. I suggest the words "kempt," "kemptness," and "unkemptness" be made available to us for descriptive purposes.

Now, people vary in the degree of kemptness in which they keep their home, garden, office, clothes, hair, or personal hygiene. They also vary in how kempt their language is, in how frequently they employ unkempt terms, or how easily they lose emotional control and allow the unkempt to bubble up to the surface. This is rather like a kempt barometer. Douglas links the kempt factor with a theory about linguistic socialization developed by sociolinguist Basil Bernstein.

Bernstein saw speech as a set of specific codes that regulated a child's verbal acts. He identified two different codes (but gave them unfortunate names that got him into a lot of trouble). His "restricted" code is deeply enmeshed in the social structures of the context, and shaped by the positions and roles available in that context. The "elaborated" code is different in that it primarily enables complex thoughts to be processed and expressed. It allows the speaker to move away from a fixed pattern of roles toward greater autonomy and individuality. (There are up- and downsides to both codes, which are not relevant to our point here; nor are the academic implications for children from restricted code environments who are thrust into school as an elaborated code environment.)

What we have here is cross-fertilization. Douglas the

anthropologist borrowed from Bernstein the linguist. Most importantly, she worked with his notion of the codes within positional-role-structured families (restricted) and personal-role-structured families (elaborated). Then the anthropologist in her applied the codes as a lens through which to view the larger unit of a society:

> A positional role society would be a strictly ordered society where each person's position in the structure determines their rights and duties. A personal role society would be a society where the individual's abilities and ambitions are important in deciding their future career and thus their rights and duties.

As Victorian society leaned strongly toward a positional-role structure—exerting a high degree of conscious control—among mainstream groups who purportedly carried Victorian values, we would expect to find a high degree of antagonism toward behaviors that suggest a loosening of self-control, such as swearing. I am referring to the public face of the "upper" of the Two Nations, as Disraeli called them, not to the lower reaches of Victorian society, nor to the underbelly of the upper level.

Numerous studies of Victorian society, including Victorian erotica, have left no doubt about the passions that seethed behind those staid pronouncements and demure exteriors. No surprise, then, that "extreme Victorian reticence and restraint produced all manner of perversion." A classic example of perversity is homosexual acts between men being illegal, but not those between women: apparently, "no one could think of a way to explain to Queen Victoria what homosexual acts between women were."

The structural frame does offer a way to compare swearing across cultures, though the comparisons are best made not in absolute binary terms but in the greater relativity and subtlety of a continuum. It's not a case of positional roles favoring hyper-control, as opposed to personal roles favoring greater individual freedom. Rather, we're thinking of a more finely calibrated concept along a gradient, with different societies positioned as orienting toward one end or the other. Douglas's theory has predictive power at two levels. First, it predicts that we could expect to find different public attitudes toward swearing across different kinds of societies. Second, it suggests that among different members of the one society, we can expect to find a range of attitudes.

Let's bring the notion of kemptness back into the picture, and include within it not only control over the external face that one shows the world, but also control over the language one uses. We can assume that the people at the core of the mainstream of a society are likely to have neat gardens and watch their language in public situations. As cornerstones in the social structure, they're expected to take a great deal of care in their appearance and language. Conversely, a homeless person living on the periphery of society can be expected to be disheveled both in appearance and in language. If your investment in the given structures of society is zero, as in the case of the long-term unemployed or the homeless, you have little to lose in letting go of the reins of maintenance and control.

Incidentally, Douglas's purity principle seems akin to Erving Goffman's notion of leaking and flooding out, where individuals struggle not to compromise their poise and face in public situations. For Goffman, the abuse contained in swearing is the disrespect shown to the face of another, so interpersonal poise might be defined as the mutual upholding of each other's face.

Douglas's theory can also apply to different groups within the one society, such as the corporate lawyer or the long-term unemployed. These might be thought of as levels of application. But there is yet another level at which we can apply it, a level that intermeshes with the aspect of linguistics known as "register."

Register is a system of variation within a language. Unlike dialect or gender-lect, it is based not on relatively permanent differences between speakers, but on temporary differences within the same speaker's language. Here the differences derive from the fluctuating circumstance of situation. This aspect of social structure also has implications for swearing.

We generally expect to find more swearing in informal than in formal circumstances. This is not, as is sometimes thought, a matter of laziness but a question of register. In the context of solidarity—for example, when coworkers go for a drink after work—language is used less for transactional purposes (the giving and receiving of information) and more for interpersonal reasons (the nourishing and maintaining of personal connections). In this case, swearing both signals and builds in-group membership. In the university expedition to arctic Norway that we looked at earlier, we saw the swearing quantum increase among the men once the women left. This was not laziness or uncouthness coming to the fore but a demonstration of how social swearing serves as a social lubricant and solidarity builder.

11

BOOTLEGGERS AND ASTERISKS

"It does so fucking look like her!"

—PABLO PICASSO

Shakespeare has his rather wise Juliet say, "O, swear not by the moon, the inconstant moon . . ." To which the lovestruck, hormone-infused Romeo asks, wide-eyed, "What shall I swear by?" And Juliet famously responds, "Do not swear at all."

In cautioning Romeo against swearing, Juliet might well be thought of as the universal voice of prohibition. The fact is that the taboo against swearing permeates almost every human society.

The word "taboo" was introduced to English by Captain Cook in 1777, but of course that was not when taboos started. In fact, so ancient is the notion and so widespread the habit that one wonders what word served before Cook and the Tongans gave us the gift of *tabu*.

What is of more interest here is the amazing failure of the taboo on swearing to achieve its goal—namely, to restrain or suppress or eliminate swearing. What the taboo has done is generate a massively rich lexicon of swear words as well as avoidance strategies by which people can still swear but get away with it. It is this notion of avoidance that we're concerned with. Impunity comes with a price tag of obliqueness, though this, too, is variable, and given the service that swearing provides, a touch of the oblique would seem to be well worth the trouble.

Banning things doesn't get rid of them, as was admirably demonstrated in the 1920s by Prohibition. People will go to extraordinary lengths to accomplish whatever they have been forbidden to do. Paradoxically, if an activity is powerful and pervasive enough to warrant one, then it's doubtful that any prohibition will be forceful enough to stamp it out.

As with alcohol, so, too, with swearing, though generally with less violence and bloodshed, and certainly fewer movies. Yet the extraordinary inventiveness that unfurls from the swearing taboo provides enough data and research opportunities for a truckload of linguists working full-time over a couple of life spans.

Diversity is the primary feature. While the taboo on swearing is pretty universal, the form or shape that the taboo takes varies enormously. One category of variance is the "who" factor, most particularly, who's doing the swearing. This is a question of sanctioned permission, which relates partly to role and the formality of the setting. No one really expects rock stars to stifle their natural language even when they're onstage collecting an award. On the other hand, the priestly class, across almost all cultures, is expected to uphold the taboo at all times.

Even in the liberal West, it's perverse to think of a minister of religion—and by that I mean a cleric of any religion—delivering a sermon embroidered with choice expletives. "Fucking Moses, he bloody well went up the side of that damn mountain" . . . no, not likely. Certain extraneous factors can mitigate lapses, however, such as if the cleric is "indisposed" (a fever-induced delirium) or "not himself" (intoxicated), or "distressed" (overly emotional). Such variables allow outbreaks from the constraints of role.

But the question "who's swearing?" doesn't provide us with sufficient information. We need to think in interactional terms—that is, not only "who's speaking?" but also "who's being spoken to?" Most language is produced with a receiver (or audience) in mind, apart from the odd Shakespearean soliloquy or two, or the toe-stubbing situation, which Montagu calls a case of the "solitary swearer."

The essentially social nature of swearing means that the swearer will sometimes adopt oblique acoustic devices such as turning down the volume to sotto voce; sending out an advance warning—"pardon my French" (which sometimes brings up the rear as a hasty afterthought); or performing a deft U-turn following an initial swear-cueing consonant ("shit!" becomes "sugar!"). They are all ways by which swearers manage to have their swearing cake and eat it, too. Or break the taboo but get away with it.

It's not that a member of the priestly class cannot swear at all. It's in the performance of their priestly duties that the prohibition most strongly applies, and even clerics remove the garb of their role, signaling perhaps a switch in register and a relaxation of the taboo. It's not impossible to imagine a minister (again, of any faith), relaxing in an out-of-work and out-of-public-domain setting and finding the odd expressive expletive passing his or her lips. The important factors are the setting, who is being addressed, and who might overhear.

My daughter has been an accomplished swearer from her earliest toddlerdom. But even as she picked up the odd taboo word—mostly through osmosis at home—she also learned the rules. Restraint was needed in the company of grandmas, headmistresses, basically anyone old-looking. So, and I say this proudly, as well as picking up the odd swear word, she also acquired the rules of use, rather like acquiring a new piece of technology, reading the instruction manual, and using it properly. This is the stuff of the competent or accomplished swearer.

Cultures differ not only in the basic constraints of who is allowed to swear, to whom, and under what circumstances, but in the particular range of experience that they choose to swear by. Over time, some words in a language become accepted as the conventional vehicles of swearing. Some Australian Aborigines call upon the name of a long-deceased relative as an exclamation in a moment of surprise or shock, perhaps akin to "Holy Moses!," "My sainted aunt!," or "Jesus, Mary, and Joseph!"

In biblical times, it was not unheard of to swear allegiance on the king's testicles. I presume the "on" was metaphorical, not literal. The ancient Greeks and Romans preferred former rulers, deities, or famous people—understandable, really, as they were blessed with such a huge repertoire of gods, goddesses, mythological characters, and creatures. Some of them, by Jove, have lasted a very long time.

However, it's not only gods and celebrities of yore that furnish languages with swear words. Sometimes a plant or a part of the body can be conscripted to swearing duty. A famous oath of ancient Ionia translates as "By the cabbage!"; Socrates swore "By the dog"; and Pythagoras—perhaps eccentrically, although not illogically—swore by the number four. And if gods, flora, fauna, and numbers don't appeal, you can make up your own. To achieve his thrill, the poet Robert Southey (1774–1843) resorted to the nonsense word "Aballiboozobanganovribo," which to my ears sounds like a forerunner of the expletives Walt Disney used for his animal characters in moments of extreme emotion. Arabic and Turkish are famous for their elaborate and ritualized swearing expressions—"You father of sixty dogs," "You rider of a female camel"—which are by no means confined to antiquity, as we shall see.

An interesting study by Abd el-Jawad of swearing sequences (termed "oaths") in Jordanian Arabic catalogs the range of swear-by options that Jordanians use. Oaths are sworn by Allah; the Koran or other holy books; prophets and messengers; important historical figures; family members, holy places and times; all of Allah's creatures and creations; and moral values such as honor, chastity, dignity, and honesty. Some oaths are male-only, such as the so-called repudiation oath, whereby the user swears to divorce his wife as a preface to a speech act of some sort.

Jordanian women, especially the older and uneducated, rarely swear by Allah but more often by the life and well-being of loved ones, using rhymed oaths that are elaborate, alliterative, and lyrical: "by the sunset and the breaking of hearts," "by the life of the flying birds and the walking beast," "by the life of this quiet darkness and the angels calling." Both men and women sprinkle oaths widely on many speech acts: declarations, invitations, suggestions and offers, promises and pledges, requests, apologies and excuses, threats and challenges, complaints, praising and blaming. El-Jawad concludes that such conversational swearing is a dominant feature of daily exchanges, to the extent that an interaction would be rare if it did not contain at least one oath.

Many Western cultures are neither as rich in oaths nor as permissive in their use. Queen Elizabeth II's famous namesake and ancestor may have inherited the Tudor facility with a neatly turned oath, but consider for a moment her extraordinary deployment of the Latin *annus horribilis* in her Christmas message to the United Kingdom and the nations of the Commonwealth in December 1992. Yes, it had been a rotten year by anyone's standards, with so much public airing of dirty laundry. Extramarital affairs, eating disorders, suicide rumors, and intimate phone calls, every salacious detail salivated over by a ravenous press. Much of the year had been spent in damage control. In the public perception, the palace had lost a good deal of its grip. There was no way Elizabeth could roll out an updated version of her usual speech, in which snippets of text are interwoven with happy faces of smiling royals in various poses—formal-regal public and relaxed public, pretend private.

For the sake of the shreds of credibility that the House of Windsor had at the time, the queen and her speechwriters had a formidable task ahead of them. They had to acknowledge what a bad year it had been, but in language befitting a royal personage in a public role. "A bloody rotten year" wasn't good enough. Enter Latin *qua* salvation.

Annus horribilis was a brilliantly inventive and studied off-shoot of the more standard *annus mirabilis.* Its effect was aided by the proximity of the Latin *annus* to the English "anus," from which it was a short step to those parts of the body that generally furnish less royal souls with a lexicon of swearing. *Annus horribilis* was as close as a queen might come to swearing without tarnishing her dignity. One can only imagine what the PR bill for that exercise might have come to, but hey, dignity is too important to worry about price tags. (Then again, the queen might have a surprisingly fluent turn of swearing phrase, having been brought up in a naval household and being married to a notoriously fluent swearer.)

Montagu does a scattershot inventory of swearing among peoples of antiquity—the ancient Egyptians, the Jews and the early Christians, the Greeks and the Romans. Where he found lengthy and forceful ordinances against swearing, such as in the Old Testament, he wisely surmised—and it's a logical step—that the people for whom the ordinances were conceived must have been "accomplished and frequent swearers." God would not go to the trouble of detailed verbal injunctions against swearing if it weren't rife among the folk in question.

The swearing that is frowned on here is using God's name in the taking of an oath or maliciously misusing God's name. The classic prohibition is the Third Commandment in Exodus 20:7—"You shall not swear falsely by the name of the Lord your God; for the Lord will not excuse one who swears falsely by His name."

The Old Testament does not address the issue of foul language directly. However, the frequent use of euphemisms signals a preference for the oblique. Robert Dessaix states that to understand how a euphemism works, we need to grasp the fundamental Old Testament message: "There will be less unpleasantness all round, less killing, less quarrelling, less hate and distress if we learn early on not to say what we mean." For example, words for "defecate," "rape," "excrement," "urine," and even "hemorrhoids" are avoided either by a gentle paraphrase ("cover one's legs" for "defecate") or by changing a letter or two, as in the hemorrhoids example, where *afalim* became *tehorim,* presumably to soften the offensive sound. Naively, I've tended to think that events recorded in the Old Testament would be far too momentous for there to be a need to discuss hemorrhoids, but it seems I was wrong.

Montagu concludes that:

> The whole history of swearing bears unequivocal testimony to the fact that legislation and punishments against swearing have only had the effect of driving it under the cloaca of those more noisome regions, where it has flourished and luxuriated with the ruddiness of the poppy's petals and the blackness of the poppy's heart.

Different cultures, it would seem, have deployed different processes and procedures to mandate, sanction, curtail, control, and corral swearing behaviors. These might be thought of as modes of prohibition, and while they're all systematic (to differing degrees), they vary in how organized and institutionalized they are. Broadly, they all might be thought of as ways in which taboo behaviors are made subject to restraint.

Take, for instance, how the print media handles words like FUCK and CUNT. One approach, and perhaps the easiest, is the total ban. Another is to allow it in certain circumstances—for example, in a quotation. Another is to cue the word, as in "the F-word" or "the C-word," which can lead to peculiar developments in the spoken language, such as the emergence of "effing" as an adjective. When Norman Mailer wrote *The Naked and the Dead,* he sidestepped existing censorship laws by writing "fug" instead of "fuck." Mae West, on being introduced to Mailer at a party, reportedly exclaimed, "Oh, you're the guy who can't spell 'fuck'!"

At the time of writing, both *The Sydney Morning Herald* and the Australian Broadcasting Corporation did not censor the "appropriate" use of coarse language, provided it was not used "gratuitously." Ultimately, the decision about what is or isn't gratuitous—or appropriate—is a discretionary one. Robert Dessaix has pointed out the curious fact that characters on the British police show *The Bill* do not in fact swear; they break just about every other commandment, but they don't swear. The decision to wash out all their mouths with soap was a viewer-sensitive one.

An earlier method of censorship by sanitizing was to purge all swear words from a text. The first to do this was a wealthy Scottish physician, Thomas Bowdler, who, at the start of the Victorian era, set himself the task of writing *The Family Shakespeare,* creating versions of the original "in which nothing is added to the original text; but those words and expressions are omitted which cannot with propriety be read aloud in a family." Bowdler gave us, as well as a clean Shakespeare, his name, eponymically. The purging process is called "bowdlerization," which I once might have been forgiven for thinking had something to do with a more literal kind of purging.

Bowdler wanted to create a family-friendly Shakespeare by removing the *pas devant les enfants* words. There is a long-standing notion that children should be protected from the contaminating influence of adult swearing. The author Mark Haddon commented on the different realities of child and adult upon the publication of his first novel, *The Curious Incident of the Dog in the Night-Time,* which in Australia was published simultaneously as an adult and as a children's book. The covers were different, but the content the same, except in the Dutch children's version, where the swearing was bowdlerized.

Of the English-language version, which retained the swearing, Haddon said, with pleasure:

[We've] out-Dutched the Dutch by leaving the swearing in. . . . The swearing is important. If you read books for kids, there's that little invisible ring of safety. You know that, if horrible things happen, the author will look after you. I don't think the ring of safety is there with this book, and the swearing is one of the signals of that.

A contemporary episode in the deliberate misspelling of FUCK is the branding of the clothing company French Connection United Kingdom. Their name just happens to form the arresting acronym "FCUK," which they clearly enjoy emblazoning across much of their apparel. Of course, you don't have to be dyslexic to read FUCK for "fcuk." You realize the misordering only after FUCK has registered. The company no doubt revels in the association, the risqué element, the apparent avoidance through misordering, the in-your-face-ness of FUCK, which they appear to sidestep but in fact highlight—in the way a judge reinforces, rather than minimizes, something when she or he instructs the jury to wipe it from their consideration.

Another swearing-curtailing device is to allow the taboo word but disenvowel it, so that FUCK and CUNT become "f-ck" and "c-nt." An alternative to the dash is the asterisk. As the taboo on FUCK has relaxed, for example, we have seen "f***" become "f**k" and then "f*ck." Though this is more than minimally absurd in a monosyllabic word, someone in a powerful position imposed the asterisk factor, deciding that there was a correspondence in rigor between the number of asterisks and public perception of the prohibition's gravity.

After a while, the circumstances and modes of imposed restraint become naturalized. We see "c*nt" in a newspaper and know exactly what it means (we might even mouth the word, for a cheap thrill), but mostly, we give not a second thought to the imposed restraint. Fish don't see the water they swim in. Our Martian anthropologist, on the other hand, would no doubt have a field day.

The asterisk, then, is a minimal and not very systematic form of imposed restraint, although the symbol's underlying meaning (what we call its "semiotics") is well and widely understood. Other cultures use other means to restrain comparable behaviors. Sometimes these restraints take the form of allowing organized opportunities for swearing to take place, which would suggest that someone has realized swearing is important or inevitable or primal in some way, and a total ban is not going to work; in fact, it might backfire. So the society finds a way to allow in some swearing behaviors.

The concept of organized swearing may be as odd to us as that of organized laughter opportunities—where groups of people get together at a set time for a set period, for the specific purpose of laughing, in order to generate both physiological and psychological benefits and promote well-being. Certain Indian and Japanese laughing groups have been well documented, and there's at least one in the Australian city of Adelaide, which I came upon by accident—quite a shock, I can tell you—on an early-morning jog. I'm told that the Japanese also provide formalized situations where employees can go and vent their anger at effigies or images of their executives, which sounds like an excellent opportunity for psychosomatic release.

Well-respected anthropological literature exists on organized swearing in nonliterate communities. Ashley Montagu reports on the work of Donald Thomson, who spent three years among the Australian native tribes of the Cape York Peninsula and wrote extensively about the systematic nature of their swearing behaviors. These were intimately connected with the kinship relationships among tribal members: Their swearing behavior, like all their other linguistic and nonlinguistic behaviors, could not be understood outside of kinship.

Briefly, different relationships are associated with different degrees of freedom and prohibition. (This is not unlike our own society—as we have seen previously, my daughter's growing competence in swearing involved her knowing with whom such behavior was permissible.) In Cape York, the strictest taboos govern the relationships of the speaker to his wife's immediate family of origin (father, mother, and brothers), and the greatest freedom is allowed between grandchildren and grandparents, and among members of one's own sex. We're talking about communities vastly different from our own—or are we?

Within the general constraints of these kinship regulations, swearing behaviors among the Cape York Peninsula tribes are classified as unorganized and organized. The unorganized variety includes all kinds of foul expressions said in the context of anger or for the purpose of provoking physical attack. Organized or "licensed" swearing, as Thomson calls it, accords strictly with the kinship rules—that is, it strictly prescribes who is to be included or excluded—and is carried out in public. It is more than permissible; it is obligatory. It has nothing to do with swearing as the stubbed-toe response or as an incitement to anger. Rather, it's playful and jocular.

Montagu refers to the sanctioned swearing within the kinship network as "joking relationships." Thomson's native informants assured him of the intention to make everyone happy, and he concludes that licensed swearing induced a state of euphoria. This is why I see it as similar to the laughter clubs (though, to my knowledge, these don't have kinship regulations).

It also reminds me, speaking as an outsider, of a group of Australian men having a beer or two with their mates after work. The similarities are startling: the regulation on who's allowed in and who's not, on what language is considered appropriate, and the positive goodwill (that is, unless too much alcohol affects the dynamic) among the participants. We might consider this a contemporary Western instance of licensed swearing.

Montagu also researched the swearing behavior of Australian Aborigines. He characterizes their socialized swearing, and a comparable version among the Eskimos, as a "licitly provided escape valve"—that is, an efficient device for the preservation of social equilibrium. He evaluates it as a far more sophisticated outlet than the cruder expression of the same need in Western societies: bachelor parties, dirty jokes, obscene limericks, and pub talk.

Instead of banning swearing outright, and driving hard-core swearers underground, as it were, these so-called primitive peoples have tried to understand it and, on the basis of their insight, have organized their societies to accommodate it. In recognizing the usefulness of swearing, they have availed themselves of the benefits of licit emotive expression, in certain controlled circumstances, and thereby have avoided the psychopathology that accompanies suppression. The cost saved in community disruption, loss of productivity, law and policing, substance abuse rehabilitation, and psychiatrists' fees must be enormous.

From a historical perspective, the constraints on swearing might be thought of as divisible into three developmental stages. The earliest restrictions were local, familial, and communal, where, as we have seen with some Australian Aborigines, taboos on certain behaviors were defined, proscribed, and conflated within existing kinship patterns. As organized religion took hold, the constraints

on swearing, mostly as blasphemy, assumed a particular religious dimension. The third stage brings us to the contemporary secular-legal sanctions that exist in Western societies
today, best thought of as an influential collection of aware-
nesses that effectively govern social relationships through
etiquette.

These days we don't look for guidance to family from
tribal elders, or from clerical authority; rather, restrictions
on speech come minimally from the courts and maximally
from social mores. However, as we shall see, the energies
invested in constraint are matched by the energies invested
in protecting freedoms. Dooling waxes lyrical about this:
"What is the First Amendment if not an attempt to confer
civil rights on words, which provide the currency of exchange in the bond markets of human interaction?"

Naturally, these three stages are not strictly linear. While
the church has lost a good deal of its clout, it still wields a
subtle influence in subtle ways. Despite the separation of
church and state, religious believers are wont to protest
publicly when their beliefs are disrespected. Such protests
can lead to self-censorship, often motivated by commercial
concerns. For example, in 1997, the shoe manufacturer
Reebok bowed to public protests over the name it had proposed for a new line of sneakers, the Incubus. It withdrew
the shoe, apologized to the public, went away and licked its
wounds, and probably commissioned a report into the
damage wrought to the brand name. You would think that
someone would have advised their marketing department
that an incubus is a demon who has sex with a sleeping
woman or, at the very least, that someone would have
looked it up.

Naturally, different peoples around the world are affected in different measure by any or all of the three stages outlined above. In some Moslem countries where church and state are indivisible, the involvement of clerical power in the suppression of language deemed offensive, especially blasphemy, would resemble presecular Western societies. And with increased contact among peoples through globalization or technology, the influence of organized religion can reach across borders, as in the famous case of the fatwa proclaimed against Salman Rushdie.

We won't concern ourselves here with the constraints that courts impose on speech crimes such as making obscene phone calls or resisting arrest using indecent or offensive language. I am more interested in the less visible, less easy to define, more nebulous, but enormously powerful deterrent that exists through the channels of social etiquette. If the courts impose fines or prison terms, social etiquette punishes those who violate the social rules with what Timothy Jay calls "social punishments"—scorn, banishments, nasty looks, ridicule, or public condemnation.

Ironically, the social punishment is often averted through the power exerted by self-censorship, as happened in 2003 when Sydney's Channel 7 closed down the interview with *Macquarie Dictionary*'s Sue Butler after she let "fuckwit" slip out—albeit in the context of her discussing taboo word use and issues of appropriateness and offensiveness. In hypersensitive damage control, they feared they would be seen as not being sufficiently protective of their viewers' sensibilities.

Perhaps the best enforcers of social standards through self-censorship are parents, a logical choice given their major input to the socialization of the young. Some friends of mine, in a mixed Australian-Japanese marriage, are bringing up their two boys bilingually and biculturally. When a swear word is inadvertently dropped in their home, the sanctioned punishment is to administer (more usually, the threat to administer) a dose of the Japanese mustard, wasabi. In fact, taboo words are now called, in a jocular way, "wasabi words." Everyone in the home knows what this means, and swearing guests, like me, soon find out. It's a form of the secret code that intimates have, which allows them to short-circuit long descriptions and explanations of frequent events.

To understand censorship, both other- and self-imposed varieties, we need to appreciate that the conventions of etiquette—which make you wipe your swearing feet at the metaphorical door—are underpinned by the crucial notion of face. We meet this word mostly in the expression "to save face" and "to lose face," both terms conveying the precious commodity of public esteem.

Indeed, we can go so far as to say that the notion of face underpins social interaction, governing linguistic and non-linguistic behaviors from the most formal and public—such as a eulogy at a funeral—to the most informal and private: a morning-after-the-night-before chat between new intimates. The notion of face is based on the work of sociologist Erving Goffman, who derived it from the anthropologist Emil Durkheim. Penelope Brown and Steven Levinson drew on the work of both to set the foundation for their universal theory of linguistic politeness.

Their central principle is what Brown and Levinson call "the mutual vulnerability of face," a tenet that governs all human communication. Simply put: In conventional human interactions, speakers seek to maintain face (their public self-image) and to avoid making anyone else lose face. This can be achieved through an infinite number of ways, mostly linguistic, from openly admiring your neighbors' rose garden (making them feel good that you have recognized all their hard effort) to *not* asking those same neighbors for a loan of their car for the evening (an inappropriate request that would no doubt be met with discomfort and would generate considerable unease between you). In general, energy invested into face-work is designed to prevent, minimize, or make up for any such unease among people who are in some sort of contact.

The rules of etiquette, as we know, touch all aspects of social life, as is well evidenced in an old and quaint book on my shelves called *Manners for Millions: A Complete Guide to Courteous Behaviour.* Swearing etiquette is a subset of rules of conduct that fits neatly within the larger paradigm of face maintenance and avoidance of face threat. Swearing is a kind of symbolic verbal violence that imposes uncomfortably on another person, so swearing at somebody violates his or her face, while simultaneously losing face for the swearer through breaking the rules.

This mutual vulnerability is the key to the maintenance of social equilibrium. You can swear wildly when you stub your toe if you know you're not going to be overheard. But in a public and social setting, you may have to forgo the relief from a momentary release of a short, sharp expletive if your social self deems the release to be face-violating. There are many gradations between suppression and release, and the swearer intuitively calibrates the cost-benefit ratio in every circumstance.

Face-work and the etiquette of swearing might be thought of as a game. Participants enter into the game knowing the rules and mostly choosing to abide by them. On occasion, participants may flout the rules, often intentionally. While on her honeymoon with Arthur Miller, Marilyn Monroe was in England filming *The Prince and the Showgirl* with Laurence Olivier, who had unconcealed contempt for her. One day Olivier shouted at Monroe, "Can't you ever get yourself here on time, for fuck's sake?" Marilyn responded—sweetly, I guess—"Oh, do you have that word over here, too?" She stepped outside the parameters of the rules—which, following Olivier's intentions, would have been to embarrass and intimidate her—and responded to the word sans its magic. Touché, Marilyn.

A similar example occurs in the film *A Fish Called Wanda*. In this exchange, the caricatured American Otto tries to insult the caricatured Englishman Archie by calling him a "pompous, stuck-up, snot-nosed, English, giant twerp, scumbag, fuckface, dickhead arsehole!" To which Archie responds, "How very interesting. You are a real vulgarian, aren't you?"

Both incidents deliberately flout the rules of the game of swearing. This is different from unintentional flouting. My nonnative-English-speaking mother once got herself into deep water by answering the question "How are you?" with the innocently intended rejoinder "Pretty fucked, actually." She'd heard me say this most nights as I came home late from studying at the university library, and in her prag-

matic understanding, it meant "very tired," which of course
it did and does. It wasn't an unexpected phrase for a young
university student to use, but it had a completely different
effect emerging from the respectable personage of a portly
sixty-year-old woman with Polish-accented English. For-
tunately, accents can sometimes generate more permissive
allowances, and no serious loss of face was suffered.

This anecdote also indicates the arbitrary nature of
words and meanings. "Fucked" didn't *sound* like a bad word
to my mother, and even after the incident, it continued to
lack magic for her, though once she'd learned the rules, she
played by them—mostly.

Many nonnative English speakers find they can swear in
English with greater personal freedom than they can in
their own language. This is not because, for instance, English is more liberal than other languages. Rather, it's because the nonnative swearer has not been socialized into
the inhibitions that usually constrain usage. In such cases,
as one middle-aged Swedish speaker told me, swearing can
be quite liberating.

Even when swearing is deliberately used to flout the
system, there are rules involved. As the receiver of swearing, you can choose whether to play by the rules—that is, to
be offended or angered or outraged—or step outside the
rules and thus divest the taboo words of their supposed
magical wounding power, as Marilyn did so deftly with
Olivier.

Swearers are not always constrained by etiquette. In a
road-rage situation, for example, the swearer has no interest in the polite maintenance of civilized behavior. Anger
has taken over, and the road-rager has, for the duration,

chosen to absent him- or herself from the rules that govern normal interaction. I am not dealing here with instances of social swearing, which actually build rapport, as with in-group conversations where swearing happens by mutual consent and fosters an atmosphere of acceptance and solidarity.

It's clear that euphemism—or language used as shield, in the terms of Keith Allan and Kate Burridge—is a sophisticated and highly variegated technique by which potential harm to another's face is avoided through a softening of the language or an obliqueness of approach. The variety comes from the fact that euphemisms have a short shelf life. Pretty soon they become tainted by association with the very smells they try so hard to camouflage. Steven Pinker calls this "the euphemism treadmill." Still, for the duration that they serve, they work as a kind of linguistic Lourdes.

The thousands of indirect and hedged ways we have developed for referring to bodily functions are all designed to take the threat of face attack out of the picture. It's as if we all have tacitly agreed to abide by the rules of public poise and composure, and to avoid behaviors that lead to rupture and discomposure. For the most part, this generalized understanding works well.

A euphemistic alternative for "fucking," as an emotionally intensifying adjective, is the now rather old-fashioned "frigging," usually spelled "friggin'," as in "you friggin' liar, tell me the truth, dammit." Because its association with FUCK caught up with it, "friggin'" itself became tainted and, perhaps for this reason, faded from use. After all, if "friggin'" won't work for you as a euphemism, it's better to either find a fresh one or go back to the full-force FUCK. There's a good chance we might lose "friggin'" altogether over time, though language has its own organic and mysterious ways of rolling oldish words into new arrangements. Take "frigmarole," for instance, meaning "a rigmarole, only more so," as in "sorting through the laundry basket for a clean pair of socks again—same old frigmarole." Then there's "kenoaf," a euphemism in the *Macquarie Dictionary of Slang,* derived from "fucking oath."

A young cousin of "frigging" is "freaking," as in "it's just too freaking bad," where the phrase "too bad" has been prised open and "freaking" inserted (à la "absofucking-lutelyawful"). The delightfully forthright Ivana Trump is quoted as describing her ex-husband's disapproval of her affair with a man nearly half her age as "just too freaking bad." We seem to have gone from frigging to freaking in the Great Fucking Bypass.

So far we have looked at the organized and overt ways that societies have evolved for the efficient management of some aspects of the human impulse to violate swearing taboo. There are also less systematic, less planned, less institutional ways. These are covert and more bottom-up (as distinct from top-down) linguistic means and measures by which people manage to break the taboo on swearing with relative impunity.

One of these involves phonological and grammatical distortions that emerge as disguised variants of the original taboo word. DAMN, for instance, used to have the very strong ecclesiastical meaning of "excommunicate," a significant threat at a time when the church held the reins of power over life and death and burning at the stake was not something to be taken lightly. With the waning of clerical authority and the rise of the secular era, DAMN has evolved over the centuries and oceans to the quite mild and now quite unecclesiastically connected "darned," which today has the diluted, slightly quaint, and rough equivalence of a toe-stubbing expletive.

According to some reports, but contested by others, "bloody" began as "by our lady," but along the developmental path, it accrued various polite evasions such as "ruddy," "blooming," "bleeding," and the truncated "b," as in "the b thing is broken." As these examples illustrate, new forms often show a rhyming or alliterative influence.

An interesting development of "bloody" was to replace it with its class name, "adjective." Dickens, for example, had one of his characters say, "I won't have no adjective police and adjective strangers in my adjective premises!" Peter Carey does the same in *True History of the Kelly Gang*. Through Ned's voice, Carey uses "adjectival" as a replacement for almost all swear words, as seen in this sampling: "I aint your adjectival mate," "you adjectival fool," "you adjectival b——," "the adjectival mare."

Sometimes euphemistic substitutions grow legs and take off. Eliza Doolittle's scandalous ejaculation "Not bloody likely!" became the sensation of the 1914 theater season and was later christened "the Ascot expletive." Swearers wishing to emulate Miss Doolittle were furnished with a built-in euphemism—"Not *Pygmalion* likely!"—with which a whole generation gratefully availed themselves.

Some decades later, the Tynan incident generated a similar euphemism. In 1965, the British theater critic Kenneth Tynan dropped FUCK during a live BBC interview. The ensuing blitzkrieg of headlines—THAT WORD ON TV, INSULT TO WOMANHOOD, IS THIS MORAL?, THE WAR ON BBC-NITY, SACK 4-LETTER TYNAN—assured that his name would be associated forever with the offending word. So much so, apparently, that the jocular "Shut the Tynan door" happily replicated "Not Pygmalion likely!" and became the euphemism of the decade.

There is even a one-size-fits-all euphemism in the form of "blankety," which *Collins* defines as "a euphemism for any taboo word."

The device of the truncated letter is seen also in variants of FUCK, with "the "F-word" morphing into its own independent word, as in "eff off" and "effing." I've even come across an article in the *London Review of Books* called "Effing the Ineffable." A peculiar metaphorical extension here is the use of "F-word" to stand for the archetype of taboo. A headline in the parents' newspaper *Sydney's Child* recently introduced a feature article on the risks of permissive upbringing: "Why 'No' is the New F-Word."

A common avoidance strategy is to retain the initial sound of the taboo word ("d," as in DAMN, and "sh," as in SHIT) but sideslip into a more innocent word, a tactic that has been labeled "remodeling." This explains how "damned" moved to "darned" and "drat" and describes a continuing experience. People (well, nowadays, mostly refined old ladies who otherwise don't swear, or mothers of toddlers with big ears) still say "sugar," "shoot," and "shucks"—depending on your regional dialect of English—as a way of hinting at but avoiding SHIT. A recent one I heard on American TV was "H-o-l-y Shi-ite Moslem!!!" I suppose the temptation of the scatalogically promising "sh" bundled in with religion was just too much.

Two words, more than any others, have generated enough euphemisms to fill a dictionary. One is CUNT, for which Farmer and Henley's *Dictionary of Slang and Its Analogues* (first published in 1904) gave approximately seven hundred synonyms. The other is "God," as we have already seen in some detail.

Perhaps the most famous of the disguise mechanisms—although relatively recent, starting from about 1840—is the euphemistic subclass of Cockney rhyming slang. These have their own conventions, like a predilection for adopting place-names (for example, "Bristol cities" for "titties") and pub names ("Elephant and Castle" for "arsehole"). Nothing stands still in language, and even the rhyming slang variant moves on, for example in reduced versions, such as "Bristols" and "elephant" for "titties" and "arsehole," respectively. Another feature of evolving rhyming slang is the way in which the reduced forms gradually grammaticize. For example, "I don't give a Friar Tuck" (for FUCK), and "you stupid Berk" (from "Berkeley Hunt," for CUNT).

There are many other devices employed in the avoidance of taboo words. In their seminal work dedicated to this topic, Keith Allan and Kate Burridge travel the length and breadth of English language used as "shield" (euphemism) and "weapon" (dysphemism). They expose dozens of linguistic measures by which we avoid taboo terms

202   Expletive Deleted

through a range of euphemistic devices. We can slip into formal language ("excrement" for "shit") or the opposite, colloquial language ("period" for "menstruation"), or even archaic ("Cupid's measles" for "syphilis"). We can hide behind vagueness ("nether regions" for "genitals," or "chest" for "breast"). We have countless circumlocutory paraphrases for "toilet" ("little girls' room") and what we do in there ("powder the nose"). We can also do the opposite of circumlocution, when we reduce the offensive word to a semiotic symbol by using letters to stand for words ("SOB" for "son of a bitch," "pee" for "piss," or "jeez" for "Jesus").

And when in doubt, we can turn to Latin, as the queen did to good effect with her *annus horribilis*. Latinate words seem particularly adept at taking the edge off—think of "copulate" and "labia." Indeed, until not so long ago, Latin served as a stand-in language when English became too risque. For example, in Alfred Hollis's 1905 work on the customs of the Masai people, the author resorts to Latin when English gets too hot to handle. For example, at the point of describing the Masai belief that coitus is a metaphor for the relationship of sky to earth—as the earth receives warmth and water from the sky, so, too, is a woman fertilized by a man—Hollis retreats into Latin.

In the same spirit, Latin has served as a face-saver for dictionary writers—well, those who chose to include the offending word rather than leave it out altogether. Latin protected the innocent while also saving the lexicographer's face. One can appreciate that *pudendum muliebre* has it over CUNT, hands down.

In the 1959 edition of *Manners for Millions,* author

Sophie Hadida complained that words such as HELL and DAMN, formerly used only by society's "degenerates," were being used "by persons in all grades of society," and as a result, "indecent words are creeping into the vocabulary of otherwise fine boys and girls." Perhaps a refresher course in Latin would have helped.

12

CROSS-CULTURALLY FOUL

"I said, no fucking violence!"

—GANDHI

In Cantonese, an all-purpose swear expression translates literally as "go trip over in the street and die." In Norwegian, the word for "devil" is the rough practical equivalent of the English "fuck." In Indonesian and Arabic, you'd be well advised to avoid calling someone a donkey. In Latvian, it's abusive to tell someone to go take a crap. When operating in French and wishing to insult, remember that whatever you call your target, you can reinforce the insult by preceding it with *espèce de* ("a kind of"). Apparently, being called a kind of something, for the French, is worse than just being called the something.

In Russian, Robert Dessaix tells us, all swear words are sexual, so subtitlers of American films are often stuck on the excreta and private body parts, as these are "no more taboo to a Russian than an elbow." According to Bill

Bryson, if you happen to wake a Finn with a wrong number at two in the morning, and she or he stubs a toe getting to the phone, you should expect to hear a word that translates as "in the restaurant" (*ravintolassa*). Where an English speaker turns to the monosyllabic, four-letter SHIT or FUCK, *ravintolassa* apparently serves the Finns as a handy, all-purpose, one-size-fits-all expletive. Semantics clearly come in a poor second to catharsis.

It's just possible that the way the Finnish say their *ravintolassa* has a particularly sweary sound to it. A Finnish journalist, after all, has this to say about her language's word for CUNT:

> I confess that I, too, use *vittu* . . . The charm of the word lies on the one hand in its aggressive phonetic quality, in which the two "t"s force the tongue to push against the alveoli, and on the other in its vulgarity. It is heavy low style, which takes speech for a moment to the gutter.

Let's look more closely into the nature of a sweary sound. A surprisingly common folk-linguistic belief is that swear words are universally patterned on the basis of sound. You hear remarks like "Every language has swear words with the /f/ sound and/or the /k/ sound." The logic here is that it is the satisfyingly cathartic effect of these sounds that renders them so nicely for the demands of their swearing function.

Notwithstanding this notion's intuitive attractiveness, I have a few difficulties with it. First, I'm inclined to think a word's semantics, so closely linked as they are to a society's taboos, will carry more weight than its phonological elements, although I grant that there's no reason why the semantic and the phonological could not both contribute to the overall impact. Second, as we have already seen, the cathartic function of swearing is important, but it is only one of three macrofunctions. Third, I couldn't find enough evidence cross-lingually to arrive at a definitive statement about any one allegedly universal sound. Fourth, it's hard to make the universal-sound hypothesis work even internally within English. Consider SHIT and ASS—not an /f/ or a /k/ sound between them; and while they do have an S in common, it's the same letter but not the same sound.

Last, the notion goes against a major principle in language that the relationship between a word and the thing it refers to is arbitrary. There's no logical connection between the word "dog" and the four-legged creature. A vertical, or historical, approach allows us to trace the word's etymology, note when it entered the language, and how it connects to "canine," etc. But a horizontal approach, in which we try to connect the signifier with the signified, puts us on shaky ground. Yes, a childish part of us *wants* there to be a logical, intrinsic connection between the label and the thing. It's part of the natural, intelligent seeking of order in our Dr. Seuss universe. It's also part of creative wordplay, an activity that young children relish but relinquish all too soon, probably under the weight of homework, which conceptually must be the antithesis of play.

Just roll "doggy" around in your mouth for a moment, over and under your tongue. Great, isn't it? Of course we want to forge a visceral association between dogginess and dog. It feels right. Dogs are more doggy than, say, cats or birds. That's why they're dogs. "It's no wonder pigs are called 'pigs,'" said the little girl on her first visit to a farm. "They're just so dirty."

Perhaps if we could establish a pattern across the Dirty Dozen of English—FUCK, CUNT, SHIT, PISS, BASTARD, BITCH, and ASS, with DAMN, HELL, FART, CRAP, and DICK —then we might be on to something we could run with. The first pattern that jumps out relates to syllabic structure and rhythm. Eleven of our twelve terms are monosyllabic. The one that isn't—BASTARD—has a strongly stressed first syllable followed by a weak-stress syllable. This also applies to ASSHOLE and FUCK in its "fucking" form. The rhythm pattern would seem to favor a single syllable or strong initial stress (these lend themselves nicely to the expletive circumstance) or, in longer rhythm groups, at least two stressed syllables before any unstressed ones—"abso-BLOODY-LUTely" and "YOU FUCKing SHIThead." The forcefulness of this rhythm fits perfectly with the emotional circumstance that surrounds most swearing.

A second possible pattern is the kind of consonant sound produced in either the initial or the final consonant. We classify consonants according to two criteria—where in the mouth the sound is produced (site or place of articulation) and which parts of the mouth are involved in its production (manner of articulation).

One pattern that emerges in our Dirty Dozen is a dominance of plosives (/k/, /p/, /d/, /b/, /t/) and fricatives (/f/, /s/, /sh/). With plosives, the mouth passage is completely blocked; pressure builds behind the blockage and is suddenly released when the articulating organs (the lips, in the case of /p/ and /b/) are separated. Hence the plosive effect in CUNT and PISS. With fricatives, the mouth passage is narrowed to the point where an audible friction is heard (try this out with /f/, /s/, /sh/, or /z/). The only one that lies outside this consonant pattern is HELL. The significance of this pattern is that both plosives and fricatives contribute to a harsh, emotive quality of a sound, and so lend themselves nicely for abuse.

It would be a huge task to confirm or refute a hypothesis that the pattern we've established in English applies across the board to human swearing. But we can make a start. The French for SHIT, *merde,* seems to lack the /f/ or the /k/ factor and, furthermore, begins not with a plosive but with a nasal sound. However, as a bilabial (formed by contact of the two lips), it shares its manner of articulation with the plosives /p/ and /b/. *Merde* is also monosyllabically cathartic and ends with the plosive /d/. The Japanese for "idiot," *baka,* has two syllables of equal weighting, each containing one plosive. This makes it a hard-sounding word, nicely matched to its abusive message. In Hebrew, *ben zonah* ("son of a whore") has one plosive (/b/), one fricative (/z/), one monosyllable, (*ben*) and one initial-stress bisyllabic word (*zonah*). Another Hebrew utterance, *lech tizdayen* ("go fuck yourself"), has plosives (/t/, /d/), fricatives (/ch/, /z/), and the right syllabic and stress distribution to create a sound-matching-sense effect. Hebrew also borrows Arabic swear words, like *koos* (CUNT). The Romanian equivalent is *pizda,* with a plosive at the start of each syllable (/p/, /d/), one fricative (/z/), and again the stress on the first syllable.

It would seem that there is something in the folk-linguistic notion that swear words share some common phonic elements across languages. The first, which works for the classic expletives, is a combination of a monosyllabic or initial-stressed word, featuring plosive and/or fricative consonants. The second pattern is in the rhythm, or the distribution of syllabic stress: "MOTHerFUCKer" and "COCKSUCKer" are just two examples that also conveniently feature a nice scattering of plosives to get your tongue around.

For a swear word to be accepted as such and to function effectively, it needs to fill a number of core criteria. First, it must be offensive. You couldn't introduce "table" or "tree" as swear words, because neither could offend anyone.

Second, the particular kind of offensiveness required is not the gently flippant poo/bum/fancy-a-bonk kind, which may or may not be simple instances of foul language.

Third, the utterance has to break a taboo to bring into the public domain any of those activities that are considered private.

Fourth, the swear word has to have an *intention* to shock or outrage or discomfort the hearer(s). For this reason, although the Australian film *Teesh and Trude* is saturated in foul language, I hesitate to call it all swearing—a large amount of it happens in the characters' home; it's lost its power and probably its intention to shock.

Fifth, the word must be an actual word. While science fiction writers seem to enjoy putting made-up words in the mouths of their protagonists, "Flarn!" or "Tanj!" or "Skiddlyboo!," these are really just "a futile attempt to give clean-cut stories some foul-mouthed action." They don't work because they're not actual things.

Sixth, it's not enough for the word to be an actual thing;

it must be generally agreed to be a slimy and disgusting thing.

And last, the word, whatever it is, must sound good "in the mouths of the Irish." This last comment is the view of one commentator on public language who calls himself "the Ferret" and calls the Irish "the kings of cursing." I take this to mean simply that the sound or delivery of the word (what the Ferret calls "the swear") is as crucial to its effect as the semantics.

Some languages go in for the curse in a big way and, to this end, have a number of ready-made phrases available for deployment in a range of situations. In translation, these can lose their abusive edge and even seem comic, but we must remember that when they are used in the original language among native speakers, the full force of the intended abuse is instantly grasped.

Different languages have different patterns. Bosnian curses, for example, seem to hover around the family: "May your children play in an electrical circuit" and "May your mother fart at a school meeting." If Bosnians go for family, the Dutch specialize in bad health. Their curses involve the target's contracting a disease, preferably cholera, typhus, or TB. They have the general, all-purpose *krijg de ziekte* ("get a disease"), and they also favor cancer—for a male, *kankerhond* ("cancer dog") and for a female, *kankerhoer* ("cancer whore"). Nice.

Bulgarian allegedly has this gem, with a rather quaint foreshadowing of reconciliation: "Lunge your boobs over your shoulders and travel the sacred pilgrimage to the crapper; after you feel relieved, come around and then we can talk anew." No provision made, it seems, for the boobless. Unfortunately, I was unable to obtain complete confirmation from my Bulgarian informants. One said, "This is basically true, except for the part about lunging the boobs. . . . Basically, when someone gets angry or riled up, they may say something like 'Go to the bathroom and relieve yourself and then we'll talk again.'" The second said he'd never heard it and doubted its veracity because "long swearings [*sic*] are not typical for Bulgarian—it's not Spanish or Italian." The third said it was probably true because "long strong offenses are common in Bulgarian." By this time, I realized that my search for verification was unlikely to be accomplished by asking any more Bulgarians, but I concluded that there might be an iota of truth in the boob-lunging example.

We know that swearing does not lend itself elegantly, or even effectively, to translation. The literal translation of an abusive Czech phrase for "go away" is the rather technical "don't oxidize here." Interestingly, Norwegians can insult their fellows by calling them "fucking Norwegian whale-killers!," which involves a big dollop of sarcasm (and no ideological-ecological zeal, as they have their own special way of looking at whale hunting). Insulting the mother of a Dutch person carries none of the venom that it might for a Latino.

Mostly, the words in another language lack the force that they have in the original. If the worst swear word in English is CUNT (though some would vote for its main rival, "motherfucker"), we can't presume that its dictionary translation (say, the French *con* or the Italian *conno*) works in parallel ways to the English word. While *con* is a swear word, it lacks the pragmatic force of CUNT and would equate roughly with the swear-loading of the English "prick" or "dickhead." Unpleasant, yes, but aggressively evil? Hardly.

Perhaps the favorite terms of abuse of the irate Parisian taxi driver are *connard* (roughly, "dickhead") and *connasse* (for the feminine—I restrained myself from asking my informant whether anyone worries about the practical difficulties of a female dickhead). A friend was in Paris with her schoolgirl French, pleased that she was getting around without too much to-do, and amused by the passing taxi drivers who continually called each other "duck" (*canard*). Not realizing that what she heard as "duck" was in fact "dickhead," she thought it quaint that where Australians might yell out something with FUCK in it, the French, for some inexplicable but probably deeply embedded and worthy-of-respect cultural reason, resorted to "duck."

An interesting indication of how different cultures can revere or insult the same phenomenon is the case of the mustache. The seemingly innocuous patch of male hair between nose and upper lip features prominently in Iraqi culture, among others, and finds its way comfortably into quite diverse speech acts. For example, Iraqis swear by it as a way of sealing a deal: "on my mustache" is their version of "on my mother's grave" or "you have my word on that." They also employ the mustache in the giving of a compliment, for example, "An eagle could land on his mustache" or as an exhortation, as when Saddam urged his army on with "Iraq is attached to your mustache." I surmise that in this last rather graphic expression, the pride of the homeland leaks into the pride of manhood and, thus combined, makes for a braver, better soldier.

The mustache, then, can be deftly applied as an insult or abuse. In March 2003 decorum was shattered at an Arab summit meeting in Doha when the Iraqi envoy lashed out at a Kuwaiti diplomat, "Shut up, you monkey. Curses be upon your mustache." In a region of the world where facial hair is practically a totem, cursing another man's mustache amounts to an invitation to bring it on. In Bulgaria, facial-hair insults come in handy when hurled at a female: "You have a mustache" translates literally as "You have a third eyebrow under your nose."

It would seem from these examples that a great deal about swearing conventions in particular languages is a case, for the outsider, of "Go figure!" Nonetheless, notwithstanding individually striking and colorful features, what emerges from a trawl through the swear words of diverse languages—at the Swearsaurus, or global swearing section, at www.insultmonger.com promises you can learn "how to insult, swear, cuss, and curse in 133 languages"—is the commonalities, not the differences. These are so pervasive that we might, at last, speak of universals.

The major patterns are, without doubt, sexuality and scatology, both separately and, for even stronger effect, combined. Sexually, the focus is on the sexual organs, with a marked preoccupation—surprise, surprise!—with the size and stamina of the male member. Body effluvia, especially semen, urine, and feces, are common, as are the orifices from which they emanate, with a remarkable diversity of suggestions about what might be shoved up someone's (or someone's relative's) whatever. Males are abused mostly by a variety of words for stupid or unmanly (usually through pejorative terms for gay). And a very common form of abuse is to wish a homosexual masturbatory act, or an anal experience, on the target of abuse or a family member.

Females are defined—here's another surprise—exclusively through their perceived sexual role and biological function. In fact, they are abused around the world through the accusation of promiscuity (think of the English "whore," "slut," "tart," "tramp," "slag," "bitch," etc.). As for the folk notion that CUNT's significance in English derives from a widespread and long-standing Anglo-Saxon discomfort with female sexuality, a cross-cultural comparison of swearing patterns suggests no such thing. Indeed, an assorted sample of swear words in a range of unrelated languages reveals that if using vaginally dominant swear words is a reflection of distress about female sexuality, the Anglo-Saxons are far from alone. So crowded is the bandwagon called "distress about female sexuality" that there is standing room only.

Another dominant feature is bestiality, though the actual animal with which the target of abuse is compared, or the one to which the target is recommended as a sexual partner, varies from culture to culture. In trolling through innumerable swearing websites, I've seen recommendations stretching from the rather exotic horned mountain goat to the humble farmyard chicken.

Mothers nearly everywhere come in for a beating, and in many languages, it's enough simply to mention the mother in an abusive context: for example, in Spanish, *tu madre*; among African-Americans, "yo' mama"; and among the Xhosa of South Africa, "your mother's ears," for the inference (about what action is being recommended) to be correctly taken up. In such circumstances, *tu madre* stands for the longer implied utterance "go fuck your mother," and therefore becomes an expletive itself. Compare the English "up yours." In context, no one would really have any doubt which orifice was being referred to, to whom it belonged, or what action was being recommended.

Nevertheless, many languages reserve the right to spell it out graphically. In Bulgarian, I'm told, it's not taken nicely when your mother is said to be doing it with bears in the forest; other languages specify a pig or a horse, and in Finnish, it's a reindeer (well, what else!). Other ways of bringing the mother into the picture are to give vivid descriptions of parts of her anatomy; to make reference to her hirsuteness; to describe in vividly disgusting terms various smells that emanate from her various orifices; to catalog her various consenting and unconsenting sexual partners; and to insult her for her massive size, often by describing how easily a particularly large public-transport vehicle might be said to pass between her legs.

Other ancestors can be dragged into the abusive conversation and subjected to various sexual and scatological verbal mistreatments. In Farsi, threatening to do it, or claiming to have done it, with the target's ancestors or his or her father's soul apparently works very well. In Brazilian Portuguese, you can deliver a double whammy via the father, who can be described as gay *and* a son of a bitch. While on the subject of family relations, the incest taboo might be thought of as a universal mother of all forbiddens, so it's hugely popular for swearing purposes. The target of abuse is typically told to go fuck his mother, sister, daughter, and/or grandmother.

It's only in Bulgarian, as far as my research can tell, that the target's aunt comes in for special abuse. What is it about Bulgarian aunts? one may ask. One of my Bulgarian informants said the expression *pichkata lelina* ("aunt's cunt") may be a common phrase for swearing more for the sound than for the particular meaning of "aunt." Another informant suggested that the expression would be really offensive if it involved the mother, and the use of the aunt somehow takes the edge off the abuse. It's a euphemism, in other words. A third was of the view that, as most men are to some degree oedipally complexed, they find it easier to swear by abuse of the aunt rather than the mother, as it confronts their own demons less directly. But this raises the question of why Bulgarian men might be more oedipal than non-Bulgarian men, which is not a trajectory that I feel at all inclined to pursue. Once again, I'm struck by the variety of opinion among Bulgarian informants, not only in what they say about aspects of their own foul language but also in their psychosocial explanations for the terms.

The abuse heaped on mothers in most places is not universal. The way a people swear is a mirror to their culture, and a Finnish writer had this to say about mixing mother curses into one's swearing: "The mother-curses so popular in the Catholic and Arab countries would be unthinkable in Finland. Insulting mothers would provoke only puzzlement here."

Swearing in most cultures involves varying combinations and manifestations of filth, the forbidden (especially the incest taboo), and the sacred. A particularly strong pattern involves all three areas, easily summed up in the following formulaic procedure: Take a religious figure (such as Mary or Mohammed) and liberally anoint that figure with abusive terms involving filthy and/or sexual suggestions. Consider the following for their mix of religious, sexual, and scatological reference: in English, "fucking Mary, mother of God" or "Jesus fucking Christ!"; in Spanish, *me cago en dios y en la puta virgen* ("I shit on God and the fucking Virgin"); in Lebanese Arabic, *alif air b'dinak* ("a thousand dicks in your religion").

Let's not forget an additional feature that is pervasive across swearing cultures—the inclusion of the incongruous and the bizarre. For example, one Mauritian Creole term references "your mother's dick." A lot of the recommended positions and antics make unwarranted assumptions about body parts and orifices, as well as digital and muscular flexibility. Or maybe to qualify as the target of swearing abuse, you have to be young and fit.

While it is relatively easy to recognize the bizarre in a different culture—"bizarre" itself being a highly ethnocentric notion, which perhaps is one good reason for having anthropologists—it is less easy to recognize the idiosyncrasies and eccentricities of one's own language. Bill Bryson puts forward a few fundamental profundities about English to which few English-language swearers have probably given much thought:

English is unusual in including the impossible and the pleasurable . . . when we wish to express extreme fury we entreat the object of our rage to undertake an anatomical impossibility, or, stranger still, to engage in the one activity that is bound to give him [*sic*] more pleasure than almost anything else. Can there be, when you think about it, a more improbable sentiment than "Get fucked!"? We might as well snarl, "Make a lot of money!"

It has been said that some cultures don't swear at all. The list usually consists of the Japanese, Eskimos, Malayans, Polynesians, and Native Americans. "Don't swear at all" I take to mean as lacking native swear words, a concept that I find quite baffling, even counterintuitive. If we consider the three functions of swearing with which we have been mainly concerned—namely, cathartic, abusive, and social—it is hard to imagine that a people exists that is so supremely well coordinated as to never stub a toe; so fortunate in life as to never step in dog poo; and so well humored in disposition as to never need to express momentary disappointment, surprise, anger, pain, or frustration. (Tell me where this planet is, and I'll book my passage, pronto.) Equally perplexing is the notion that even while levels of interpersonal harmony must vary enormously across societies, there is a society—other than that of *The Stepford Wives*—where people have no need, ever, to express nastiness to or about one another.

But to explore this topic thus is to set yourself up for failure. In a very real sense, the lens we use to see actually shapes what we see. If we look for versions of English, the chances are we will find that Eskimos don't swear. It's a naive way to approach the massive complexity of human culture that scores of anthropologists and linguists have exposed and explored.

I'm of the view that the binary division of "who swears?/who doesn't swear?" is the outcome of asking the wrong question: whether people/language are the same or different. A better question, I suspect, may be to ask: How are people/languages alike? How are they different? But to ask the question this way is to be willing to embrace infinitesimal differences and then deal with the ensuing complexity. I can see the neatness and the attraction of "Eskimos don't swear."

Languages do not carve up the world into the same patterns. Take the notion of color. This would seem to be a function of sight, and therefore of the human condition. One might expect to find evidence of color across all languages. In fact, color as we think of it in English is far from universally or homogenously perceived. Many languages don't have a word for color, which can mean that they afford their speakers the capacity to represent visual experiences without separating color out from *other* aspects of the experience. For example, "blue" in English tells of color alone, but "gold" and "silver" tell of color *plus* texture (shiny surface). Some languages do this quite pervasively.

Color is only one of a multitude of concepts that are realized linguistically in different ways. The fact that we see the world through the parameters or lens of our language is not something we normally spend time thinking about. Most of the time, we simply assume our way is the right way. In addition, if it's all we've ever known, the sense of "mine is normal" will be that much more entrenched.

A recent public debate in Australia touched on this very issue: specifically, on the words (or alleged lack of them) that Tasmanian Aborigines used for "land." According to

Australian historian Keith Windshuttle, the Aborigines lacked words for "land," "own," "possess," or "property" and therefore had no sense of ownership or territoriality, which meant they would not have had a notion of trespass, which in turn meant that they could not have interpreted European settlement as encroachment. In a fierce rebuttal, Henry Reynolds showed how indigenous languages of the time carried the notions of territoriality and ownership, pointing to Windshuttle's bad faith, limited research, and prejudiced agenda.

Metaphors are one way of getting a handle on cross-cultural variation. If one of the core universals across the human experience is the expression of emotion though metaphors of internal bodily images, then the metaphors that different peoples use cue us to the diversity of world-views.

Let's start with English, in which we often use the heart to express strong emotion: "my heart *sank* when I read the letter"; "I felt my heart *breaking* when she went away"; "I did it with a *heavy* heart." From this we can induce that English speakers experience a particular deep emotion by sensing their hearts sinking, breaking, and getting heavy.

Now consider Polish hearts. These are also given to *breaking,* but they can be *squeezed, cut,* and *torn* as well. Chinese hearts, too, experience the sensation of cutting, and the agent of said action, the knife, is actually specified ("My heart is *cut as if by a knife*"). Chinese hearts also *burn,* and other organs such as the intestine and the gallbladder can feel *broken.*

Speakers of Kayardild, an indigenous Australian language, feel the emotion as *cuts* and *breaks* in their stomach.

Different organs, different kinds of hurting actions, similar strong emotions. Anna Wierzbicka is, wisely, hesitant to equate emotions across cultures, and when she refers to her short list of universal emotions, she adds a "-like" to them: "anger-like," "fear-like."

If we think of the propensity to swear as being linked largely to negative emotion (this means excluding the social swearing category for our purposes), then appreciating how different cultures express negative emotions will give us some insight into if and how swearing is part of the picture. But cultural diversity is an "intra" as well as an "inter" construct. We know that expressiveness is massively variegated within cultures. To think otherwise is to fall into such stereotypes as all Englishmen are reserved, all Australians laid-back, all Americans loud, all Germans boisterous. If people vary across cultures, so, too, do they vary within a culture. We need go no further than our own families to see that.

There might be a continuum of expressiveness in negative emotion, in which the Balinese would probably be placed close to the inexpressive end. Balinese are expected to express positive feelings but to conceal negativity, which they believe weakens the life force, erodes strength, and makes the individual vulnerable to the evil of others. At the same time, they are sensitively attuned to the subtle signals that might cue negative feelings in other people. Similarly, the Chewong of Malaysia favor an inexpressive form of daily composure, so they, too, would be placed on the inexpressive end of the continuum.

At the other end are languages/peoples whose culture not only endorses but expects emotional expressiveness. At the extreme end are cultures that have a ventilationist view of emotional expression, based on the belief that suppressing emotion is unhealthy. Aristotle, by virtue of his notion of catharsis, would be happy in this company, as would many in contemporary Western societies who see counseling and talk therapy as prerequisites for mental and physical health. Some communities of the South Pacific practice an emotional-healing ritual that is geared more to the interpersonal well-being of the community than the health of the individual, but it serves all as a cathartic release.

The Ifaluk of Micronesia, for instance, have a concept of justifiable anger that has its own semiprescribed script roles for the offended and offending parties, a complementary set of emotions for each, the provision of payback via an apology or redress, and even a role for an emotional adviser whose primary function is to urge the offended party to throw out his or her bad thoughts and be calm. Not so far removed from the executive life coach, perhaps. Further up the expressive end of the continuum, we find that speakers of Russian, French, Italian, and German draw on emotionally expressive cultures and have a rich repertoire of swear words available for their use.

But even a continuum such as this leaves out as much as it states. If by "expressiveness" we mean not so much display but whether the emotion is culturally valued, then the picture changes. In rural China, for example, displays of emotion are very vivid by Western standards, though they are not valued. The emotional outburst is not considered dangerous, but neither is it thought to be useful for the achievement of any goal, so in effect, it is unimportant.

Many are the ways in which cultures engineer the expression and management of negative emotion. Take the case of the Japanese, whom a number of writers on swearing have claimed don't swear, in a language with no swear words. Certainly, many Japanese are loath to admit that they swear or that their language has a swearing vocabulary. If pushed, they may admit to the existence of *warui kotoba* ("a bad word"), then they'll urge you never to use it. And this reticence is widespread.

One of my informants, an Englishman married to a Japanese woman, asked his wife the questions I was using to elicit data about Japanese. She told him she couldn't help because she didn't know any Japanese swear words. This she said, mind you, in wide-eyed innocence to a husband who was fully aware, as she was aware that he was, from firsthand experience of her skills in that department.

As a longtime American expatriate living in Japan, Jack Seward made a study of the Japanese and their language. He writes, "I was far from . . . convinced . . . that the Japanese were incapable of insulting each other. Finally I came to realize that . . . [all the Japanese I encountered] were parties to a monstrous conspiracy to prevent us . . . from learning to insult ourselves—and them—in their language." He calls this the "Bad Word Conspiracy."

For a people who allegedly don't swear, there are many words in their language that correlate to the major preoccupations that less coy and more overtly swearing cultures display. On the Swearsaurus at www.insultmonger.com, more than two hundred Japanese swearing expressions are listed. Like any list of swear words, these are not used by everyone to anyone in all situations. Major variables here are gender, age, and hierarchical factors, such as boss to employee. Words on any such list will also date or shift in their application. Nonetheless, they afford a resource from which to draw and deploy subject to circumstance.

Let's explore some typical Japanese swearing scenarios, starting with the cathartic type. If you hit your head or accidentally cut yourself, you might say *itai!* ("ouch!"), which also has a less than polite form (*itee*). However, if someone steps on your toe in the subway during rush hour, you might emit an *itai,* but you wouldn't swear at him or her. This may be less a matter of polite consideration than a function of the crowds going every which way and all of them late for work.

A very common expression is *mazui,* which might equate to something like "Oh crap!" Here, for example, you're signing some official papers in a public situation, and you make a mistake. You emit this audible expletive, which is acceptable because you're understood to be talking to yourself. It's a stub-your-toe cathartic release aimed at no one. A similar one is *shimatta* ("darn it") or *chikkusho* ("hell!," "damn it!") for when you're halfway to the subway and you realize you forgot something important at home; or you're driving along and you become aware that you have a flat tire, and now is not a good time (when is?); or you just got your exam results and the news is not good.

In terms of a lexicon for the purpose of an aggressive verbal outlet, the Japanese have most of the usual preoccupations with excrement, effluvia, sexual organs, and sexual activities, including (but not more so than any other language) the perverse variations. If anything, their terms for these notions are more referential and less emotive than, say, the English versions. There's the usual array of terms for "fuck off!," "get fucked!," "you're fucked," "shit," and "asshole." And just as every language group has its own idiosyncracies, the Japanese have their own expressions.

They clearly don't like small-breasted women with stubby or bowlegs. Both older women and men, especially those who are not generously endowed aesthetically but who wield some authority, are particular targets. The usual attention to ugly, fat, dirty, or weird finds its expression in an array of terms, some of which may be verbally abusive, some more friendly, some now old-fashioned, some mildly rebuking, as in mother-child talk. These can sound odd when translated literally into English, for example, *kin tama* ("golden testicles"), *uchujin* ("space person," "alien"), *koroshite yaru* ("I'm going to kill you"), *heso magari* ("twisted belly button," "weirdo"). But then, as we've seen earlier, "go fuck yourself!" is also pretty weird, if only from a physiological perspective.

It's been noted that the Japanese are less obsessive about sexuality than Westerners, more candid and realistic. As Seward puts it, "To them, sex does not carry the stigma of evil, since it is not related to the question of morality. . . . Like all spheres of Japanese activity, they assign it a place and surround it with rules, but within these prescribed boundaries they pursue it with vigor and indulge in it in gusto." It stands to reason that linguistically, sexuality is less of a taboo in Japan than it has been for a good few centuries in English.

Why this should be is a matter of opinion. One view gives some credence to the Japanese creation myth, which is very straightforward. The male deity meets the female deity; they exchange information about their individual bodies and the location of the essence of their respective masculinity and femininity; and then they get it on. No distractions such as serpents, apples, ribs, and loss of innocence. They work out the mechanics, sort through the consent forms, and go for it.

To return to the subject of women, we have seen that one universal running through swearing cultures is the special abuse that females, especially mothers, seem to attract. Japanese is no exception. The word *baba* means "old woman," and it can be easily attached to a plethora of insulting adjectives (take your pick of "wrinkled," "toothless," "baboon-like," "shark-skinned," "hunchbacked," "fish-faced," "withered-up," "saggy-breasted," "rusty-holed," "prune-faced"). There's a clear predilection for the compound adjective, producing a complete do-it-yourself insult resource. One explanation for this abuse is older Japanese women's (alleged) "tendency to go to pot more quickly and thoroughly than their Western counterparts." The allegedly sharp tongues and tyrannical bearing of these older women are possibly sweet revenge for all those years they were brow-beaten by their husbands and mothers-in-law.

The most frequent and strongest expression used by Japanese in aggressive swearing scenarios is *baka,* translated literally as "stupid," "idiot," "nitwit," or "dummy." Now, the fact that *baka*'s literal meaning is rather mild in English in no way conveys its pragmatic power. Words and meanings work differently in different cultures. Remember, the French *con* is also relatively mild. The translation of the English "bastard"—*shiseeiji* ("illegitimate child")—does not carry the same shameful stigma it did in English. A stigma exists, but, as with much else Japanese, it is avoided in the language, becoming one more unmentionable term. On the other hand, words for a country person (equivalent to our "country bumpkin" or "hick") are powerful in Japanese because of the contempt held for traditional ways in a country where the miracle of postwar recovery effected a rapid transformation from a rural economy to an industrialized economic giant. So the softness of the English translations of Japanese swear words may have contributed to the folk notion that the Japanese don't swear.

The Japan Times recently reported on what it called the "*baka* explosion" across the urban landscape. In the context of rapid social change and deteriorating economic stability, the frequency of *baka* use is seen as a public irritability index. In other words, *baka* has been around for a long time, but the threshold at which it is being used has lowered. The phenomenon is linked to the loss of a sense of community, along with the accelerating influence of Western notions of individuality and autonomy. One of my informants, a longtime expat—American-born, widely traveled, multilingual, and culturally sensitive—comments sadly:

> With all the bullying that goes on at all levels of society, it's a good thing Japan has such strict gun control. *Baka* is part of that. Nobody wants to be called "stupid," but you are, from the time you can walk, perhaps till the day you die. And then afterwards too, as in the expression "he was stupid to go and die." This could just be my perspective on things and most other people would probably call me *baka*.

Social swearing has its own conventions, such as when a group of friends talks about someone else. You can expect to hear the very versatile *baka* ("idiot"), *kusotare* ("idiot"), *kusojiji* ("stupid old fart"), *ahobaachan* ("stupid old woman"). Clearly, brainpower (the lack of it) and age (too much of it) come in for special treatment. Perhaps this is not surprising in a country whose workforce is increasingly knowledge-based and whose traditional veneration for the wisdom of old age is rapidly disintegrating.

The above notwithstanding, it's been argued that Japanese still lags behind English in "the sheer beauty, sustained invention and gasp-producing force" of its swearing capability. This is written by a native English speaker, so there's a built-in bias. In the appreciation of swearing as a comparative study, the analyst's bias is an important factor. Consider what this Finnish writer has to say:

> We Finns have a fine vocabulary of cursing, I dare boast. The Turks, too, have a rich one, I hear. French curses, on the other hand, are absolutely pathetic, and I wouldn't—pardon me—give much for British or American swearing either.

You can hear the pride as she continues:

> We [Finns] have gathered our swear-words from all the directions of the compass. The traditional *perkele* is an old loan from the Baltic; it is the king of our curses, and means "devil." *Perkele* comes from deep, uncontrolled layers of the self. It echoes with the sound of the spruce-forest and the axe.

As for the claim that the Japanese don't swear or that their language lacks swear words, I say look again. A recent short survey of a typical class of young Japanese college students produced local equivalents of "shut up," "drop dead," "go to hell," and "fuck off," as well as an array of abusive terms for older people, especially women, where the allusions are to alleged easy morals and/or large behinds.

It could be argued that Japanese does not need swear words as much as English. First, religion does not hold the same sway there. Compared to the awe and dread invested in the Christian god, traditional awe and dread in Japan has been spread (diluted?) across many different deities, leading to a much reduced religious influence, and this is reflected in what is considered taboo. Indeed, the increasing postwar secularization of Japanese society means that religion holds even less sway than it did in the past.

Second, for reasons not unrelated, both institutional and dogmatic, the words that refer to body parts, functions, and products are not invested with anywhere near the same power as they are in countries where religion was institutionalized.

All this is not to suggest that the Japanese do not have taboos. Their one big taboo is being rude or insulting. The phrase "bad language" means "a language in which to be impolite." I was advised by a specialist in Japanese language and culture that Japanese swearing was breaking the taboo of politeness, and that there were many, many ways to do this in Japanese. Precisely because Japanese has its own language-specific, internally logical way of being rude and insulting, it has far less need of the category of stand-alone swear words. This, however, is a far cry from saying the Japanese don't swear.

For the Japanese, "good" language constitutes a close, ritualistic abiding by the polite formulae; "bad" language is breaking them. Perhaps the biggest challenge for an English speaker learning Japanese is to understand and implement the rules for conversational rituals in Japanese. Haruod Aoki and Shigeko Okamoto, in their book designed for American native-English speakers hoping to master Japanese while living in Japan, make it abundantly clear where the overlaps are between the two languages. Their emphasis is less on what words mean in the dictionary sense, and more on the meanings given to words in particular circumstances. This is particularly important in Japan, where the inequality of power relationships affects how assertive one is expected to be, or, as Aoki and Okamoto put it, inside the Japanese language, "a feudal system is alive and well." In a chapter devoted to guidance on choosing one's appropriate "mode of assertion," some nineteen distinct circumstances are given. Some of these are: "when you are at a loss for words," "when you want to take a low posture," "when you want to avoid commitment," "when you want to express reservations indirectly," and, lastly, my favorite, "when you want to signal that you are not dead but thinking."

In all languages, we can distinguish between socially oriented language (when the relationship is being privileged) and information-oriented language (when the task or message is being privileged). In the following exchange, I'm at my local friendly butcher's one Monday morning, after buying loads of meat for a barbecue the previous Saturday:

Me: G'day, Dennis.

Butcher: Hi, Ruth. Did the rain ruin your barbecue on Saturday?

Me: No, actually, it held out, miraculously, until after everyone left.

Butcher: Good on yer!
         Now, what can I get you today?

Of course, it's hard to know for sure if Dennis is a friendly butcher because he likes people or because he's worked out that being friendly is commercially sensible. But it doesn't matter for our purposes. In the exchange, his first remark is an example of socially oriented language, as is his second. It is only in the third that it switches to being information-oriented.

In Japanese, it is the socially oriented language that trips up speakers from other languages such as English. Socially oriented language in Japanese contains two subsets, each of which contains three levels. The first subset is called "polite language," which is oriented toward the person you're speaking to, or the "addressee." This subdivides into informal, semiformal, and formal. The second subset is "respect language," which is oriented toward the person you're talking about, called "the referent." Three levels apply here as well: pejorative, neutral, and respectful. It's not necessary to go further in this description of the complex differentiation of Japanese. Obviously, a culture that goes to such lengths to encode and prescribe accepted rituals of practice will value and enshrine these rituals. The way the Japanese have protected politeness is by making impoliteness taboo, so their complex set of rules to follow becomes a complex set of rules to break.

It might be argued that so efficiently does Japanese grammar embody the potential mechanics of abuse that swear words, as they're used in English—whether stand-alone or embedded—are actually redundant. Consider the pronoun "you" in Japanese. Let's refresh what we know about "you" in English. Union regulations notwithstanding, the English "you" works overtime, performing functions that in other languages are differentiated into a number of separate words. Our "you" can mean you singular or plural, you child or animal, you highly esteemed or feared person, you as anyone (as in the instruction "You pick up the drill in the manner illustrated"). Of course, people understand which "you" is intended, inferring much from context, and if they're unsure, they seek confirmation ("Do you mean just me, or all of us here?"). Where there is perceived to be a need for the marked plural, for example, some speech communities create words, like "youse," "y'all," or "yezall."

Japanese lexicalizes "you" so delicately that by manipulating it, one can achieve an abusive goal without ever straying into anything remotely as gross as a FUCK. We must remember that in Japanese society, "very few people are considered exactly equal." As a matter of course, fathers, husbands, bosses, and teachers talk down (respectively) to children, wives (outside the home), employees, and students. When you interact with another, your assessment of the other person's rank relative to yours is encoded in the language choices you make.

This explains the Japanese fetish for business cards and

letters of introduction as strategies for enabling people to know how to deal with one another socially. At a social gathering, it's a comfort to Japanese to know who will be attending. It's not unheard of for invitees to be given advance biographical information about anyone who will be unknown to them. In a society where relative rank is so important, it's logical to find an elaborate system of honorific prefixes by which to operate, and it's manipulation of this code that allows the Japanese to be abusive without straying into swearing as we know it in English. For example, one common way of being offensive is to use the lower rank of "you" when a higher one would be expected.

Let's imagine a scale of respect in the choice of "you" forms in Japanese, with 10 standing for a super-ranking person of godlike status or power. At about 2 or 3, we find *omae,* which is for kids and dogs and those who have low status. At 5 to 6, we have *kimi,* which is for subordinates, younger friends, girlfriends (though not boyfriends), and sometimes children. At 7 to 9, there's *anata,* which is for adult peers, customers, or adults whose name we don't know. And at 9 and 10, we have the suffix *-sama* added to the name, or perhaps the word for "customer," creating something like "esteemed customer." Where the name is not used, the honorific prefix *o* is attached. Thus, *o-kyaku-sama* is roughly "oh so honorable customer." The closest we come to this in English may be the marketing letter we get from a bank, insurance company, or some other corporation, addressed to "Dear Valued Customer."

A teacher comes in for special respect and is addressed as *sensei* (meaning "wise, learned one") attached to the surname. This is also a term added to the surname of a doctor.

A professor is addressed as *kyouju,* and a police officer is addressed as *omowarisan*—if you're trying to get out of a ticket. Call the officer *omae* at your peril—you'll get the ticket and your car searched.

There is also a very abusive form of "you," *ki sama,* which would be about minus 10 on the scale of respect. It is utterly disparaging and might be roughly considered on a par with "you fucking asshole." It is a peculiarity, or perhaps an irony, that this offensive "you" actually incorporates the highly respectful *-sama.* Perhaps the construction might be translatable roughly as "You, esteemed sir, are a fucking asshole." As one informant tells me, the grammatical options available in the forms of "you" "make for a lot of swearing. And this is where Japanese are frequently bloody rude when it suits them."

In Japanese, there is also a way of saying something where the abusive intention is almost independent of the semantic content. The following utterance—*anata wa saiteina otoko dayo ne*—translates as "You're a despicable man!," or perhaps, because of the hyperformality, "You, sir, are a scoundrel." There are elements in the internal logic here that make this a powerful abusive assault. For the strongest version, you would use what one of my informants calls "the voice from hell." This is cold, flat, direct, allows the target no way out, and you wouldn't wish it on your worst enemy (or maybe you would).

An analogous effect of tone in English might be that created by the surly teenage-muttered epithet "whatever," where rarely has more contempt been packed into a mere three syllables. The milder version of the Japanese utterance can be delivered with a tonal inflection that gives the target a way out. The target of the abuse has options. They can be consumed by rage but let the insult ride, aware that the outburst was a flash in the pan and that their own extreme response might fuel the bad vibes. This is another example of internally logical ways by which Japanese can swear.

One job that would keep you on your toes and potentially get you into hot water is simultaneous interpreting. Special attention has to be paid to linguistic expressions that convey cultural attitudes or personal feelings but do not lend themselves to literal translations. The intention and tone of a swear word or a brusque remark have to be conveyed without the interpreter being "infected." Similarly, with jokes, the interpreter needs to use a "filter" that allows the humor and fun to be passed on to the listeners without the interpreter becoming personally caught up in the laughter.

We saw earlier how cultures vary in the way their languages express the visual experience—what we in English call "color." So, too, do they vary in the ways in which their languages encode the expression of negative emotion, arguably the most powerful reason for swearing. The ethnocentric mistake to avoid is bringing to your analysis of cross-cultural swearing preconceptions that were formulated elsewhere. In other words, you cannot look at Japanese through the eyes of an English speaker. If we do this, we may well emerge with the sense that Japanese is swearing-impoverished.

As for the Eskimos, North American Indians, and Polynesians—who are also allegedly low swearers—until I have the opportunity to explore their languages, I'm holding fast to my position that there are in fact underpinning universals with local particularities. But hey, I'm willing to do the research—a six-month, fully paid sojourn on a South Pacific island engaged in hands-on linguistic fieldwork might be a logical first step. Must have a word with my publisher.

EPILOGUE

"Who's gonna fucking find out?"

—RICHARD NIXON

I love swearing," said an Australian woman I interviewed. "Fucking oath! It really lets me express myself." "Hey, it's good for you," said another. "Gets all the stress outta ya. Bloody toxic stuff, stress." "No one's gonna fuckin' tell me how I oughta speak," said a third, belligerently, both her words and tone warning me to back off.

This is the view from the street. It's the knee-jerk view that you get when you attack someone's identity, because casting aspersions on how someone speaks is, and is understood as, casting aspersions on that someone personally. The three women quoted above were being deliberately subversive. In a quieter moment, and in a one-on-one discussion, they'd all admit that they don't like it when their kids used foul language, that they wouldn't swear at a job interview, or when the boss might hear, or at their kids' school. This kind of self-censoring indicates that, despite their bravado, they have internalized society's prohibitions, hook, line, and sinker.

In any case, defenders of swearing are not voicing the views of the higher echelons—the ivory tower, the CEO's office in the skyscraper with its wraparound panoramic views, or anyone else with a vested interest in maintaining the status quo. By and large, the anti-foul-language camp has won the battle. Once the powers-that-be stigmatize a particular style of speaking, it becomes the dispreferred model. It's been well established that this has little to do with linguistic quality or purity or refinement, and everything to do with their having the power to make their own style the officially sanctioned one.

In other words, snobbery or classism is manifested linguistically. This attitude seeps down to the middle class, which invests huge amounts of energy maintaining it, because they have bought (also hook, line, and sinker) the message from above that coarse language is substandard, and because they, the middle class, are eternally upwardly aspirational. Their ambition is fueled in no small part by their fear of being identified with the great unwashed.

There is a tremendous ignorance about language that perpetuates the myths about foul language, the same ignorance that makes people receptive to unfounded prejudice, especially when it relates to issues of identity and perception and taps into their deeper needs and aspirations. People mostly have a verbal-hygienist approach to language, seeing it in good/bad, moral/immoral terms—not unlike the way people with eating disorders categorize food. The same impulse that makes people mind their grammatical p's and q's also makes them view swearing as problematic, as a weed in an exquisite garden, a rotten apple in a barrel of beauties.

As they used to say about the beat, the myths go on. After conducting vast amounts of research on swearing, and writing two books with the stated intention of changing the way swearing is understood in the communication sciences, Timothy Jay came to the rather depressing conclusion that his work was unlikely to make much of an impact on people's thinking. This was partly because people like to believe what they like to believe, regardless of evidence to the contrary. And partly because the "censoring institutions"—by which Jay means organized religion, the media, the law, government, educational authorities, the family, and the community—apply their various censoring functions to perpetuate ignorance. Orchestrated, choreographed disinformation, in other words—what Chomsky means when he refers to the "manufacture of consent." Depending on how inclined toward conspiracy theory you are, you might see this as systematic, methodical, and planned, or random, chaotic, and organic. Either way, the outcome is that the myths go on.

And what are these myths about swearing? They are perhaps best understood as notions about swearing that derive from three perspectives. The perspectives themselves are not separate and discrete; they are congruent and can coexist happily, although each individual who subscribes to them tends to lean more heavily toward one in particular.

Those who hold the first perspective are unemotional about swearing, dismissing it as unimportant: much ado about nothing. For such people—Steven Pinker is among them—swearing is not really language, it's more like the gestures of chimpanzees. Perhaps it should be called extralingual, but at any rate, it's not particularly meaningful. Remember that the next time your teenager calls you a fuckwit. (Ironically, dismissing rather than reinforcing your teenager's verbal abuse is probably the wisest course of action you could take, but that has nothing to do with whether swearing is classifiable as language.)

A second perspective, a censorial one, gets people much hotter under the collar. These people see swearing as a function of the kind of life we lead at this time in the history of *Homo sapiens*. This view is condemnatory ("swearing is bad"), concerned ("it's getting worse all the time"), focused ("teenagers are the worst offenders"), protective ("young children should be protected"), but essentially hopeful ("the condition is curable"). Part of the emotion is bound up in nostalgia for the allegedly kinder and gentler world of yesteryear. We cannot test this theory empirically, because data from those allegedly quiet and gentle times of yore are most definitely lacking. Timothy Jay suggests that those who think swearing is a modern-day pestilence should "imagine the conversation patterns . . . in brothels in the 1700s, the saloons of the American west, the Australian outback"; many other sites, I'm sure, will spring to mind.

As we've seen, should you choose to eliminate swearing from your life, there are self-help books, courses, and counseling services available to help curb your tongue and beat the habit. Swearing in these venues is treated rather like smoking, and perhaps we should not be too surprised if we see sometime soon the marketing of commercial equivalents of nicotine gum (perhaps gum-chewing will be proposed as an alternative occupation for the mouth?) or nicotine patches (perhaps an ordinary patch placed strategically over the mouth?).

The third perspective is pure linguistic snobbery. It's the same linguistic attitude that characterizes the approach of the well educated and well heeled toward the language of the less educated and less economically privileged. The fact is that all cultures have a range of registers and styles that serve different purposes. It is only the distribution of power in a culture that enables those-who-have-a-lot to label their own language as "standard" or "normal" or "neutral" and, correspondingly, the language of the have-nots as "substandard"—deviant and defective in multiple ways. This is no different from the ethnocentrism that allows one people to see their culture as the norm, and anything different as exotic or weird.

To repeat Peter Trudgill's wise words: If you don't like their vowels, it's because you don't like their values. There is nothing inherently defective or deficient in forms such as "ain't" (am not) and "youse" (second-person plural)—indeed, a very good case could be made on linguistic grounds for the inclusion of "youse" in the language, as an addition for all to enjoy. But that wouldn't help at all—after all, it is the association of these nonprestigious forms with the people most likely to use them that firms up the cement around people-like-us and people-like-them.

Consistent with this linguistically snobby perspective are a few satellite prejudices. These relate to a perception that swearers lack self-control, suffer from verbal impoverishment, and are impossibly lazy. First, lack of control. This view of the swearer is rather fanciful. The assertion is that swearing is automatic and involuntary in nature, rather like blinking or vomiting (not necessarily at the same time). The suggested antidote is discipline, a euphemism for physical violence. No one, it would seem, has thought to ask how discipline will prevent behaviors that are seen to be involuntary. Ever tried not to vomit when you need to?

A second prejudice held by the linguistically snobby is that swearers lack sufficient words (an impoverished lexicon, perhaps, to match their impoverished zip code) and have a lazy disposition (after all—runs an argument in the footsteps of Ayn Rand—surely if they were more diligent, efficient, and ambitious, they would be living at a different zip code, wouldn't they?). As Oscar Wilde observed with his trademark snobbishness, "The expletive is a refuge of the semi-literate."

But this dismissive view flows from a highly implausible model of how language is produced, which goes like this: Speakers use swear words because they're either too cognitively indolent to reach inside their minds to find the right word, or they're too lexically impoverished to have the word in the first place, making the effort at retrieval a pointless exercise. Timothy Jay illustrates the absurdity of this model by asking us to imagine that a speaker wants to say "Today there was a drop in the consumer price index." However, being impoverished or lazy, the speaker can come up with only "Today there was a drop in the fuck." The truth is that people who don't have the right word to use can (and do) signal this fact with a range of devices, such as hesitation markers ("um," "ah"), fillers ("you know"), repetitions ("the building . . . the building"), reformulations ("the place where the exhibition is on"), or vague referents ("thingy"). Or they scratch their head and admit they don't have the word they need. Or they ask for collaboration ("What do you call it when . . . ?"). What they don't do, when at a loss, is randomly swear. They may well say something along the lines of "Today there was a drop in the fucking consumer price index," but that is altogether a different thing.

The mistake, I think, is to see language as monolithic, invariant, logical, and fixed. That might be how some people want language to be, and if so, fair enough, we all have our wants. But the reality is that language is less like a cathedral than a kind of ground-covering plant. Also, it's massively varied, rule-governed (but not necessarily logical), rubbery, and shifting (no, not "shifty"). Words shift about, take on fresh nuances, realign themselves, acquire new connotations. No word is immune to these trends and influences, not even the words most foul.

Blanket, one-size-fits-all rules really don't serve much purpose. A leading Sydney socialite was anonymously reported as saying, "Nothing will label a man as much as his nonunderstanding of the swearing ethos." She went on to outline the differences between the odd swear word selected to underscore a point at a critical juncture or to add pungency or convey emotion; and thoughtless, oafish repetition that signals at best insensitivity and at worst social illiteracy.

Swear words correspond to the taboos of society. "God," "Jesus," "Mary," and "Mother of God" were swear words for such a long time because they broke the injunction about not taking the Lord's name in vain. "Hell" and "damnation" also had awfully long innings, which itself is an indicator of how long and how much power was wielded by the Christian church. In the wake of the break-down of feudalism and the crumbling of the church's investment in the state came a new era of unfaith. "God" and "Hell" and various related religious accoutrements started to lose their currency and, therefore, their power as taboos. Those of us living critical, secular, pluralist, postmodernist lives would say, "Good thing, too!" These days the most offensive of the bunch is probably "damn," which is unlikely to ruffle many clerical feathers.

However—much to their relief, I'm sure—people didn't need to scramble for long in the dust of crumbling church buildings in search of new taboos, because sex and bodily functions and products jumped into first place in line and quickly became the premier taboo of choice. The taboo du jour, except that the jour went on for a few centuries. Before you knew it, Queen Victoria was enthroned, and Victoriana had arrived. This age of prudery, prissiness, and hypocrisy poured fuel on the fire of taboo, generating a host of euphemisms so that people could sidestep the land mines and still make their meanings.

As we have seen, as long as taboos serve their purpose, they enjoy currency. In 1887, Gilbert and Sullivan were obliged to change the spelling of their opera *Ruddygore* to *Ruddigore,* because even a euphemism for "bloody" was enough to cause public outrage. Nearly thirty years later, Shaw's Eliza dropped her "not bloody likely," and the rage came out again. Then the world wars took over, and wars do great things for the spread of swear words. In 1941 an English newspaper published an unexpurgated "bloody" (instead of the usual "b——y"): "I really loathe the bloody Hun." In any case, by the start of the second half of the twentieth century, it was pretty clear that the general hysterical response to swearing would not long outlast the authentic experience of two world wars.

Over the next few decades, sexuality gradually slid off its taboo pedestal, not so much because of overexposure to words such as FUCK, but because the old notions of virginity, sexuality, and sin had had their day. At the start of the new millennium, it's generally agreed that a FUCK today is nothing like it was twenty years ago. So once again, we're in the market for a new taboo. And once again, there's no problem to speak of.

The "new" taboo is personal vilification of the "-ist" kind—especially relating to race, ethnicity, religious affiliation, sex and sexual orientation, and able-ism. A good example of this shift can be noted in the reactions over time to the phrase "a Jew bastard." Fifty years ago, any perceived offense would have been about the sexual innuendo of "bastard." Today it's about the word "Jew." Indeed, many non-Jews are reluctant to use the word "Jew," for fear of offending, and are more comfortable with "Jewish," presumably because the suffix "-ish" takes the allegedly harsh edge off "Jew." As for Jews, some are fine with the word "Jew"; some like the "-ish" better; some think that "-ish" actually means less Orthodox and more secular-cultural— and maybe it does come down to the latter, in reality.

The point is that people worry about the word, and the worry bespeaks an undercurrent of anxiety about the words we use and the impact they have on others, including others' perceptions of us. An incident akin to the "Jew bastard" example mentioned above took place some years ago in South Africa in the context of sport. The Afrikaans-

speaking coach of the Springbok team had allegedly referred repeatedly to "fokken kaffirs." Now, "kaffir" is
known in South Africa as "the K-word," and of the two
words, "fucking" and "kaffir," there was no question that
the K-word was the source of the offensiveness.

In Australia (but not exclusively so), there is no shortage
of incidents involving swearing as rule-breaking behavior.
Increasingly, they come to attention in the media, less because of the words used than because of the erratic legal responses. Charges of using offensive language are dismissed
or accepted depending on the magistrate's discretion—or
whim. In September 2002 a Sydney magistrate dismissed
an offensive-language charge against a man who had told
police to fuck off, on the grounds that the man's tone had
not been offensive. It was reported under the headline
PUTTING THE "F" BACK INTO FRIENDLY. A week later, the
same magistrate upheld the same charge against a young
man who'd said to a policeman, when asked what he was
doing, that he "was just fucking going home." The headline
for the latter report read PERHAPS THE -ING MADE ALL THE
DIFFERENCE.

However, the domain given the most sensationalist appeal by the mass media is the nexus of swearing and sport.
Every now and again, an incident involving swearing bursts
into the public arena. One such occasion was in January
2003, during a series of one-day cricket matches between
Australia and Sri Lanka, when the Australian cricketer Dar-
ren Lehmann was overheard to have used the infamous
phrase "black cunt." It was less the sexuality than the racial
vilification that caught Lehmann out. There's no doubt
that "racial and ethnic swear words have become the true

obscenities today," a view that places "black cunt" in the same group as "Jew bastard" and "fokken kaffirs." And "nigger," according to Christopher Darden, deputy district attorney on the O. J. Simpson case, "is the dirtiest, filthiest, nastiest word in the English language, and it has no place in a courtroom." Richard Dooling makes a good point when he writes, "For centuries 'fuck' was the most objectionable word in the English language, but now 'nigger' and 'cunt' are probably tied for that distinction, and 'fuck' has stepped down. Finally, hatred is more dangerous than sex."

There's nothing new in all this. Let's have no illusions about the Romans who brutalized Jesus en route to the site of crucifixion, or the Spanish Inquisitors who expelled Spain's Jews in 1492, or the marauding ethnic cleansers of the former Yugoslavia. What's relatively new, at least in the English-speaking West, is the taboo that surrounds the use of personally vilifying language as abuse. As *Macquarie Dictionary*'s Sue Butler has said, "Today's taboos are all about the labels you use for people. So that the sentence *'you are a . . . '* is practically a no-no. Even if [all you're saying is] *'you're a boofhead,'* because you're putting it in the same context as things which are clearly rude."

Hughes suggests that the taboo shift to -ist language (racist, sexist, chauvinist, etc.) is an outgrowth of the nationalism, mercantile expansion, imperial rivalry, and military conquest that brought different peoples into contact that was, for the most part, belligerent and hostile. In this connection, he further points out that the potency in modern swearing, in contrast to, say, that of the Victorian era, is related to group identity rather than individual morality. There is a greater cruelty in maligning someone for something outside of his or her personal control (such as skin pigment) than for actions (for example, sexual activity) that involve personal choice.

When talking about euphemism, any discussion of race, says Robert Dessaix, "gets us racing for cover in a way a Victorian would have found astonishing." It's a touchy subject. "Ethnic" was promoted as a way of legitimizing cultures other than the Anglo-Saxon-Celtic. A great deal of discomfort is experienced by colonizers and their descendants in and around a word to describe the original inhabitants. A general rule of thumb is to adopt the term that the people being referred to prefer, such as "indigenous Australians." Canada uses "First Nation," America "Native American." "Native" as a noun, with or without a capital, is a no-no for any reference to original inhabitants or their descendants. There is no greater taboo today than to break these rules, wittingly or unwittingly.

Instrumental in raising public awareness about the nature of abusive vilification is the so-called political correctness (PC) movement, very front-stage in the 1980s. So-called PCers are those who advocate greater neutrality in public language, such as "humanity" instead of "mankind." Following Deborah Cameron's usage, I say "so-called PCers" because the pro-neutral-language people do not use the term "PC" to describe their ideology or actions. The term as such was used *about* them (and unfortunately stuck fast) by the American conservative right, and it has been so contaminated by negative connotation that it tends to be used for attack purposes ("you're so PC"), as a disclaimer ("I'm not PC, but . . ."), or in irony or jokes.

The bottom line is that the appellation "PC" was hugely successful in discrediting the movement to which the label was attached. Some synonyms emerged over time, like the equally hostile "thought police" and "feminazis." Dooling's take on all of this is: "The central paradox about political correctness is that it demands diversity in everything except thought."

One huge central irony about the term "PC" is that the arguments proffered by the critics of so-called PCers (from both the right and the left) are betrayed by the rampant success achieved by "PC" in the free-lexical marketplace. The right accuses the so-called PCers of abusing the language, but they do the same thing by using the dismissive term. The left charges the so-called PCers with wasting time on trivial language issues when the real issues need attention, all the while failing to note that language issues, as seen by the massive success of "PC," are far from trivial in their effect on public consciousness.

Ever present is the scoffing tone, as when Robert Hughes questions whether being called "physically disabled" can either "fix the cripple's [sic] disability or improve their emotional state." Richard Dooling is even more savage in his critique. He writes that people think they can "remedy ancient hatreds with a little word surgery, a logosectomy to remove offensive words and the hateful thoughts lurking behind them. Maybe we should remove all the religious slurs and racial epithets from all the dictionaries in Bosnia and see if the civil war ends."

It also didn't help that "PC" quickly came to be associated with priggishness and moral self-righteousness rather than with a liberal movement to raise awareness of en-

demic, naturalized, and institutionalized prejudice and dis-
crimination. The anti-PC detractors launched a scoffing attack that used humor to great effect. Partly this had to do
with taking so-called PC principles to their logical but absurd extreme—such as suggesting that Paul Newman
change his name to "Paul Newperson."

Then there were a few unfortunate incidents that were
inherently comic and made so-called PC the risible target
of mockery. For example, in the early 1990s, a California
newspaper that had computer-automated its so-called PC
language policy inadvertently printed "a plan for putting
Massachusetts back in the African-American." The subse-
quent public correction informed readers that "back in the
black" was what had been intended. The incident is redo-
lent with irony, not the least of which relates to this use of
the word "black." English is riddled with negatively associated meanings for "black" (think of "black-and-blue,"
"blackmail," "black box," "Black Death," "black money,"
"black hole"), but ironically, it's better to be "in the black"
than "in the red."

The so-called PC movement was responsible for the
production of an alternative set of linguistic denoters to replace the ones that were considered politically incorrect.
The idea was to avoid terms with built-in judgments, or
terms that had accrued a social stigma. The preference was
for "an artificial currency of polysyllabic abstract substitutions." "Drug addiction" became "substance dependence";
"blind" became "visually impaired," "deaf" became "hearing-impaired"; "sex worker" replaced "prostitute." The
only exception to this trend was the widespread use of
"dead white European males," which blatantly broke the

PC rule about emotive, prejudiced language in a defiant example of double standards.

Despite criticism, the so-called PC movement's influence has been profound. Perhaps not on what people think, but certainly on what they say in public. And its influence continues, despite the scorn. A recent report in the media referred to an international attempt to ban certain signs that the hearing-impaired use in their sign language, specifically, representations of Jews, Asians, gays, and the disabled. Some of the barred signs include making a hooked nose ("Jew"), a limp wrist ("gay"), slanting eyes ("Chinese"), and pointing to a spot on the forehead ("Indian"). Less offensive alternatives (like drawing a triangular shape to signify the subcontinent of India) have been recommended. In a rather ironic echo of the mainstream debate, spokespeople for various deaf groups denied that the existing signs were intentionally offensive. They explained that signing is based essentially on the visual, that offense can be easily avoided by spelling out the word; finally, they asserted that the hearing world had no right to impose its views on the deaf. I found myself wondering what the sign for "deaf" is.

Without wading too deeply into the murky and emotional waters that lash the shores of the island of so-called PCness, there's little doubt that the PC movement, along with the surrounding publicity and controversy, did raise public consciousness about the offensiveness of negatively loaded words, which had hitherto been registered as such only by women and minorities, who knew from their own authentic personal experiences that the language describing them was contributing in significant ways to the raw deal

they were being served. Increasing this awareness contributed to the emergence of the taboo on calling someone
a (whatever).

So vilifying language has stepped up into the place
where sexual obscenity used to stand, but as we have seen
in the South African example ("fokken kaffirs") and the
Australian cricket example ("black cunt"), there's no law
against the double whammy. Not yet, anyway.

ACKNOWLEDGMENTS

I owe thanks to the many people who have been involved in the production of this book. Mark Cherry and Barbara Lasserre have been the guiding lights from the outset. They laughed with me during the up times, stuck by me through the down times, infecting me with their enthusiasm. I thank them for their spirit of generosity.

I have been fortunate indeed in my publishers at Allen & Unwin. They have been a great team—Richard Walsh, Jo Paul, and Emma Cotter. Their dealings are unfailingly professional and expert. It helps, too, that they're unfailingly nice. I thank them for their belief in me and their support throughout. I'd like also to thank the team at Free Press, especially Amy Scheibe and Maris Kreizman for their work on the American edition.

To put this jigsaw puzzle of a book together, I called on the knowledge of many people. Sometimes I was in need of their first-language knowledge; other times, more general insights into language, behavior, and society. I am grateful to them all. They are: Dimitri Akhmetov, Libi Burman, Anna Dash, Nic Farrow, Louise Haynes, Jeremy Jones, Matthew Kenny, Marcel Khoury, Andrew Klonowski, Sheila Man,

Evelyn Mike, Mayumi Nito, George Rizk, Arnel Santos, Sergio Sergi, Andrew Spaille, Sasha Wajnryb, Marguerite Wells, Victor Yee, and many others whose names are sprinkled through the notes.

As, too, are those of some serious researchers and writers on foul language, who provided a foundation for my own thinking on the subject. They are: Lars-Gunnar Andersson and Peter Trudgill, Keith Allan and Kate Burridge, Richard Dooling, Geoffery Hughes, Timothy Jay, Angus Kidman, and Ashley Montagu.

NOTES

Prologue

"If all science …" (p. 1)   Jay, 1992:113.

"If English were …" (p. 2)   Taylor, 1975:17.

"the most conventionalized …" (p. 2)   Goffman, 1981:90.

"Others have commented …" (p. 2)   For Kidman's criticism of the notion of swearing as intuitively obvious, see his Honours thesis (1993).

"Researcher …" (p. 3)   Dooling, 1996:130.

"inextricably bound …" (p. 3)   Ibid.

1. Falling Foul

"The editors of *The Random House* …" (p. 5)   See Bryson (1990) for a fascinating trip through the history of lexicography.

"We're going to have to ditch …" (p. 6)   Bryson, 1990:219.

"one Burges Johnson …" (p. 6)   Bryson, 1990:218.

"the Cuss Control Academy …" (p. 7)   For further enlightenment, see http://www.cusscontrol.com.

"James V. O'Connor …" (p. 8)   O'Connor's book, *Cuss Control: The Complete Book on How to Curb Your Cussing,* is published by Three Rivers Press (2000).

"O'Connor then goes on …" (p. 8)   For a full version of O'Connor's arguments, see the transcript of Sharon Bloyd Peshkin's interview with him, titled "Swearing Off Foul Language" at http://www.chicagoparent.com/CPpages/archive/Interview%20Archive/Int0500.htm.

"one Australian journalist …" (p. 9)   *Sydney Morning Herald,* 22 December 2003, p. 16.

"Non bestemmiare per l'onore ..." (p. 9)　　Montagu, 2001:24–25.

"In another advice column ..." (p. 10)　　Found at
　　http://www.spiked-online.com/articles/00000006D9A6.html.

"We live ... in an age ..." (p. 11)　　Phillips (2002).

"trickle-down effects ..." (p. 12)　　Personal communication from
　　Natalie Kent to the author, March 2004.

3. Foul Is as Foul Does

"In his massive survey ..." (p. 26)　　See Crystal (1987).

"the secondary meaning ..." (p. 27)　　*Collins* (2003).

"Why are you crying ..." (p. 28)　　Montagu, 2001:72.

"Crying and swearing ..." (p. 28)　　For Pinker's comparison of hu-
　　man language with other animals' communication systems, see
　　The Language Instinct (1994).

"ipsa hominis essentia ..." (p. 28)　　This tag comes from Arango's
　　Dirty Words (1839) and is cited in Dooling, 1996:54.

"Our psychosocial equilibrium ..." (p. 29)　　Montagu, 2001:72.

"our relief valve ..." (p. 29)　　Montagu, 2001:79.

"Releasing an expletive ..." (p. 30)　　See the reference to Campbell,
　　Hughlings, Jackson, and Steinhoff in Montagu, 2001:83.

"annoyance swearing ..." (p. 30)　　Two researchers who use this
　　term are Burridge (2002) and Montagu (2001).

"It's not for nothing ..." (p. 31)　　For an interesting discussion of
　　"fighting words," see Jay (1999).

"two schools of thought ..." (p. 32)　　Jay, 1999:212.

"Some writers, including ..." (p. 33)　　Montagu, 2001:53.

"One way of distinguishing ..." (p. 33)　　Montagu, 2001:35.

"Generally speaking, the more relaxed ..." (p. 34)　　Burridge,
　　2002:229.

"the integrated adjective ..." (p. 35)　　Hughes, 1998:24.

"A Book About Australia ..." (p. 35)　　Edited by T. Inglis Moore and
　　published in 1961 by Collins UK.

"a phenomenon explored ..." (p. 36)　　See Eble (1996).

"While such swearing ..." (p. 36)　　For a discussion of swear words
　　as loose intensifiers, see Andersson & Trudgill, 1990:61.

"Social swearing is a great ..." (p. 36)　　Holmes et al. (1996).

"What Cruise seems to have ..." (p. 38)　　See Jess Cagle's article
　　"About Tom," in *Time,* 1 July 2002, emphasis added.

4. Where the Fuck?

"The use and overuse of ..." (p. 41)   *Collins,* 2003:655.

"partly perceived influences ..." (p. 42)   See Tony Thorne's introduction to the *Bloomsbury Dictionary to Contemporary Slang* (1991), p. iv.

"eight categories of use ..." (p. 43)   Hughes, 1998:31–32.

"Angus Kidman offers an alternative ..." (p. 45)   Kidman cites J. L. Austin (1967) in Kidman (1993).

"a lewd term ..." (p. 45)   Greer, 1971:41.

"I have a love interest ..." (p. 46)   This quote was originally taken from an interview in *Playboy,* January 1988, and is cited in Crawley (ed.), *The Wordsworth Dictionary of Film Quotations* (1991).

"Wayland Young contends ..." (p. 47)   Young is cited in Montagu, 2001:314–15.

"a transitive verb ..." (p. 48) Montagu, 2001:305.

"If only our social masters ..." (p. 48)   See http://www.users.bigpond.com/burnside/obscene.htm.

"[w]e lack a language ..." (p. 48)   C. S. Lewis is here being cited in Hughes, 1998:1.

"any explicit reference to sexuality ..." (p. 48)   See Hughes, 1998:241.

"the virtues of brevity ..." (p. 48)
http://www.users.bigpond.com/burnside/obscene.htm.

"Research into sexual naming ..." (p. 48)   See Cornog (1986), cited in Jay, 1999:86.

"Alan Ayto suggests ..." (p. 50)   Ayto, 1999:462.

"We didn't always have ..." (p. 50)   Personal communication from Jeffrey Mellefont to the author, March 2004.

"the twitching lace curtain ..." (p. 51)   Mike Carlton in the *Sydney Morning Herald,* 17–18 April 2004.

5. The Wild Thing

"some people might ..." (p. 53)   Hughes, 1998:27.

"combining the vocalism ..." (p. 53)   Montagu, 2001:307.

"a widespread Germanic form ..." (p. 53)   Dooling, 1996:32.

"Anglo-Saxon terms ..." (p. 54)   Goffman, 1981:114. See also Hughes, 1998:35.

"why precisely procreation ..." (p. 55)   Hughes, 1998:24.

"word gestapos ..." (p. 55)   A term coined by Dooling, 1996:32.

"the first widespread use of ..." (p. 55)   This reference comes from Flexner's 1976 book, *I Hear America Talking* (which might as well have been called *I Hear America Cursing*), cited in Jay, 1992:74.

"it was an incomparable ..." (p. 56)   Montagu, 2001:314.

"Its naturalism inflamed ..." (p. 56)   Malmberg, http://www.kaapeli.fi/flf/malmber.htm.

"a statement of quality ..." (p. 57)   Montagu, 2001:314.

"In his book ..." (p. 57)   Wayland Young's picturesque example is quoted in Montagu, 2001:314–15.

"this unashamedly raunchy poem ..." (p. 58)   This uninhibited offering is cited by Montagu (2001:308) as an example of Scots' innate frugality in all things, even swearing.

"taking especial care ..." (p. 60)   Montagu, 2001:304.

"an instinctive repugnance ..." (p. 60)   Partridge, cited in Montagu, 2001:306.

"the three thousand most frequently used ..." (p. 61)   Hughes, 1998:270.

"An alternative view ..." (p. 62)   Hughes, 1998:271.

"the wearisome reiteration ..." (p. 63)   Farmer & Henley, *Slang and Its Analogues,* seven volumes (1889–1904), cited in Hughes, 1998:271.

"if you don't like their vowels ..." (p. 63)   Trudgill, 1975:29.

"Warning! usu.considered obscene ..." (p. 64)   Dooling, 1996:26.

"perhaps the face ..." (p. 64)   Robert Dessaix in *Lingua Franca,* Radio National, "Swearing": http://www.abc.net.au/rn/arts/ling/stories/s1154069.htm.

6. A Cunt of a Word

"the worst name ..." (p. 66)   Greer, 1971:39.

"a publicly acceptable term ..." (p. 67)   A suggestion found in Hughes, 1998:20.

"This would seem to fit ..." (p. 67)   McDonald, 1988:35–36.

"In women the neck ..." (p. 67)   This quote from Lanfranc's *Science of Chirurgie* also comes from McDonald, 1988:36.

"the quintessential physical ..." (p. 67)   This quotation from Partridge is found in McConville & Shearlaw (1984:45), and for what it's worth, they follow the claim with an exclamation mark.

"the likely but problematic ..." (p. 67)   Hughes, 1998:27.

"A variant of ..." (p. 68)   Hughes, 1998:20.

"What is a cunt ..." (p. 69)   Lawrence [1928], 1960:234.

"The tension between these two ..." (p. 70)   Jay, 1992:10–11.

"were being progressively …" (p. 71)   Haggard (1961) cited in Hughes, 1998:193.

"With great taxonomic precision …" (p. 72)   For Hughes's eight categories of use, see Hughes, 1998:30–31.

"one important exception …" (p. 74)   Despite its alleged inflexibility, one respondent claims that "cunting" is used quite prolifically in the north of England, particularly Yorkshire, to the extent that it is almost interchangeable with FUCKING.

"The C word …" (p. 76)   Spectrum, *Sydney Morning Herald*, 6–7 September 2003.

"the way to change …" (p. 77)   Saunders, http://www.shoal.net.au/~sandral/WIF6.html.

"Some women actively cultivate …" (p. 77)   Saunders, http://www.shoal.net.au/~sandral/WIF6.html.

"the battlefield where she fights …" (p. 77)   Greer, 1999:106.

"begin to like the word …" (p. 78)   Saunders, http://www.shoal.net.au/~sandral/WIF6.html.

"*Vittu* is … an ancient …" (p. 78)   Malmberg, http://www.kaapeli.fi/flf/malmber.htm.

"women still find themselves …" (p. 79)   McConville & Shearlaw, 1984:23.

7. Shit Happens

"I've been told …" (p. 82)   Personal communication from Alan Stennett to the author, October 2003.

"his joking counterpoint …" (p. 83)   Jay (1999).

"the semantics of disgust …" (p. 84)   Jay, 1999:200.

"Disgust, incidentally …" (p. 84)   Rozin & Fallon (1987), cited in Jay, 1999:199.

"Shitting is pure …" (p. 86)   Dooling, 1996:137.

"How could a child …" (p. 86)   Jay, 1999:200.

"Hershey squirts …" (p. 86)   Mechling (1984), cited in Jay, 1999:200.

"poor little words …" (p. 87)   Burridge, 2002:221.

"the rather quaint …" (p. 90)   Hughes, 1998:29.

"over sixty word combinations …" (p. 90)   Partridge, 1984:1052–54.

"to discard in a speedy …" (p. 90)   Gaines, 1948; Gilliland, 1980.

"a major function …" (p. 91)   Eble (1996).

"hands-down winner …" (p. 91)   Dooling, 1996:150.

"A predominantly American …" (p. 93)   *Macquarie Dictionary of Australian Colloquialisms,* 1984:276–77.

"toadying parasite ..." (p. 94)   Hughes, 1998:29.
"a database of 'shitty' ..." (p. 95)   Kidman (1993).
"Metaphorical uses need ..." (p. 96)   Kidman, 1993:
    http://www.gusworld.com.au/nrc/thesis/ch-3.htm#3.4.
"the written 'shit' ..." (p. 98)   Dooling, 1996:130.
"David Crystal comes at it ..." (p. 99)   Crystal (1987).
"Never doubt the potency ..." (p. 102)   Burridge, 2002:220.

8. In the Name of God

"There's a particular ..." (p. 107)   Andersson & Trudgill, 1990:35–37.
"They're always crying out ..." (p. 109)   Hill, 1992:214.
"Apropos offendedness ..." (p. 110)   Dessaix, in *Lingua franca,* Radio National, July 2004, "Swearing,"
    http://www.abc.net.au/rn/arts/ling/stories/s1154069.htm.
"the seven modes of swearing ..." (p. 111)   Michael's categories are analyzed in Montagu, 2001:122.
"the church banned profanity ..." (p. 111)   Jay, 1999:191.
"how seriously one treats ..." (p. 111)   Jay, 1999:107.
"Today devout Jews ..." (p. 113)   I am grateful to Rabbi Fred Morgan for his insight and advice, personal communication, January 2004.
"multiple interpretations ..." (p. 113)   Allan & Burridge, 1991:37.
"euphemistic expletive versions ..." (p. 114)   Hughes, 1998:13.
"The range ..." (p. 115)   Allan & Burridge, 1992:38–39.
"speak of the devil ..." (p. 116)   Dooling, 1996:43.
"Christian panoply ..." (p. 117)   Dessaix, in *Lingua Franca,* Radio National, July 2004, "On the Euphemism,"
    http://www.abc.net.au/rn/arts/ling/stories/s1154074.htm.
"an age of unfaith ..." (p. 117)   Dooling, 1996:13.
"Nonetheless, the sheer quantity ..." (p. 117)   Montagu, 2001:200–201.
"the notion of taboo-loading ..." (p. 118)   Taylor, 1975:17.
"God is dead ..." (p. 119)   Jay, 1992:167.
"garlic in the stew ..." (p. 119)   Dooling, 1996:115.
"the landscape of Hell ..." (p. 119)   Dooling, 1996:115.
"entire civilizations ... have lived ..." (p. 119)   Ibid.
"a less antisocial alternative ..." (p. 120)   Montagu, 2001:57–58.
"Good and beautiful Proserpina ..." (p. 121)   Crystal, 1987:61.
"Indeed, internal attribution ..." (p. 124)   Seligman (1990).
"It is when a people ..." (p. 125)   Montagu, 2001:48.

"the need to swear ..." (p. 125)   Dooling, 1996:11.
"the vocal calls of primates ..." (p. 125)   Dooling, 1996:10.
"Swearing has been with us ..." (p. 125)   Ibid.
"The power to damn ..." (p. 129)   Montagu, 2001:281.
"London would be known as ..." (p. 129)   Montagu, 2001:282–83.
"Very glad see you!" (p. 130)   Captain Hall's memoirs of his travels are cited in Montagu, 2001:356.
"they allow 'the speaker ...'" (p. 130)   Jespersen (1962:229), cited in Hughes, 1998:7.
"However, with time ..." (p. 130)   Montagu, 2001:298.
"An unconfirmed report ..." (p. 131)   Cited in Montagu, 2001:298.
"a word is not a crystal ..." (p. 131)   Justice Oliver Wendell Holmes, cited in Dooling, 1996:24.
"The words are there ..." (p. 132)   Montagu, 2001:68.

9. Son of a Bitch

"the semantics of deterioration ..." (p. 134)   Hughes, 1998:223.
"the opposed exemplars ..." (p. 138)   Delaney (1974), cited in Hughes, 1998:218.
"Eve, the stained-mistress ..." (p. 138)   Hughes, 1998:218.
"The dichotomy is one ..." (p. 138)   Summers (1977).
"Margaret Atwood has pointed out ..." (p. 140)   Atwood (1982:198), cited in Hughes, 1998:209.
"But if it's a mere step ..." (p. 140)   Kidman (1993), personal communication with Cliff Goddard.
"a mass psycholinguistic phenomenon ..." (p. 140)   Hughes, 1998:228.
"women should be obscene ..." (p. 140)   Groucho Marx, quoted in Dooling, 1996:93.
"for they were mere troopers ..." (p. 141)   Montagu, 2001:23.
"*fucking* was used as an adjective ..." (p. 141)   Dooling, 1996:9.
"a nation capable of sending ..." (p. 141)   Allan Walker Read, cited in Dooling, 1996:10.
"A soldier going over the top ..." (p. 141)   Montagu attributes this to Kingsley Amis, Montagu, 2001:328.
"because men are congenitally incapable ..." (p. 142)   Dooling, 1996:8.
"the resource of weeping ..." (p. 144)   Montagu, 2001:87.
"Resilience, or acquired ..." (p. 144)   Tyler (1997).
"these beliefs have been subjected ..." (p. 145)   Kidman, 1993, Section 5.1.

"A recent study …" (p. 145)   J. Coates (1998).

"One finding consistently emerges …" (p. 146)   Kidman, 1993,
     Section 5.1.

"Some forty years ago …" (p. 146)   This experiment is discussed in
     some detail in Montagu, 2001:87–89.

"One inference to be drawn here …" (p. 147)   Montague, 2001:88.

"this word offends …" (p. 148)   Jay, 1992:178.

"men and women have …" (p. 149)   Jay, 1992:179.

"Sexual harassment is …" (p. 149)   Jay, 1999:165.

"fewer women harass …" (p. 150)   Some might say, to put it baldly,
     that we live in "a phallocentric cockocracy" (Taylor, cited in
     Hughes, 1998:206).

"Women are allowed to …" (p. 150)   A good example of relevant
     studies of young people's talk is Vincent (1982), cited in Eckert &
     McConnell-Ginet, 2003:181–82.

"Women are now talking …" (p. 150)   Critic Rosalind Coward,
     writing in *New Statesman and Society* in 1989, cited in Hughes,
     1998:211.

"Restraint is lifted …" (p. 150)   Eckert & McConnell-Ginet,
     2003:183.

"This is why male …" (p. 150)   Personal communication from
     Richard Walsh to the author, June 2003.

"swearing usage in Australia …" (p. 151)   Kidman, 1993, Section
     5.1.

"the Australian film …" (p. 151)   Released 2003, directed by
     Melanie Rodriga, written by Vanessa Lomma, based on stage play
     by Wilson McCaskill.

"at the lower end …" (p. 151)   Review of *Teesh and Trude* by Sandra
     Hall, *Sydney Morning Herald,* 18 September 2003.

"a flavourless diet …" (p. 152)   Sandra Hall, in her review of the
     film for the *Sydney Morning Herald.*

"men swear more than women …" (p. 152)   Jay bases this conclu-
     sion on his research in the United States (1992, 1999).

"As with the case of love …" (p. 153)   Jay, 1992:181.

"an interesting piece of comparative …" (p. 153)   Jay, 1999:166–67.

"the overall conclusion …" (p. 153)   Jay, 1999:166.

"In Australia …" (p. 153)   Amy Cooper, *Sunday Life,* 4 April 2004,
     p. 10.

"South African findings …" (p. 154)   De Klerk, 1992.

"an important gender difference …" (p. 154)   Dooling, 1996:5.

"rude negators …" (p. 154)   linguist@tamvi.bitnet. June 2003,
     week 5.

"With each choice …" (p. 156)   Eckert & McConnell-Ginet, 2003:307.

"We'd like to hire you …" (p. 157)   Thorne & Henley, cited in Jay, 1999:165.

"NO SWEARING …" (p. 157)   Montagu, 2001:87. Montagu gives his source as the Philadelphia *Evening Bulletin,* 16 September 1942.

10. Born to Be Foul

"a rare and puzzling …" (p. 160)   Jay, 1999:3.

"In the 1994 documentary …" (p. 160)   Laurel Chiten's 1994 award-winning film, *Twist and Shout,* is distributed by New Day Films.

"What is intriguing …" (p. 161)   Jay, 1999:6.

"So the grammatical rules …" (p. 163)   Andersson & Trudgill, 1999:61–62.

"Compiling a list of marginal elements …" (p. 164)   Andersson & Trudgill, 1999:65–66.

"Flyting was a feature …" (p. 166)   Hughes, 1998:119.

"In Scotland, flyting …" (p. 166)   Hughes, 1998:119–20.

"Variations of this kind …" (p. 167)   William Labov (1972), *Language in the Inner City,* cited in Andersson & Trudgill, 1999:66.

"This style is also …" (p. 167)   Burridge, 2002:230.

"There is an argument …" (p. 167)   Andersson & Trudgill, 1999:66.

"The comic has to respond …" (p. 167)   A study of the verbal patterns in comic-heckler interactions was published in an article entitled "You're Ugly, Your Dick Is Small and Everybody Fucks Your Mother: The Stand-Up Comedian's Response to the Heckler" (Conway, 1994).

"May you marry …" (p. 168)   Chaikin, 1982:112–13.

"One theory …" (p. 168)   Reported by Andersson & Trudgill, 1999:62–63.

"There are five levels …" (p. 169)   Following Andersson & Trudgill, 1999:62–63.

"two points of relevance …" (p. 171)   Andersson & Trudgill, 1999:64.

"social behavior or 'style' …" (p. 171)   Douglas (1966, 1973), cited in Andersson & Trudgill, 1999:64.

"linguistic socialization …" (p. 172)   Bernstein (1970) in Gumperz & Hymes.

"A positional role …" (p. 173)   Douglas taken from Andersson & Trudgill, 1999:65.

"Numerous studies of Victorian ..." (p. 173)   A good example is
     Pearsall (1969).

"Victorian erotica ..." (p. 173)   See Hughes, 1998:155.

"extreme Victorian reticence ..." (p. 173)   Hughes, 1998:155.

"no one could think of a way ..." (p. 174)   Pearsall, 1969:474.

"As cornerstones in the social structure ..." (p. 135)   Douglas, cited
     in Andersson & Trudgill, 1999:65.

"Erving Goffman's notion of leaking ..." (p. 175)   Goffman (1981).

11. Bootleggers and Asterisks

"The word 'taboo' ..." (p. 177)   Hughes, 1998:8.

"solitary swearer ..." (p. 179)   Montagu, 2001:1.

"the conventional vehicles of swearing ..." (p. 180)   Crystal (1987).

"Some Australian Aborigines ..." (p. 180)   Montagu, 2001:17.

"An interesting study ..." (p. 181)   Abd el-Jawad (2000).

"such 'conversational swearing' ..." (p. 182)   Abd el-Jawad,
     2000:237.

"a scattershot inventory ..." (p. 183)   Montagu, 2001:5–34.

"the frequent use of euphemisms ..." (p. 184)   Dessaix, in *Lingua
     Franca,* Radio National, July 2004, "On the Euphemism,"
     http://www.abc.net.au/rn/arts/ling/stories/s1154069.htm.

"Naively ..." (p. 184)   Again, I am grateful to Rabbi Fred Morgan
     (personal communication, March 2004) for his help in consult-
     ing *The Encyclopedia Judaica,* vol. 6:959–62.

"The whole history of swearing ..." (p. 184)   Montagu, 2001:25.

"Ultimately, the decision ..." (p. 185)   Personal communication,
     March 2004, Michael Visontay, re: ABC editorial policies, Syd-
     ney, 2002.

"the curious fact ..." (p. 185)   Dessaix, in *Lingua Franca,* Radio Na-
     tional, July 2004, "Swearing,"
     http://www.abc.net.au/rn/arts/ling/stories/s1154069.htm.

"in which nothing is added ..." (p. 185)   Bowdler, quoted in Mon-
     tagu, 2001:235.

"the different realities ..." (p. 186)   Mark Haddon, in an interview
     for the *Sydney Morning Herald*'s Spectrum, 24 January 2004, p. 15.

"Well-respected anthropological literature ..." (p. 188)   For a full
     description of Donald Thomson's work, see Montagu, 2001:345.

"the sanctioned swearing ..." (p. 189)   Montagu, 2001:12.

"Thomson's native informants ..." (p. 189)   Thomson (1935),
     cited in Montagu, 2001:9–15.

hemism …" (p. 244)   Crystal, 2003:173.

…" (p. 244)   Ibid.

nt akin to …" (p. 245)   Hughes, 1998:277.

THE F BACK …" (p. 246)   *Sydney Morning Herald,* 6 Sep-
2002, no byline.

THE -ING …" (p. 246)   *Sydney Morning Herald,* 14 No-
2002, no byline.

ethnic swear words …" (p. 246)   Burridge, 2001:2.

ger' …" (p. 247)   Dooling, 1996:18.

aries …" (p. 247)   Ibid.

ussion of race …" (p. 248)   Dessaix, in *Lingua Franca,* Ra-
ational, July 2004, "On the Euphemism,"
www.abc.net.au/rn/arts/ling/stories/s1154069.htm.

d PCers …" (p. 248)   Cameron (1995b).

's take on all this …" (p. 249)   Dooling, 1996:167.

trivial in their effect …" (p. 249)   Cameron (1995a).

esent is the …" (p. 249)   R. Hughes (1993).

re savage in his critique …" (p. 249)   Dooling, 1996:18.

is riddled with …" (p. 250)   Cameron (1995b); Wajnryb
).

cial currency …" (p. 250)   Hughes, 1998:276.

"the swearing behavior of Australian Aborigines …" (p. 190)   See
Montagu (1937) referenced in Montagu, 2001:345.

"licitly provided escape …" (p. 190)   Montagu, 2001:13.

"In recognizing the usefulness of swearing …" (p. 190)   W. La
Barre (1939), cited in Montagu, 2001:345.

"What is the First Amendment …" (p. 191)   Dooling, 1996:27.

"social punishments …" (p. 192)   Jay, 1999:206.

"the notion of face …" (p. 193)   The work of both Erving Goffman
and Emile Durkheim set the foundation for this universal theory
of linguistic politeness developed by Penelope Brown and Steven
Levinson (1978).

"an old and quaint …" (p. 194)   Hadida, 1959:124.

"Marilyn Monroe …" (p. 195)   *Sydney Morning Herald,* 2 September 2003, no byline.

"language used as shield …" (p. 197)   Allan & Burridge (1991).

"the euphemism treadmill …" (p. 197)   Stephen Pinker, *New York
Times,* 5 April 1994, cited in Dooling, 1996:46.

"a kind of linguistic Lourdes …" (p. 197)   R. Hughes (1993), cited
in Dooling, 1996:44–5.

"same old frigmarole …" (p. 198)
http://www.pseudodictionary.com/search.php.

"it's just too freaking bad …" (p. 198)   *Sydney Morning Herald,* 19
March 2004, p. 18.

"I won't have no adjective …" (p. 199)   Dickens, cited in Hughes,
1998:12.

"the euphemism of the decade …" (p. 200)   Hughes, 1998:195.

"Effing the Ineffable …" (p. 200)   *The London Review of Books* online at http://www.lrb.co.uk/v21/n23/newe01_.html.

"Why 'No' Is the New F-Word …" (p. 200)   Jane Carafella in *Sydney's Child,* August 2003:12–13.

"a tactic that has been labeled 'remodeling' …" (p. 200)   Allan &
Burridge, 1992:15.

"Farmer and Henley's …" (p. 201)   A full reference to Farmer &
Henley's *Dictionary of Slang and Its Analogues* can be found in the
bibliography in Hughes (1998).

"Another feature …" (p. 201)   For a fuller discussion of rhyming
slang, see Hughes (1998).

"the avoidance of taboo words …" (p. 201)   See Allan & Burridge
(1991).

"the customs of the Masai …" (p. 202)   A full reference to Alfred
Hollis's work can be found in Allan & Burridge (1992).

"*pudendum muliebre* …" (p. 202)   See Nathan Bailey, 1730, *Dictionarium Britannicum,* cited in Hughes, 1998:163.

12. Cross-Culturally Foul

"In Russian … all swear words are sexual …" (p. 204)   Dessaix, in *Lingua Franca,* Radio National, July 2004, "Swearing," http://www.abc.net.au/rn/arts/ling/stories/s1154069.htm; V. Erofeyev (2003).

"if you happen to wake a Finn …" (p. 205)   Bill Bryson, 1990:210.

"I confess that I, too …" (p. 205)   Malmberg, http://www.kaapeli.fi/flf/malmber.htm.

"a futile attempt …" (p. 209) http://www.theferrett.com/showarticle.php?Rant=34.

"one commentator on public language …" (p. 210)   Ibid.

"The mustache, then …" (p. 213)   Jess Cagle, "About Tom," *Time,* 17 March 2003, p. 15.

"The mother-curses …" (p. 216)   Malmberg, http://www.kaapeli.fi/flf/malmber.htm.

"English is unusual …" (p. 217)   Bill Bryson, 1990:211.

"The list usually …" (p. 218)   Two good sources here are Montagu (2001) and Hughes (1998).

"How are people/languages alike …" (p. 219)   Lofland, cited in Planalp, 1999:195.

"Some languages do this …" (p. 219)   Wierzbicka, 1999:273–74.

"According to Australian historian …" (p. 219)   Windshuttle, 2002:110; Reynolds (2003).

"If one of the core …" (p. 220)   Wierzbicka, 1999:297.

"These are also given …" (p. 220)   Wierzbicka, 1999:298.

"Chinese hearts …" (p. 220)   Chun (1997), cited in Wierzbicka, 1999:301.

"Speakers of Kayardild …" (p. 220)   Evans (1994) cited in Wierzbicka, 1999:302.

"Anna Wierzbicka is, wisely …" (p. 221)   Wierzbicka (1999).

"Balinese are expected …" (p. 221)   Wikan (1990), cited in Planalp, 1999:210, 221.

"At the other end …" (p. 221)   Planalp, 1999:220.

"Some communities of the South Pacific …" (p. 222)   Planalp, 1999:222–23.

"The Ifaluk of Micronesia …" (p. 222)   Kluz (1998), cited in Planalp, 1999:228.

"In rural China …" (p. 222)   Potter (1998), cited in Planalp, 1999:206.

"As a longtime American expatriate …

"To them, sex does not carry …" (p.

"the Japanese creation myth …" (p. 2

"tendency to go to pot …" (p. 226)

"sweet revenge …" (p. 226)   Seward

"*baka* explosion …" (p. 227)   Ashby

"The phenomenon is linked …" (p. 2

"With all the bullying …" (p. 227)   Pe
LH, October 2003.

"Japanese still lags behind …" (p. 228)

"We Finns have …" (p. 228)   Malmbe
http://www.kaapeli.fi/flf/malmber.ht

"I was advised …" (p. 229)   Marguerite
cation, 20 March 2004.

"For the Japanese …" (p. 230)   Ibid.

"the overlaps … between the two langua
Okamoto, 1988:218.

"We must remember that …" (p. 232)   S

"the grammatical options available …" (p.
munication, March 2004.

"One job that would keep you …" (p. 235)
the European Parliament,
http://www.aiic.net/ViewPage.cfm/page

Epilogue

"Once the powers-that-be …" (p. 238)   Tru

"a verbal hygienist approach …" (p. 238)   C

"censoring institutions …" (p. 239)   Jay, 199

"manufacture of consent …" (p. 239)   Herr
(1995). The phrase was coined by America
Lippmann, who said in 1921 that "the art o
requires … the manufacture of consent."
http://www.zpub.com/un/chomsky.html.

"myths about swearing …" (p. 239)   Jay (199

"imagine the conversation patterns …" (p. 240

"If you don't like …" (p. 241)   Trudgill (1975)

"a highly implausible model …" (p. 243)   Jay,

"Nothing will label a man …" (p. 243)   *The Su
May 2002, p. 21.

"These days the most offensive …" (p. 244)
http://expage.com/4letterwords1.

REFERENCES

Abd el-Jawad, H. 2000. A linguistic and sociopragmatic and cultural study of swearing in Arabic. *Language Culture and Curriculum* 13 (2): 217–40.

Allan, K., and K. Burridge. 1991. *Euphemism and dysphemism: Language used as shield and weapon.* New York: Oxford University Press.

———. 1992. "Raising gooseflesh": "Dirty" words and language change. *La Trobe University Working Papers in Linguistics* 5:31–43.

Andersson, L.-G., and P. Trudgill. 1990. *Bad language.* London: Penguin Books.

Aoki, H., and S. Okamoto. 1988. *Rules for conversational rituals in Japanese.* Tokyo: Taishukan Publishing Company.

Arango, A. C. 1989. *Dirty words: Psychoanalytic insights.* Northvale, N.J.: Jason Aronson.

Ardo, Z. 2001. Emotions, taboos and profane language. *Translation Journal* 5 (April). http://accurapid.com/journal/16review.htm.

Ashby, J. 2003. Does "*baka* explosion" indicate identity crisis being in Japan? *The Japan Times,* October 9.

Ayto, John. 1999. *Twentieth century words.* Oxford: Oxford University Press.

Bernstein, B. 1970. A socio-linguistic approach to socialisation. In *Directions in socio-linguistics.* Ed. J. Gumperz and D. Hymes. New York: Holt, Rinehart & Winston.

Bragg, M. 2003. *The adventure of English 500 AD to 2000: The biography of a language.* London: Hodder & Stoughton.

Brown, P. 1990. How and why women are more polite: Some evidence from a Mayan community. In *Language and gender: A reader.* Ed. J. Coates, 81–99. Oxford: Blackwell.

Brown, P., and S. Levinson. 1978. Universals in language usage: Politeness phenomena. In *Questions and politeness: Strategies in social interaction.* Ed. E. Goody. Cambridge: Cambridge University Press.

Bryson, B. 1990. *Mother tongue.* London: Penguin.

Burridge, K. 2001. Ma's out, Pa's out. Let's talk rude: Pee-poo-belly-bum-drawers. *Ozwords* 7 (2). http://www.anu.edu.au/ANDC/ozwords.

———. 2002. *Blooming English: Observations on the roots, cultivation and hybrids of the English language.* Sydney: ABC Books.

Cagle, J. 2002. About Tom. *Time,* July 1.

Cameron, D. 1995a. Words, words, words: The power of language. In *The war of the words: The political correctness debate.* Ed. S. Dunant, 15–34. London: Virago.

———. 1995b. *Verbal hygiene.* New York: Routledge.

Chaikin, E. 1982. *Language: The social mirror.* Rowley, Mass.: Newbury House.

Claire, E. 1983. *A foreign student's guide to dangerous English.* Fairlawn, N.J.: Eardley Publications.

Coates, J. 1990. *Women, men and language: A sociolinguistic account of sex differences in language.* London: Longman.

Coates, J., ed. 1998, 1990. *Language and gender: A reader.* Oxford: Blackwell.

Collins Australian dictionary. 2003. 5th ed. Glasgow/Sydney: Harper-Collins.

Conway, A. 1994. You're ugly, your dick is small and everybody fucks your mother. The stand-up comedian's response to the heckler. *Maledicta: The International Journal of Verbal Aggression* 11.

Cornay, M. 1986. Naming sexual body parts: Preliminary patterns and implications. *The Journal of Sex Research* 22 (3): 393–98.

Crawley, T., ed. 1991. *The Wordsworth dictionary of film quotations.* Hertfordshire: Wordsworth Editions.

Crystal, D. 1987, 2003. *The Cambridge encyclopedia of language.* 2nd ed. Cambridge: Cambridge University Press.

Defoe, D. 1966. Of academics. In *The English language: Essays by English and American men of letters, 1490–1939.* Ed. W. F. Bolton, 91–101. Cambridge: Cambridge University Press.

de Klerk, V. 1992. How taboo are taboo words for girls? *Language in Society* 21: 277–89.

Delaney, S. 1974. Womanliners in The Man of Law's Tale. *Chaucer Review* 9 (1): 68.

Dooling, R. 1996. *Blue streak: Swearing, free speech and sexual harassment.* New York: Random House.

Douglas, M. 1966. *Purity and danger: An analysis of the concepts of pollution and taboo.* London: Routledge & Kegan Paul.

————. 1973. *Natural symbols: Explorations in cosmology.* London: Barry and Jenkins Ltd.

Dunant, S., ed. 1995. *The war of the words: The political correctness debate.* London: Virago.

Eble, C. 1996. *Slang and sociability: In-group language among college students.* Chapel Hill: University of North Carolina Press.

Eckert, P., and S. McConnell-Ginet. 2003. *Language and gender.* Cambridge: Cambridge University Press.

Encyclopaedia Judaica. 1972. Vol. 6. Jerusalem: Keter Publishing House.

Erofeyev, V. 2003. Letter from Moscow: Dirty words. *The New Yorker,* September 15, 42–48.

Foote, R., and J. Woodward. 1973. A preliminary investigation of obscene language. *The Journal of Psychology* 83:263–75.

Gaines, Irvin J. 1948. Talking under water: Speech in submarines. *American Speech* 23 (1): 36–38.

Gilliland, C. Herbert. 1980. United States naval slang: *"shitcan."* *American Speech* 55 (2): 153–54.

Goddard, C. 1989. Issues in natural semantic metalanguage. *Quaderni Di Semantica* 10 (1): 5–64.

————. 1991. Anger in the Western Desert: A case study in the cross-cultural semantics of emotion. *Man* (n.s.) 26 (2): 265–79.

Goffman, E. 1981. *Forms of talk.* Oxford: Basil Blackwell.

Gray, P. 1993. Oaths and laughter and indecent speech. *Language & Communication* 13 (4): 311–25.

Greer, G. 1971. *The female eunuch.* London: Paladin.

————. 1999. *The whole woman.* London: Doubleday.

Gritten, D. 2002. *Fame: Striping celebrity bare.* London: Allen Lane.

Hadida, S. 1959. *Manners for millions: A complete guide to courteous behavior.* New York: Barnes and Noble.

Herman, E. S., and N. Chomsky. 1995. *Manufacturing consent: The political economy of the mass media.* London: Vintage.

Hill, D. 1992. Imprecatory interjectional expressions: Examples from Australian English. *Journal of Pragmatics* 18:209–23.

Holmes, J., M. Stubbe, B. Vine, and M. Mara. 1996. Language in the workplace. Research project, Victoria University, Wellington, New Zealand.

Hughes, G. 1988. *Words in time: A social history of the English vocabulary.* Oxford: Basil Blackwell.

————. 1998. *Swearing: A social history of foul language, oaths and profanity in English.* London: Penguin.

Hughes, R. 1993. *Culture of complaint: The fraying of America.* New York: Oxford University Press.

Hughes-Warrington, M. 2001. *Fifty key thinkers on history.* London: Routledge.

Humphries, R. 1995. American-English taboo words and Japanese learners. *Journal of Humanities* 18:25–43. Kobe: Association for the Study of Humanities.

Inglis Moore, T., ed. 1961. *A book of Australia.* London: Collins.

Jay, T. 1992. *Cursing in America: A psycholinguistic study of dirty language in the courts, in the movies, in the schoolyards and on the streets.* Philadelphia: John Benjamins.

———. 1999. *Why we curse: A neuro-psycho-social theory of speech.* Philadelphia/Amsterdam: John Benjamins.

Kidman, A. 1993. How to do things with four-letter words: A study of the semantics of swearing in Australia. Unpublished BA Honours thesis, Linguistics, University of New England. Online at http://www.gusworld.com.au/nrc/thesis/intro.htm.

Lakoff, R. 1975. *Language and woman's place.* New York: Harper & Row.

———. 2001. *The language war.* Berkeley: University of California Press.

Lawrence, D. H. 1928, 1960. *Lady Chatterley's lover.* Harmondsworth: Penguin.

Macquarie dictionary of Australian colloquialisms. 1984. Sydney: The Macquarie Library Pty Ltd.

Macquarie learners dictionary. 1999. Sydney: The Macquarie Library Pty Ltd.

Manne, R., ed. 2003. *Whitewash: On Keith Windshuttle's fabrication of Aboriginal history.* Melbourne: Black Inc. Agenda.

McArthur, T. 1992. *The Oxford companion to the English language.* Oxford: Oxford University Press.

———. 2002. *The Oxford guide to world English.* Oxford: Oxford University Press.

McConville, B., and J. Shearlaw. 1984. *The slanguage of sex: A dictionary of modern sexual terms.* London: Macdonald.

McDonald, J. 1988. *A dictionary of obscenity, taboo and euphemism.* London: Sphere Books.

Mercury, R. 1995. Swearing: A "bad" part of language; a good part of language learning. *TESL Canada Journal* 13 (1): 28–36.

Montagu, A. 2001. *The anatomy of swearing.* Philadelphia: University of Pennsylvania Press.

Newey, G. 1999. Effing the ineffable. *The London Review of Books,* November 25. http://www.lrb.co.uk/v21/n23/newe01_.html.

Nias, J. 1987. *Seeing anew: Teachers' theories of action.* Victoria: Deakin University Press.

Partridge, E. 1984. *A dictionary of slang and unconventional English.* 8th ed. Ed. Paul Beale. London: Routledge & Kegan Paul.

Pearsall, R. 1969. *The worm on the bud: The world of Victorian sexuality.* London: Weidenfeld & Nicolson.

Phillips, M. 2002. Swearing: The sickness in society. *The Daily Mail,* February 27.

Pinker, S. 1994. *The language instinct: The new science of language and mind.* London: Penguin.

Planalp, S. 1999. *Communicating emotion: Social, moral and cultural process.* Cambridge: Cambridge University Press.

Reynolds, H. 2003. *Terra nullius* reborn. In *Whitewash: On Keith Windshuttle's fabrication of Aboriginal history.* Ed. R. Manne. Melbourne: Black Inc. Agenda.

Rieber, R., C. Wiedemann, and J. D'Amato. Obscenity: Its frequency and context of usage as compared in males, nonfeminist females and feminist females. *Journal of Psycholinguistic Research* 8 (3): 201–23.

Risch, B. 1987. Women's derogatory terms for men: That's right, "dirty" words. *Language in Society* 16:353–58.

Seligman, M. 1990. *Learned optimism.* Sydney: Random House Australia.

Seward, J. 1968. *Japanese in action.* John Weatherhill: Tokyo.

———. 1992. *The Japanese.* Chicago: Passport Books.

Sheidlower, J. 1999. *The f-word.* New York: Random House.

Summers, A. 1977. *Damned whores and god's police: The colonisation of women in Australia.* Harmondsworth: Penguin Books.

Takeshi, Y. 2003. *Baka no kabe* (trans. as *The wall of a fool*). Tokyo: Shincho Shinsho.

Taylor, B. A. 1975. Towards a structural and lexical analysis of "swearing" and the language of abuse in Australian English. *Linguistics* 16 (4): 17–43.

Thomson, D. 1935. The joking relationship and organised obscenity in Northern Queensland. *American Anthropologist* 37.

Thorne, T. 1991. *The Bloomsbury dictionary of contemporary slang.* London: Bloomsbury Publishing.

Trudgill, P. 1975. *Accent, dialect and the school.* London: Edward Arnold.

Tyler, M. 1977. Why ladies don't swear. Paper presented at the 16th meeting of the Southeast Conference on Linguistics, North Carolina.

Wajnryb, R. 2002. Strong language: The language of racism. *(R)U?* 3:48–51.

Wierzbicka, A. 1999. *Emotions across languages and cultures: Diversity and universals.* Cambridge: Cambridge University Press.

Windshuttle, K. 2002. *The fabrication of Australian history.* Vol. 1, *Van Dieman's land 1803–1947.* Sydney: Macleay Press.

INDEX

Dr. Ruth Wajnryb is an applied linguist, researcher, and writer. She has a weekly column in *The Sydney Morning Herald* in which she explores linguistic topics.